OECD ECONOMIC SURVEYS

1993-1994

UNITED STATES

ORGANISATION FOR ECONOMIC CO-OPERATION AND DEVELOPMENT

ORGANISATION FOR ECONOMIC
CO-OPERATION AND DEVELOPMENT

Pursuant to Article 1 of the Convention signed in Paris on 14th December 1960, and which came into force on 30th September 1961, the Organisation for Economic Co-operation and Development (OECD) shall promote policies designed:

- to achieve the highest sustainable economic growth and employment and a rising standard of living in Member countries, while maintaining financial stability, and thus to contribute to the development of the world economy;
- to contribute to sound economic expansion in Member as well as non-member countries in the process of economic development; and
- to contribute to the expansion of world trade on a multilateral, non-discriminatory basis in accordance with international obligations.

The original Member countries of the OECD are Austria, Belgium, Canada, Denmark, France, Germany, Greece, Iceland, Ireland, Italy, Luxembourg, the Netherlands, Norway, Portugal, Spain, Sweden, Switzerland, Turkey, the United Kingdom and the United States. The following countries became Members subsequently through accession at the dates indicated hereafter: Japan (28th April 1964), Finland (28th January 1969), Australia (7th June 1971), New Zealand (29th May 1973) and Mexico (18th May 1994). The Commission of the European Communities takes part in the work of the OECD (Article 13 of the OECD Convention).

Publié également en français.

Table of contents

3

Boxes

Tables

Diagrams

BASIC STATISTICS OF THE UNITED STATES

THE LAND

Area (1 000 sq. km)	9 373	Population of major cities, including their metropolitan areas, 1991:	
		New York	19 384 000
		Los Angeles-Anaheim-Riverside	14 818 000
		Chicago-Gary-Lake Country	8 339 000

THE PEOPLE

Population, 1993	258 291 000	Civilian labour force, 1993	128 035 000
Number of inhabitants per sq. km	27.6	*of which:*	
Population, annual net natural increase		Employed in agriculture	3 074 000
(average 1986-91)	1 854 600	Unemployed	8 726 667
Annual net natural increase, per cent (1986-91)	1.00	Net immigration (annual average 1986-91)	730 400

PRODUCTION

Gross domestic product in 1993		Origin of national income in 1993	
(billions of US$)	6 343.3	(per cent of national income[1]):	
GDP per head in 1993 (US$)	24 559	Agriculture, forestry and fishing	1.8
Gross fixed capital formation:		Manufacturing	17.7
Per cent of GDP in 1993	13.7	Construction and mining	5.0
Per head in 1993 (US$)	3 355.3	Government and government enterprises	14.8
		Other	60.7

THE GOVERNMENT

Government purchases of goods and services,		Composition of the 103rd Congress 1993:	
1993 (per cent of GDP)	18.1		

	House of Representatives	Senate
Revenue of federal, state and local governments, 1993 (per cent of GDP) — 31.1		
Federal government debt held by the public (per cent of GDP), FY 1993 — 51.6		
Democrats	256	56
Republicans	178	44
Independents	1	–
Vacancies	–	–
Total	435	100

FOREIGN TRADE

Exports:		Imports:	
Exports of goods and services as		Imports of goods and services as	
per cent of GDP in 1993	10.4	per cent of GDP in 1993	11.4
Main exports, 1993 (per cent of merchandise exports):		Main imports, 1993 (per cent of merchandise imports):	
Food, feed, beverages	8.8	Food, feed, beverages	4.7
Industrial supplies	22.3	Industrial supplies	15.0
Capital goods (ex. automotive)	39.5	Capital goods (ex. automotive)	25.7
Automotive vehicles, parts	11.4	Automotive vehicles, parts	17.4
Consumer goods (ex. automotive)	11.9	Consumer goods (ex. automotive)	22.6

1. Without capital consumption adjustment.
Note: An international comparison of certain basic statistics is given in an annex table.

This Survey is based on the Secretariat's study prepared for the annual review of the United States by the Economic and Development Review Committee on 12th September 1994.

•

After revisions in the light of discussions during the review, final approval of the Survey for publication was given by the Committee on 10th October 1994.

•

The previous Survey of the United States was issued in November 1993.

Introduction

When the Committee last met in September 1993 to review economic developments in the United States, the recovery had firmed somewhat compared to its early days, but output growth was expected to pick up only modestly to about 3 per cent in 1994. This was not expected to eliminate the slack in labour and product markets that was then seen as likely to persist into 1995. In the event, the expansion has gathered much more momentum than then predicted, with underlying GDP growth accelerating to about 4 per cent and the unemployment rate falling another percentage point (abstracting from the changes in Survey methods). Nevertheless, despite the quickening pace of activity, broad measures of inflation continued to decline at least until the end of 1993 and have remained subdued thus far this year. But the risks of an uptick in inflation have increased as markets have continued to tighten.

The short-term outlook is for slowing output growth, as Federal spending restraint continues, pent-up demand for housing and consumer durables is satisfied and higher interest rates begin to bite. But with accelerating real income gains bolstering consumption, still-rapid growth in business fixed investment and improving export market prospects, the slowdown will probably be gradual, and real GDP could still rise nearly 3 per cent in 1995 after a $3^3/4$ per cent gain this year. This might not be enough of a slowdown to prevent a modest pickup in wage and price inflation from getting under way, as unemployment heads somewhat below its full-employment level in 1995. The current external deficit may continue to widen, albeit at a slower pace, reaching $2^1/4$ per cent of GDP in both 1994 and 1995. These developments, both in the recent past and in prospect, are discussed in Chapter I; particular emphasis is placed on assessing the risks of higher inflation.

In recent months the Federal Reserve has substantially reversed the policy stimulus provided by unusually low short-term interest rates. Chapter II reviews the reasons for and market reactions to this shift in policy. It then moves on to examine recent budgetary outcomes and proposals for 1995. While last year's deficit-reduction package has helped to put the deficit on a downward path, the medium-term outlook is less favourable, especially if real interest rates stay at recent higher levels. Looking further out, spending pressures are likely to grow, and the issue of adequate financing of the Social Security system will come to the fore.

The Administration has put before the Congress a wide variety of draft legislation to reform some of the most basic services provided by the public sector. A detailed look at three of these initiatives is provided in Chapter III. Various bills emanating from the National Performance Review attempt to make the Federal government operate more efficiently overall. The Health Security Act proposed to provide universal health-care coverage to all Americans at a social cost the economy can bear and to brake the upward spiral of health spending over the medium term. The Work and Responsibility Act is the Administration's response to the President's promise to "end welfare as we know it" by making work more attractive than staying on welfare and by providing its recipients with the means to upgrade their human capital in order to enter the labour market successfully.

Chapter IV surveys the strengths and weaknesses of the current education system and assesses recent policy initiatives. Primary responsibility for the education system lies with State governments, who, in turn, often delegate control to local school districts. The role of the Federal government is limited: in recent years it has provided less than 7 per cent of the financing of primary and secondary education. Over a period of many decades, local control has helped to foster a system characterised by wide disparities in education quality across different communities and by a low degree of standardisation in education outputs. The Federal government has been seeking to alter this situation by co-ordinating and facilitating national development of "voluntary" education standards. Overall conclusions are presented in a final chapter.

I.   Recent trends and prospects

The economic expansion in perspective

The current expansion of economic activity differs in several important ways from past experience. The sources of growth have been very different: monetary easing contributed, as in previous recoveries (Diagram 1) (Romer and Romer, 1994) – but in most past recoveries, fiscal policy was not contractionary, and substantial inventory-building accompanied the recovery of final expenditure. In contrast, the current recovery occurred in the face of the biggest retrenchment of Federal purchases in over twenty years, and despite sharp cut-backs in business inventories relative to sales. Partly for these reasons, as well as because of the shallowness of the preceding recession, the pickup in output growth has been much more gradual than usual. In the year after the trough, GDP growth averaged only 1.6 per cent; in the four quarters ending mid-1993, growth averaged 3.2 per cent; and only since then has average growth surged to 4 per cent. In contrast, over each of the previous five recoveries output growth was at its fastest in the first two years after the trough. Even after including the three strong quarters of growth in late 1993 and 1994, average real GDP growth since the 1991 trough remains far lower than in past recoveries. In several previous business cycles strong inflationary pressures were already building at this point in the expansion; there has been no such price acceleration as of the summer of 1994, though inflation may soon pick up a little.

Low interest rates played a major role in the first two and a half years of the current expansion. Corporate cash flow improved, allowing firms to pare bank debt substantially relative to income (Table 1). This corporate balance-sheet improvement and increased cash flow provided some of the stimulus for a take-off in business investment. Initially, most of this increased spending went into purchases of computers – partly because corporate ''re-engineering'' required

Diagram 1. **SOME CHARACTERISTICS OF THE CURRENT EXPANSION**

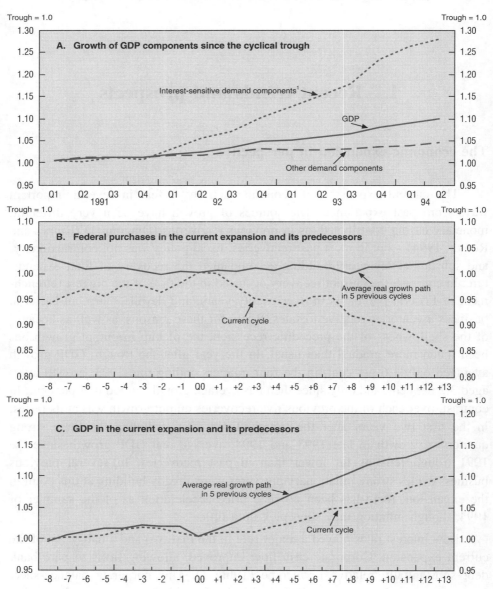

Trough = 1.0

A. **Growth of GDP components since the cyclical trough**

Interest-sensitive demand components[1]

GDP

Other demand components

Q1 Q2 Q3 Q4 Q1 Q2 Q3 Q4 Q1 Q2 Q3 Q4 Q1 Q2
1991   92   93   94

B. **Federal purchases in the current expansion and its predecessors**

Average real growth path in 5 previous cycles

Current cycle

-8 -7 -6 -5 -4 -3 -2 -1 Q0 +1 +2 +3 +4 +5 +6 +7 +8 +9 +10 +11 +12 +13

C. **GDP in the current expansion and its predecessors**

Average real growth path in 5 previous cycles

Current cycle

-8 -7 -6 -5 -4 -3 -2 -1 Q0 +1 +2 +3 +4 +5 +6 +7 +8 +9 +10 +11 +12 +13

1. Fixed investment plus consumption of durable goods.
Source: Department of Commerce and OECD.

Table 1. U.S. household and business-sector liabilities

	1980	1981	1982	1983	1984	1985	1986	1987	1988	1989	1990	1991	1992	1993 Q1	1993 Q2	1993 Q3	1993 Q4	1994 Q1
Household liabilities as % of disposable income [1]	70.4	69.3	68.4	69.5	71.4	77.6	82.1	84.3	86.9	90.5	90.4	91.1	88.9	90.4	90.7	92.6	93.5	93.4
Mortgages	45.7	45.0	43.9	44.0	45.1	47.9	51.9	55.3	58.2	61.5	62.8	64.3	63.4	64.6	64.9	65.9	65.9	65.9
Consumer installment	17.3	16.6	16.4	16.9	18.4	20.0	20.8	20.4	20.3	20.6	19.7	18.5	17.2	17.1	17.1	17.6	18.2	17.9
Other	7.4	7.7	8.2	8.5	7.9	9.6	9.4	8.6	8.3	8.4	8.0	8.3	8.3	8.7	8.7	9.2	9.5	9.6
Household assets ratio to disposable income																		
income	5.42	5.31	5.34	5.30	5.20	5.41	5.61	5.62	5.60	5.83	5.51	5.77	5.59				5.75	
Tangible	2.29	2.28	2.26	2.19	2.18	2.20	2.24	2.26	2.22	2.25	2.12	2.16	2.05				2.09	
Financial	3.12	3.04	3.08	3.12	3.02	3.21	3.37	3.36	3.38	3.57	3.39	3.61	3.53	3.63	3.59	3.66	3.67	3.62
Household net worth: ratio to disposable income [2]	4.71	4.62	4.66	4.61	4.48	4.63	4.79	4.77	4.73	4.92	4.61	4.86	4.70				4.82	
Business liabilities [3] as % of business GDP	86.5	87.9	92.0	90.3	94.8	98.7	103.9	103.7	104.3	105.9	104.9	101.5	95.8	94.7	94.9	94.6	93.7	93.5
Corporate bonds	15.8	15.5	16.3	15.4	15.7	17.1	20.0	20.4	21.4	22.0	22.2	23.2	23.0	23.1	23.4	23.6	23.6	23.6
Commercial paper	1.2	1.7	1.5	1.3	1.9	2.1	1.8	1.9	2.1	2.5	2.6	2.1	2.1	2.2	2.4	2.4	2.3	2.5
Bank lending [4]	37.9	37.2	39.7	39.3	41.1	42.3	44.8	44.5	43.2	43.0	41.3	39.1	34.9	34.1	33.8	33.6	32.8	32.5
Trade debt	17.4	17.3	17.2	16.6	16.5	16.5	16.2	16.1	16.5	16.5	16.6	16.3	15.8	15.6	15.7	15.9	15.9	15.6
Other [5]	14.2	16.2	17.3	17.7	19.7	20.6	21.1	20.8	21.2	21.9	22.2	20.8	20.0	19.7	19.6	19.1	19.2	19.4
Memo:																		
Growth rate of mortgage and other bank debt, non-farm, non-corporate business (%)		4.5	4.5	10.9	13.4	4.8	15.7	11.8	4.6	7.5	-1.3	-3.2	-5.5	-6.3	-1.9	-4.2	1.8	0.8

1. Year-end liabilities, relative to fourth-quarter disposable income, BEA definition. Quarterly figures are end-of-quarter liabilities versus quarterly income.
2. Assets minus liabilities: assets include financial assets plus current-cost net stocks of consumer durables, residential structures and land.
3. Business liabilities exclude foreign direct investment. Business GDP = GDP minus government employee compensation minus indirect business taxes plus substantial less surplus of government enterprises.
4. Including mortgages and bank lending not elsewhere classified.
5. Includes finance-company loans, public lending, and other miscellaneous liabilities.
Source: Federal Reserve, *Flow of Funds Accounts, Z.1 and C.9 releases*, September 1994.

increased computer intensity, and also because computer price declines of 10 to 18 per cent annually (corrected for quality improvements) allowed firms to stretch their investment dollars further *via* computer purchases. Gross computer investment thus increased 26 per cent in 1992 and a spectacular 54 per cent in 1993. But price increases for other forms of business equipment were by no means rapid: 1.4 per cent in 1992 and 2.1 per cent in 1993. Thus, with continuing balance-sheet improvements and rising sales, non-computer equipment invest-ment took off in the second quarter of 1992, about a year after the business-cycle trough. Over the past two years, overall gross equipment investment has increased to record levels relative to GDP.[1] Net of depreciation, the rise in share of equipment investment in GDP was not as imposing, but it was sufficient to boost the overall stock of equipment relative to output in 1993.

Compared with the booming demand for producer durable equipment, spending on non-residential structures has been noticeably slower to recover. A glut of commercial office space held down construction and overall output growth until end-1992; by early 1993, though, office construction activity had become so small that overall non-residential construction was dominated by swings in other components. Over the last three quarters of 1993, strong growth of investment in factories and utilities halted the decline in overall investment in non-residential structures. However, the absolute levels of structures investment remain modest, and the stock of non-residential structures is not increasing nearly as fast as business output. Thus, overall business capital intensity continued to decline in 1993, despite the equipment investment boom.

Over the past two or three years, households did not take the opportunity afforded by low interest rates to reduce debt in the same way as businesses did. After a brief period of deleveraging in 1992, household debt returned to histori-cally high levels relative to income at the end of 1993. However, the decline in mortgage rates during 1993 allowed large numbers of consumers to improve cash flow lastingly by refinancing mortgage debt at much lower rates, more than offsetting the drag from the 1993 tax increase on high-income households. The improvement in cash flow (along with a very high average age of the auto stock) was a major factor behind the hefty growth in consumer spending on durable goods from the trough. Overall consumer spending rose noticeably faster than disposable income, which was slowed by higher tax rates and the effects of summer flooding.[2] Thus, the household saving rate (OECD definition) fell from

5.2 per cent in 1992 to 4.6 per cent last year – a disappointingly low figure, given that cash flow improvements dried up in early 1994 as mortgage rates began to move back up.

The recession of 1990-1991 left a considerable amount of pent-up demand for housing: the number of households in 1991 was probably about a million below trend, given demographic developments. But in 1992-93, low mortgage rates, moderation in housing prices and recovery in real incomes made houses more affordable, allowing faster household formation in both years. Home sales therefore picked up, and the volume of single-family residential construction rose 20 per cent in 1992 and 10 per cent in 1993.[3] Low interest rates and rising demand for housing also brought to an end the seven-year collapse in multi-family construction which followed the overbuilding of the mid-1980s. Over the past four quarters, annualised growth in multi-family construction has averaged 21 per cent.

In most previous recoveries, Federal purchases have been a significant contributor to growth – but they were never a driving force for recovery in this expansion: defence downsizing pulled down real Federal purchases both in 1992 and 1993. The last two years have seen the biggest annual declines in real Federal purchases since the aftermath of the Vietnam War twenty years ago. Defence employment has fallen sharply, and starting in fiscal 1994 sharp cuts have also been occurring outside of defence (see the discussion of the National Performance Review in Chapter III). State and local government spending on construction has picked up sharply in recent years, as school and prison popula-tions have risen, but State operating deficits are on average quite high relative to the tax base. Thus, State governments pared employment growth during and immediately after the recession. Faster growth of the tax base in 1993 allowed an increase of 1 per cent or so in State employment, but many State governments are still encouraging early retirement and moving toward contracting out work.

Over the past year or two, manufacturing inventories have stagnated in the face of very rapid growth of manufacturing output. Improved technology and ''just-in-time'' inventory management most likely explain the rapid fall in the inventory-sales ratio since the early 1980s. Still, the decline since 1992 goes well beyond the trend declines of the 1980s, and overall inventories look quite lean relative to sales – even after the surge in the second quarter of 1994. In 1993, the ratio of inventories to final sales of domestic business fell below the previous record low of the mid-1960s (Diagram 2).

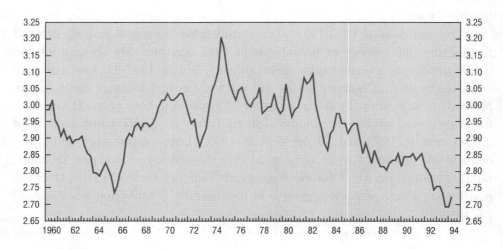

Diagram 2. **BUSINESS INVENTORY/FINAL SALES RATIO**
Months of supply, 1987 prices

Source: Bureau of Economic Analysis.

Table 2. **Current account**
$ billion, seasonally adjusted annual rates

	1992	1993	1993				1994	
			Q1	Q2	Q3	Q4	Q1	Q2
Current account balance	−68	−104	−79	−102	−111	−122	−129	−148
Exports of goods, services and income	731	756	740	756	746	780	779	814
Imports of goods, services and income	767	827	790	829	827	863	880	932
Balances								
Goods	−96	−133	−117	−135	−146	−133	−148	−67
Non-factor services	56	57	59	59	57	53	51	59
Investment income	5	4	7	3	8	−2	−3	−10
Private transfers	−13	−14	−13	−14	−14	−14	−15	−16
Official transfers	−19	−18	−16	−15	−16	−26	−13	−14

Source: U.S. Department of Commerce, *Survey of Current Business.*

Foreign activity was relatively weak in 1993. Although export markets softened significantly in Western Europe, Mexico and Japan, U.S. manufacturers gained market share abroad, notably in industrialised countries such as Canada and the United Kingdom: thus, overall export volumes increased at a 4 per cent rate. However, the pickup in U.S. total domestic demand and continued weak import prices led to a surge in imports, and the foreign balance was a net drag on GDP growth, as in 1992. Indeed, last year's drag on overall growth was the most substantial since 1984. With a decrease in net factor income from abroad (in fact, the balance has been negative since the final quarter of 1993) due to the continuing rise in foreign indebtedness as well as the unfavourable cyclical movement in relative rates of return, the current-account deficit increased to 1.6 per cent of GDP in 1993, up from 1.1 per cent in 1992 (Table 2).

Tightening labour markets but still-slowing inflation

Much has been made in the popular press of a revolution in productivity taking shape in recent years. As discussed later in this chapter, there may indeed have been an increase in trend productivity growth in the 1990s, but this increase is probably less than a half percentage-point economy-wide. The improvement seems focused on supervisory workers, and especially on workers in the manufacturing sector. At the same time, however, measured productivity in the service sector is increasing rather slowly relative to past experience. Aside from any true underlying gains from restructuring and the information revolution, manufacturers have, to some extent, saved on non-wage labour costs by replacing their own permanent employees with those of temporary agencies (who count as employees in the service sector). However large the underlying increase in trend productivity, most of the shifts in output per hour in the 1990s have been cyclical. From early 1991 through the first quarter of 1994, output per hour in the non-farm business sector increased sharply, as is typical in the early stages of a recovery, and productivity returned more or less to trend levels. Productivity rose above trend at the end of 1993 and stayed above trend in early 1994, though once again, much of the surge was cyclical. Second-quarter data show that productivity fell noticeably, leaving it at mid-year once more in line with the OECD Secretariat's estimate of long-run trend.

17

The average workweek is currently rather high relative to the early 1990s, but the August level of 34.5 hours per week is by no means out of line with the figures from the expansion of the late 1980s. Establishment employment growth during 1994 has largely parallelled hours growth, but household employment has lagged significantly. (Seasonal adjustment problems may have distorted the household numbers for the first half of the year.) What employment growth has occurred has done very little to encourage increased labour force participation as yet. From mid-1992 to end-1993, both prime-age male and female participation rates were surprisingly slow to recover, even if one assumes that the trend increase in female participation is essentially over (Diagram 3). This year, the prime-age white male labour force participation rate has been very weak, even with the late-summer surge in labour force growth. Thus, despite the January 1994 changes to the household survey (see Box 1) which boosted the measured amount of joblessness, the unemployment rate has moved down to the 6 per cent range. At the same time, those who remain out of work have on average been out of work for an unusually long time. The median duration of unemployment has not shown the normal downturn usually seen this far into an expansion (though the high level as of mid-1994 is by no means unprecedented – Diagram 4). The high median duration of unemployment may have implications for likely wage growth in coming quarters, as discussed below.

From late 1991 until March 1993, growth of employee compensation per hour (as measured by the employment cost index) showed no signs of slowing, despite a significant excess of unemployment over even the higher estimates of the inflation-neutral rate, or "non-accelerating-wage rate of unemployment" (NAWRU). However, compensation growth eased slightly beginning in the second half of 1993 – consistent with a labour-market gap that at that point had not yet quite closed. The deceleration is reflected in a sharp reduction in the growth of employee benefit costs – especially health insurance. At about the same time that compensation per hour was slowing in the second half of 1993, price inflation was also easing. The 1993 rise in the GDP deflator was the smallest in nearly 30 years. Excluding food and energy, consumer price growth slowed from 3.7 per cent in 1992 to 3.3 per cent in 1993, and 2.7 per cent in the first four months of 1994. However, core consumer price inflation seems to have returned to a pace of about 3 per cent in recent months.

Diagram 3. **LABOUR-FORCE PARTICIPATION RATES**

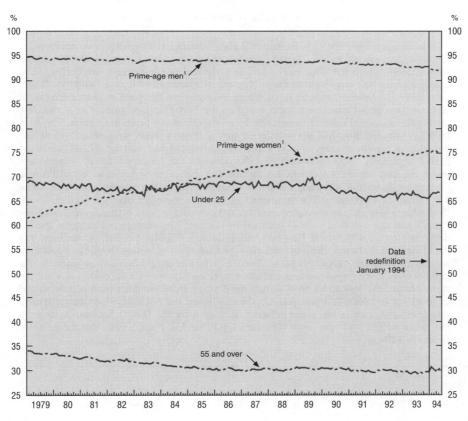

1. 25-54 years old.
Source: Bureau of Labor Statistics.

At the end of last year, GDP growth surged to an extraordinary 6.3 per cent rate. In comparison, the 3.3 per cent figure for growth for GDP in the first quarter of 1994 might appear to mark a slowdown. However, appearances are a bit deceptive in this case. The California earthquake and unusually cold weather combined to reduce incomes (notably because of losses to insurers from the earthquake) and delay construction activity. Both corporate cash flow and profits tailed off sharply in the first quarter, due in part to these natural disasters. At the same time, increased demand started to push up the prices of business equipment. However, investment in producer durables remains strong, both for computers and for other equipment, though computer investment growth did slow from 1993's 54 per cent rate to 16 per cent in the first quarter and 10 per cent in the second quarter.

Increases in household cash flow eased markedly in early 1994, for several reasons: income growth slowed a bit from end-1993 rates, the mortgage refinancing bonanza ended, and upper-income households felt the bite of higher tax rates. However, households reacted in a rather unexpected way: auto sales and overall consumption surged in the first quarter, and the personal saving rate plunged to 3.6 per cent. Such a low rate has not been sustained over any quarter in the past five years. Correspondingly, the strong growth in auto sales and overall con-

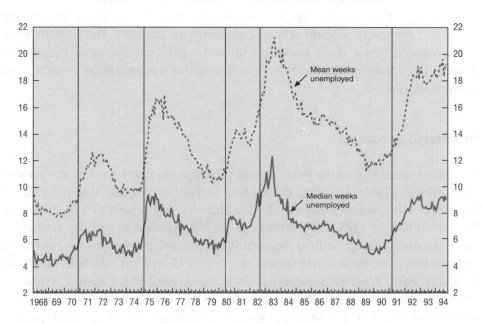

Diagram 4. **AVERAGE DURATION OF UNEMPLOYMENT**

Mean weeks unemployed

Median weeks unemployed

Note : Vertical lines mark business cycle troughs. New survey as of January 1994.
Source: Bureau of Labor Statistics.

sumption during the first quarter was not likely to be sustained indefinitely: some pickup in the saving rate was seen in the second quarter, and more is likely in the second half of 1994. Final demand experienced a much-discussed slowdown during the spring and early summer, with less of a deceleration in aggregate supply. The result was a significant build-up in inventories, especially at the retail level, through July. That stockbuilding added 2.6 percentage points to real GDP growth in the second quarter, a substantial part of the overall rate of 4.1 per cent achieved. Private consumption growth eased to 1.3 per cent from its torrid pace of over 4 per cent on average in the previous three quarters. Public consumption recorded its third straight quarterly decline, led by another substantial fall at the Federal level. With housing starts having reached an apparent plateau below 1.5 million units at an annual rate, residential investment continued to slow, although with a lag; further deceleration is in store for the remainder of the year.

Business fixed investment growth was still robust, even though growth fell below a double-digit pace for the first time since 1992. Exports continued their recent sawtooth patten with a sharp rebound of nearly 16 per cent. But imports once again outpaced their trade cousins with a 19 per cent increase, despite the slackening in domestic demand. No doubt much of the additional imports went into inventories.

Near-term prospects

In the latter half of the year, several factors seem likely to slow the pace of GDP growth (Table 3). First, the OECD Secretariat projects that the Federal funds rate will rise to $5^{1}/_{4}$ per cent by the end of this year and to $6^{1}/_{4}$ per cent in the second half of 1995. Long-term rates are not expected to rise any further, as these increases appear to have been fully discounted by the financial markets. Overall, however, interest rate increases since 1993 will cut into household and corporate cash flow, slowing durables consumption and housing – and in 1995 even equipment investment growth should slow from double-digit rates. Second, the boom in auto sales and single-family construction in recent quarters will soon push the stock of autos and single-family housing near desired levels: some cyclical slowing in these sectors would probably have occurred over the next few quarters even in the absence of interest rate increases. Inventory accumulation contributed noticeably to growth in the second quarter, as businesses moved to replenish depleted stocks. Less of a contribution is expected from inventories in the third quarter and beyond, although stocks of autos probably rose a bit over the summer, as sectoral supply problems were overcome. And, as in the past two years, Federal purchases will be pruned. The result is a projection of real GDP increasing by nearly 3 per cent in 1995, after $3^{3}/_{4}$ per cent this year. This should allow a narrowing of the Federal deficit by $87 billion in 1994 and another $7 billion next year, reaching $147 billion on a national-accounts basis.

On the positive side, construction activity (apart from single-family housing) is very likely to pick up, since current investment levels are barely sufficient to maintain the existing net stock of business structures, much less increase in line with sales.[4] As activity rebounds in Europe and Japan, U.S. exporters are well positioned to exploit low unit labour costs and the weakness of the dollar

Table 3. **Near-term outlook**

Percentage change from previous period, seasonally adjusted at annual rates, volume (1987 prices)

	1993	1994	1995	1993		1994		1995	
				I	II	I	II	I	II
Private consumption	3.3	3.4	2.7	2.8	3.6	3.6	2.9	2.8	2.4
Government consumption	-0.8	-1.0	0.4	-2.5	0.8	-2.9	0.9	0.3	0.0
Gross fixed investment	11.3	11.8	6.1	11.3	13.6	13.0	7.7	6.1	4.3
of which:									
Residential	8.2	8.6	-0.6	6.1	9.2	13.4	-0.8	-0.4	-0.7
Non-residential	12.5	12.9	8.4	13.3	15.2	12.9	10.8	8.4	6.0
Final domestic demand	3.7	3.9	2.9	3.1	4.6	3.9	3.3	2.9	2.3
Stockbuilding [1]	0.3	0.5	-0.2	0.5	-0.3	1.2	-0.2	-0.2	-0.1
Total domestic demand	3.9	4.4	2.7	3.6	4.3	5.1	3.0	2.7	2.2
Exports of goods and services	4.1	7.8	10.1	3.1	5.3	7.2	11.6	9.9	8.9
Imports of goods and services	10.7	11.8	7.3	11.1	11.3	13.4	9.0	6.8	6.7
Foreign balance [1]	-0.8	-0.6	0.2	-1.0	-0.8	-0.9	0.1	0.2	0.2
GDP at constant prices	3.1	3.8	2.9	2.6	3.5	4.2	3.2	3.0	2.4
GDP price deflator	2.2	2.1	2.8	2.7	1.3	2.4	2.3	2.9	3.1
GDP at current prices	5.4	6.0	5.8	5.4	4.8	6.8	5.6	6.0	5.6
Memorandum items:									
Private consumption deflator	2.5	2.3	3.4	2.8	1.7	2.0	3.3	3.4	3.5
Unemployment rate	6.8	6.2	5.8	7.0	6.6	6.4	6.1	5.8	5.7
Household saving rate	4.6	4.0	4.2	5.2	4.0	3.9	4.1	4.3	4.2
Three-month Treasury bill rate	3.0	4.2	6.0	3.0	3.0	3.6	4.8	5.8	6.3
Ten-year Treasury note rate	5.9	7.0	7.5	6.1	5.6	6.6	7.5	7.5	7.5
Net lending of general government									
$ billion	-215	-130	-121	–	–	–	–	–	–
Per cent of GDP	-3.4	-1.9	-1.7	–	–	–	–	–	–
Current account balance									
$ billion	-104	-147	-161	–	–	–	–	–	–
Per cent of GDP	-1.6	-2.2	-2.3	–	–	–	–	–	–

1. The yearly and half-yearly rates of change refer to changes expressed as a percentage of GDP in the previous period.
Source: OECD estimates.

against the yen and Deutschemark. Real goods and services exports are thus expected to increase at about a 10 per cent rate until the end of 1995. However, imports will still grow vigorously in the rest of 1994. Domestic demand growth is expected to slow about 2½ percentage points by year-end from the torrid rates of the past three quarters, but it will still be strong enough to support import growth in the 9 per cent range. By 1995, with domestic activity slowing further, import growth will no longer keep pace with that of exports, and the foreign balance may even become a net positive contributor to growth. The current-account deficit is thus expected to stabilise in the second half of next year – averaging 2.3 per cent of GDP for 1995 as a whole.

Prospects for wage and price inflation

Labour markets appear to have tightened markedly in recent quarters. The unemployment rate fell 0.3 percentage point in the fourth quarter of 1993, and since the switch to a new survey in January, it has fallen another 0.6 percentage point. Around the second quarter of this year, labour markets probably tightened sufficiently to start putting slight upward pressure on wage growth (though some would disagree, for reasons discussed below). And demand for labour will continue to increase faster than the labour force until 1995, when growth slows closer to potential rates. By mid-1995, the unemployment rate is projected to fall to below 5¾ per cent. This tightening in labour markets should put increasing upward pressure on wage inflation. However, employee compensation does not typically respond at once to tightness in labour markets. For most workers, wages are adjusted once a year, and some union wage contracts extend over more than one year (though the rapid rate of U.S. job turnover does speed up the pace of wage adjustments somewhat). Increases in the employment cost index for civilian workers' hourly compensation are expected to pick up gradually, rising from 3.1 per cent in the first half of 1994 to 4 per cent in the second half, reaching 4.8 per cent in the second half of 1995.

The projected pickup in wage inflation is likely to put upward pressure on prices over the next year or two – though the rate of price inflation may not immediately reflect the entire increase in growth of unit labour costs.[5] Production is bumping up against limits of available capacity in a few manufacturing industries, and some sectors have reported a pickup in producer price growth.[6] However, evidence on the overall extent of capacity pressures is mixed, as discussed below. Capacity constraints are not projected to put widespread upward pressure on business margins over labour costs before year-end. Thus, inflation, as measured by the GDP deflator, is expected to pick up gradually from 2.4 per cent in the first half of 1994 to 3.1 per cent in the second half of 1995.

Risks to the inflation projection

The above projections, incorporating a moderate pickup in wages and price inflation over the coming year or so, are probably not out of line with views of many business economists and economic forecasting firms. However, not all recent indicators consistently point toward the same timing or extent of wage and price increases. There is considerable risk of even faster price acceleration through end-1995 – or even of no pickup at all. The most widely discussed indicators, in themselves, do suggest an upcoming pickup in inflation. By May, the aggregate unemployment rate had fallen to 6.0 per cent – not far from most estimates of the NAWRU. Even earlier, in the fourth quarter of 1993, capacity utilisation had risen to a level which in the past triggered a slight increase in growth of price mark-ups. The "output gap" – in a sense a summary measure combining the extent of capacity and labour-market slack – is estimated by the OECD Secretariat to have closed by the second quarter of 1994[7] (Diagram 5).

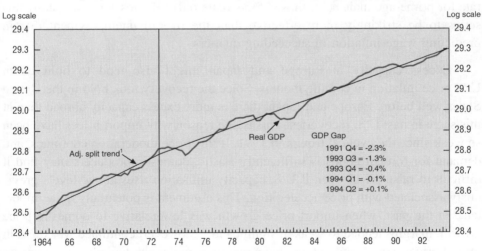

Diagram 5. **ONE MEASURE OF POTENTIAL GDP AND THE GDP "GAP"**

1. Implied potential real GDP growth from Q2 1973 onward is 2.44 per cent per year.
Source: OECD.

25

However, it may be that none of these traditional leading indicators of inflation is reliable at this point in time. There are a variety of caveats, which are reviewed below.

First, the properties of the new unemployment data since January are not at all clear. In the Bureau of Labor Statistics' preliminary tests in 1993, aggregate unemployment rates using the new survey averaged about $1/2$ percentage point higher than the old measure, but the differences varied substantially from month to month; more recent BLS estimates point to an average difference of about $1/4$ point. The new seasonal factors are not yet known and may not be close to the old ones, as the BLS has assumed for lack of any obvious alternative. Even under the old definitions, demographic shifts made it difficult to pin-point an aggregate unemployment rate at which wage inflation starts to increase: the definitional change since January 1994 compounds the problem. Tests reported in the annex confirm that the aggregate unemployment rate is indeed a bad measure of labour-market slack. That is, the unemployment rate is a poor predictor of wage inflation, until one corrects for demographic changes and other structural shifts. Even when such considerations are taken into account, the aggregate NAWRU is difficult to calculate and not very stable. A better measure, less affected by demographic shifts and the January 1994 survey change, is the unemployment rate for prime-age males (*i.e.* those 25-54 years old).[8] Regression tests[9] show this series to be strikingly more effective than the overall unemployment rate in predicting wage inflation in succeeding quarters.

Excess capacity in Europe and Japan might also tend to hold down U.S. price inflation in coming months. Since the recovery took hold in the United States well before Europe and Japan, there is more excess capacity abroad than at this stage in past U.S. recoveries. This is one reason why import prices have been so weak since the cyclical trough in 1991. If this price moderation continues, and demand for foreign goods is sufficiently elastic, domestic producers may find it difficult to raise prices even if U.S. capacity utilisation rises above levels previously associated with price acceleration. This argument is potentially quite important: in the past, when import price growth was low relative to domestic price growth, margins tended to weaken significantly. However, continued weakness in import prices would tend to hold down mainly manufactured goods prices: excess capacity abroad will do little to hold down growth of U.S. construction costs or service prices, which will be more sensitive to any pickup in the growth of domestic unit labour costs. Furthermore, recent weakening of the dollar may boost import price growth later this year, creating *upward* pressure on margins at year-end and in 1995.

Over the past year, the non-employment rate (1 – (employment/working age population)) has not improved nearly as much as the unemployment rate. At this stage of the business cycle, more workers normally re-enter the labour force to search for jobs. On this occasion, however, a surprising number of workers remain sufficiently discouraged about job prospects that they still do not bother searching for work. Such "discouraged workers" tend to have less effect in bidding down wage growth than do active jobseekers. However, if these discouraged workers start to look for work in greater numbers, and if the female labour force participation rate resumes its past upward trend, the unemployment rate could stabilise at a level which would not put significant upward pressure on wage rates.

The number of long-term unemployed remains rather high for this stage of the recovery.[10] Some might argue that this should increase downward pressure on wages, because once unemployment insurance benefits lapse, the reservation wage of the unemployed should fall. Alternatively, others have suggested that the long-term unemployed tend to behave a lot like discouraged workers – and are part of the labour force in name only. If the long-term unemployed constrain overall wage growth less than the short-term unemployed (as in Layard and Nickell, 1986), the current difference between the aggregate unemployment rate and past estimates of the NAWRU may in this respect *understate* nascent wage pressures. This caveat turns out to be an important one. In the regression tests reported in the annex, the ratio of long-term to total unemployment was positively and significantly related to wage inflation.[11] Thus, when the proportion of long-term unemployed to overall unemployment is high, as in the first half of 1994, the effective NAWRU is also higher.

The job-vacancy rate, as measured by the Conference Board index of help-wanted ads, has risen significantly in recent months. However, by past standards it still remains at a rather low level relative to total employment. Medoff (1994) emphasises that today's unemployed have fewer job opportunities than did job-seekers prior to 1987. At that time, the Beveridge curve, which measures the relationship between job vacancies and the unemployment rate, began to shift inward (Diagram 6). Medoff suggests this is due in part to the trend toward

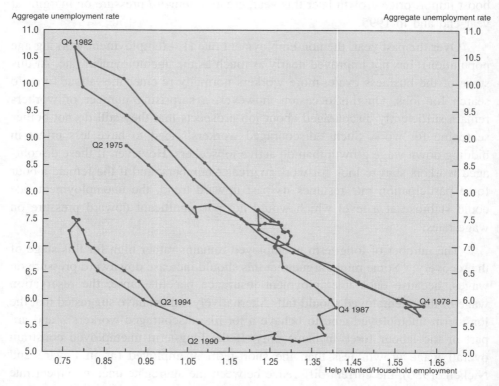

Diagram 6. **THE BEVERIDGE CURVE**
1975-1994

Aggregate unemployment rate

Aggregate unemployment rate

Help Wanted/Household employment

Note: The observations for 1994 have been shifted due to the new Current Population Survey as follows:
the unemployment rate has been reduced by 1/4 percentage point and the help-wanted ratio by 1.1 per cent.
Source: Bureau of Labor Statistics; The Conference Board.

downsizing by large U.S. corporations.[12] He argues that in light of today's low job-vacancy rate, wage inflation will not pick up despite the low unemployment rate. While the job-vacancy rate is more significant than the aggregate unemployment rate in explaining wage growth, this is not necessarily relevant, since even the job-vacancy rate is completely dominated by the prime-age male unemployment rate in empirical tests (see Annex I). The econometric tests reported below provide no support for the assertion that current low job-vacancy rates will hold down wage inflation over the next year or so.

Capacity utilisation rose a bit above historical norms during the fourth quarter of 1993, but manufacturers' deliveries from vendors[13] did not slow down much at all until the first quarter of 1994, and the pace of slowing did not become unusual until the second quarter – thus price mark-ups may be slower to increase than capacity utilisation might suggest (Diagram 7). This point is important, since manufacturing capacity utilisation is normally taken to be a good predictor of future changes in business price mark-ups.[14] In the past, mark-ups typically started to creep upward as this utilisation measure rose above its historical norm of 80 or 81 per cent. It is, thus, a bad omen for inflation that manufacturing capacity utilisation rose above 84 per cent during the summer of 1994. However, empirical tests reported in Annex I suggest that vendor performance has in the past been as reliable an indicator of future mark-ups as manufacturing capacity utilisation, both for the overall business sector and manufacturing in particular.

Diagram 7. **MANUFACTURING CAPACITY UTILISATION AND VENDOR PERFORMANCE**

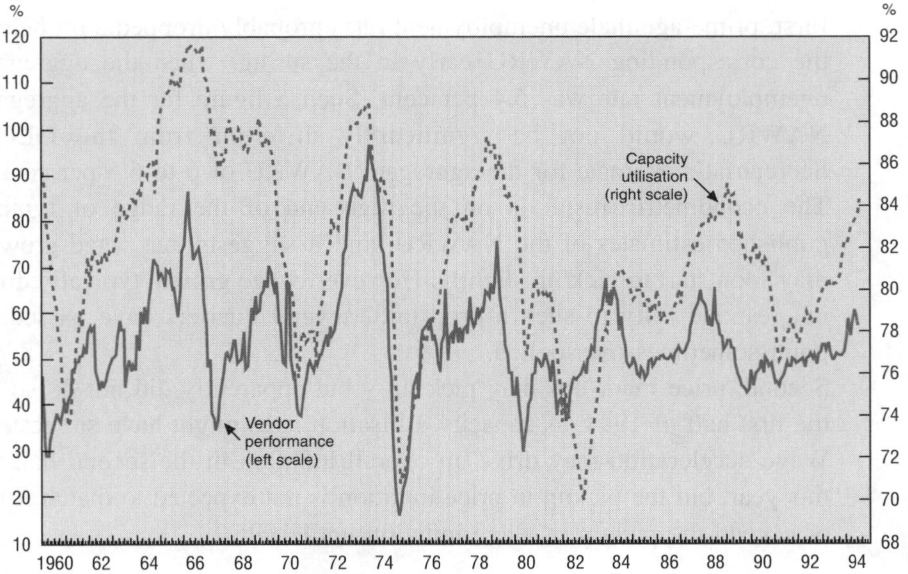

Note: Vendor performance is the percentage of respondents reporting slower deliveries from vendors.
Source: Federal Reserve Board; National Association of Purchasing Managers.

And in the past, mark-ups reacted to each of these indicators with a similar lag: mark-ups typically respond most strongly after one quarter or so to changes in either measure.

Growth of the money supply has been quite slow this year, both for M1 and M2, and M2 velocity has continued to rise rapidly. Prior to the 1990s, such a rise in velocity might have signalled lower inflationary pressures to come, as in the "P-star" model – and even now, a few economists still point to the high and rising velocity of money to suggest that monetary policy was already sufficiently restrictive before the 1994 increases in the Federal funds rate. Even in the heyday of the P-star model, however, its supporters would have admitted that the velocity gap *per se* was less important in predicting future inflation than the output gap.[15] And in recent years, the link between inflation and the velocity gap has been quite weak.[16] Thus, the Federal Reserve Board no longer relies heavily on velocity as a predictor of future inflation, and velocity is not an important factor in this Survey's projection for inflation.

Combining the results of all of the above-mentioned statistical tests yields two conclusions:

- First, prime-age male unemployment rates probably dropped a bit below the corresponding NAWRU early in the spring, when the aggregate unemployment rate was 6.4 per cent. Such a figure for the aggregate NAWRU would not be significantly different from the OECD Secretariat's estimate for the aggregate NAWRU of 6 to 6½ per cent.[17] The econometric result is on the high end of the range of typical published estimates of the NAWRU, and it suggests that wage growth may soon start to pick up slightly. However, wage growth typically does not respond fully to such a drop until several quarters have passed, a point sometimes overlooked.
- Second, price mark-ups may pick up – but apparently did not do so in the first half of 1994, as capacity utilisation rates might have suggested. Wage acceleration may drive up overall inflation in the second half of this year, but the pickup in price inflation is not expected to match fully or exceed the pickup in wage inflation until 1995.

II.   Macroeconomic and structural policies

Monetary tightening gets underway

Low interest rates were clearly the most important factor supporting the economic recovery in the early 1990s. Favourable financial conditions facilitated balance-sheet restructuring by firms, households and banks. Businesses issued substantial amounts of bonds and new equity[18] in order to pay down older, higher-cost debt and undertake productivity-enhancing investments, primarily in information technology. Households also reduced borrowing and refinanced outstanding mortgage and consumer loans and used the interest savings to increase spending on a variety of items, but especially on interest-sensitive durable goods and housing. As a result, indicators of financial stress among non-financial agents, such as loan-default rates and bankruptcy filings, improved significantly in 1993. And banks and other depository institutions strengthened their financial positions by exploiting the steepness of the yield curve to improve profitability and by issuing new equity and subordinated debt to boost capital ratios.[19] Their losses on collateral in the form of commercial real estate were also reduced by the flattening out in that market in many areas of the country. Most vestiges of the so-called "credit crunch" were eliminated, and the recovery of the financial system was substantially completed. Overall, the mission of monetary policy in the early 1990s – to guide the economy back to a growth path with full employment and low inflation by offsetting what Chairman Greenspan often referred to as the "headwinds" facing it – was largely accomplished by the end of 1993.

A move toward "neutrality"

Even though there was no evidence of any meaningful upward pressure on inflation, the Federal Reserve recognised that the longest period of stability in official interest rates since the Second World War had to come to an end. After

31

finding itself tempted to raise rates in the late spring and summer of 1993 (when a so-called "biased directive" was in effect), it decided against such a course of action, preferring to wait until trends became clearer. But the Federal Open Market Committee (FOMC) recognised that it could not afford to wait until inflationary tensions were clearly visible before withdrawing the stimulus provided by low rates. The case for not overstaying an accommodative stance was becoming clearer all the time: underlying output growth had accelerated far beyond the economy's potential rate, bringing the unemployment rate rapidly down toward levels which would begin to risk a pickup in wage inflation; commodity prices began to move upward quite sharply around the beginning of 1994; long-term interest rates stopped falling in October 1993 and started to rise, at first rather modestly, indicating a possible trend reversal in inflation expectations; financial markets started to show some signs of excessive leverage-based speculation; and some credit aggregates accelerated noticeably (see below).

The result was a series of decisions to tighten reserve conditions in order to raise the Federal funds rate. Rather than risk destabilising the markets with a sharp rise right off, it was decided to move gradually at the outset. Thus, the first three decisions (in February, March and April) led to ¹/₄ point rises in the funds rate; both the fourth (in May) and last (in August) boosted it ¹/₂ point and were combined with similar increases in the discount rate, the first in that symbolic rate since February 1989.[20] The Federal Reserve described its action as a "move toward a posture of policy neutrality – that is, a level of real short-term rates consistent with sustained economic growth at the economy's potential". Real short rates had indeed been very low by historical standards (Diagram 8), and it was only after the May increase to 4¹/₄ per cent that monetary accommodation was described as "substantially removed" and after the August rise that policy might possibly be described as slightly restrictive. However, while real short rates are a useful guide to assessing short-term monetary strategy, the equilibrium value of real short rates – whatever it is at any point in time – is consistent with any rate of inflation, and accordingly they cannot be relied upon as a target to achieve longer-term objectives of price stability.

The market's reaction

While the FOMC no doubt expected some rise in long-term interest rates in response to their policy change – long-term rates have tended to rise less than

Diagram 8. **REAL SHORT-TERM INTEREST RATES**

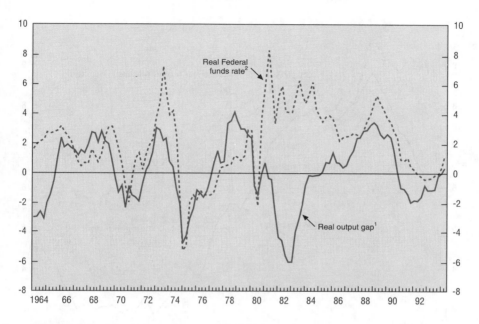

1. Defined as a deviation of actual from trend GDP as in Diagram 5.
2. Deflated using the change in the CPI excluding food and energy over the preceding four quarters.
Source: OECD.

half as much as short rates – the hope was that the reaction would be muted, drawing on the central bank's credibility. In the event, however, what transpired was one of the sharpest three-month declines in the bond market in history (Diagram 9).[21] Ten-year government note rates surged more than 1½ percentage points by early May (compared with a rise of only 1¼ percentage points in the Federal funds rate), bringing their total rise since the October 1993 trough to over 2 percentage points. Further upward pressure emerged in July. The response of the 30-year bond was only slightly more damped. Thus, instead of flattening as it has done most often in the first year of a tightening phase, the yield curve actually steepened, with the spread of two-year notes over three-month bills, for example, reaching its highest level since 1987.[22] Bond markets abroad also declined substantially.

33

Diagram 9. **SHORT AND LONG-TERM INTEREST RATES**

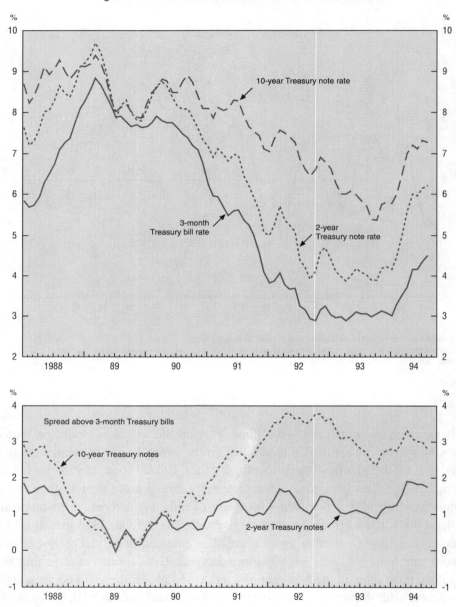

Source: Federal Reserve Board.

The reasons for such a bond-market reaction need elucidation. The most important factor was no doubt upward revisions to estimates of the momentum of underlying output growth in the United States.[23] Inseparable from this upward revision to growth prospects was the associated impact on the amount of spare capacity in labour and product markets and the resulting effect on expected inflation although survey data shows little evidence of any increase in such expectations. Real growth and especially the drop in unemployment have been at the top end or beyond the range of expectations of FOMC members[24] (Table 4). While Chairman Greenspan has called for the introduction of indexed bonds, in part in order to shed light on inflation expectations,[25] other countries have already developed markets for such securities; for the United Kingdom they show that real interest rates over a ten-year horizon rose about $1\frac{1}{2}$ percentage points over

Table 4. **Recent economic projections of FOMC members and other FRB Presidents**

Central tendencies

Date of projections	July 1992	February 1993	July 1993	Actual
	Projections for 1993[1]			
Nominal GDP	$5\frac{1}{2}$-$6\frac{1}{4}$	$5\frac{1}{2}$-6	5-$5\frac{3}{4}$	5.4
Real GDP	$2\frac{3}{4}$-3	3-$3\frac{1}{4}$	$2\frac{1}{4}$-$2\frac{3}{4}$	3.1
(implicit GDP deflator)	$2\frac{3}{4}$-$3\frac{1}{4}$	$2\frac{1}{2}$-$2\frac{3}{4}$	$2\frac{3}{4}$-3	2.2
Consumer price index	$2\frac{3}{4}$-$3\frac{1}{4}$	$2\frac{1}{2}$-$2\frac{3}{4}$	3-$3\frac{1}{4}$	2.7
Unemployment rate	$6\frac{1}{2}$-7	$6\frac{3}{4}$-7	$6\frac{3}{4}$	6.5

Date of projections	July 1993	February 1994	July 1994	Blue Chip Sept. 1994
	Projections for 1994[1]			
Nominal GDP	5-$6\frac{1}{2}$	$5\frac{1}{2}$-6	$5\frac{1}{2}$-6	6.0
Real GDP	$2\frac{1}{2}$-$3\frac{1}{4}$	3-$3\frac{1}{4}$	3-$3\frac{1}{4}$	3.0
(implicit GDP deflator)	$2\frac{1}{2}$-$3\frac{1}{4}$	$2\frac{1}{2}$-$2\frac{3}{4}$	$2\frac{1}{2}$-$2\frac{3}{4}$	2.9
Consumer price index	3-$3\frac{1}{2}$	3	$2\frac{3}{4}$-3	2.8
Unemployment rate[2]	$6\frac{1}{2}$-$6\frac{3}{4}$	$6\frac{1}{2}$-$6\frac{3}{4}$	6-$6\frac{1}{4}$	6.1

1. Percentage change, fourth quarter to fourth quarter, except for the unemployment rate which is in levels, also in the fourth quarter.
2. New basis as of February 1994 column. The difference is approximately +0.5 percentage points.
Source: Board of Governors of the Federal Reserve System, *Monetary Policy Report to the Congress*, and *Blue Chip Economic Indicators*, 10 September 1994.

the four months ending in June. If a similar increase took place in the United States, however, then there would be very little increase in nominal long-term rates which remains to be explained by higher inflation expectations.

Long rates probably also rose because of signs of recovery abroad, bringing about an expected global increase in the demand for capital: recovery in Europe and Japan seemed to be getting underway somewhat earlier and with greater vigour than had been generally expected. Heightened uncertainty of policy intentions world-wide may also have played a role, something which would also help explain the unusually high degree of international correlation of bond-market performance. One example of this was the failure of trade negotiations between the United States and Japan in February. Uncertainly also emanated from the impression that the U.S. authorities were willing to see the dollar decline (see below).[26] A further explanation lies in a correction of the probable overshooting of financial markets prior to the change (popularly described as a "bubble"). Many investors, sophisticated and unsophisticated alike, appear to have gained the mistaken impression that the returns on long-term assets such as bonds and equities were permanently high and that the variance in such returns would be lower than historical averages. Combined with low money-market and deposit rates, this false sense of security and certainty had led to a portfolio adjustment toward longer-maturity, riskier assets (especially in the form of bond and equity mutual funds which rose $281 billion in 1993). Part of this was undertaken in heavily leveraged form by so-called "hedge funds". When volatility returned, the shift was reversed, and funds flowed back into bank deposits and money-market mutual funds.[27]

Money and credit

For the most part, the monetary aggregates have continued to follow earlier trends until around April 1994. Narrow money (M1) growth remained strong through early April, as i) low money-market and deposit rates were not sufficiently attractive to entice agents to give up the liquidity advantages of transactions balances; ii) mortgage refinancings led to temporary flows through such balances; and iii) demand for currency from abroad is believed to have been robust. However, during the month of April such balances fell fairly sharply, probably in response to the drying up of mortgage refinancings. Since then modest growth has resumed. The part of M2 not included in M1 has stagnated since early 1993, leaving overall M2 growth steady below 2 per cent per year. Increases in M3 have been even more modest. While both have been just above the target ranges which the Fed is still required to fix (growth of 1 to 5 and 0 to 4 per cent, respectively for both 1993 and 1994), it is clear that little weight is being placed on them in setting monetary policy. Velocity of the broader aggregates has continued to increase rapidly, owing to the rise of short- and long-term market rates relative to sluggishly adjusting deposit rates. Bank have not pursued deposit funding aggressively, instead relying heavily on equity and subordinated debt to bolster their capital positions and support the loan growth they have experienced since the beginning of 1994.

Domestic non-Federal non-financial debt increased 3.9 per cent in 1993, up slightly from 3.3 per cent in 1992. This indicates continued private-sector deleveraging, given business sector value added growth of 5.9 per cent. This process may, however, be coming to an end in 1994. Commercial and industrial loans began to rise in January after steady declines in recent years; annualised growth has averaged about 10 per cent since then. In March the pace of loan increases quickened, and over the past few months annualised growth has been in the range of 15 per cent. Likewise, consumer credit rose 5³/₄ per cent during 1993 after three years of very slow growth, but by June 1994 the year-on-year growth rate was almost 13 per cent. Federal debt rose only 8.3 per cent in 1993, the lowest increase since 1989, bringing the increase in total domestic non-financial debt to 5.0 per cent, essentially the same rate as in 1992.

Recent pressures on the dollar

During 1993, the dollar followed a U-shaped pattern: it fell on an effective basis from early in the year until early June and then recovered thereafter, especially during the autumn, regaining its 1992-93 peak just after the turn of the year (Diagram 10). Thus far in 1994 it has been on a downward trend, having lost about 5 per cent of its value by September. However, it remains well above all of its local troughs during the 1990s; indeed it is still about 7 per cent above its lowest value as recently in the late summer of 1992. Many observers, however, tend to focus on the bilateral rates against the yen and the Deutschemark, and the dollar rate hit a record lows against the yen in June 1994. However, that combination alone gives an unduly pessimistic impression, as the dollar has risen sharply against a number of other currencies over the past two years, most

Diagram 10. **EXCHANGE VALUE OF THE DOLLAR**

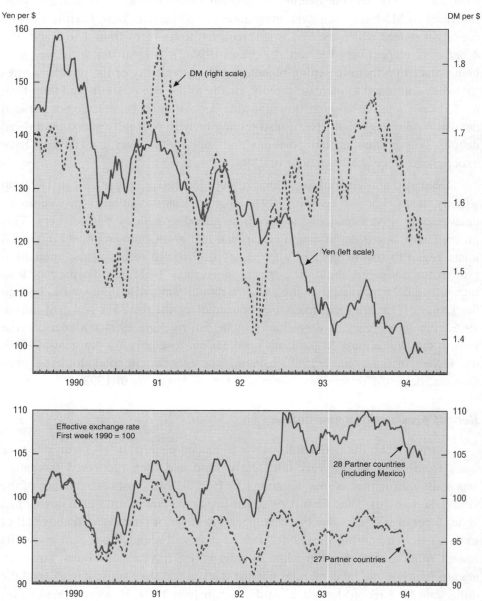

Source: OECD.

notably against its Canadian counterpart as well as the Mexican peso. Overall, the best description of the dollar's pattern on an effective basis over the last few years is that it has been trendless (at least once the peso is excluded over the period of high inflation in Mexico).

Nevertheless, the evolution of the dollar has been somewhat surprising, given the trend in interest differentials. Its failure to rise removes one channel for slowing the domestic economy and preventing a rise in inflation. Short spreads against the yen have moved up by about 2 percentage points over the past year; against the Deutschemark the narrowing has been about 3 points. At the long end the movements have admittedly been smaller. Monthly figures on the budget deficit have been much below expectations, and inflation outcomes have also been more moderate than most projections. Nevertheless, there seems to have been some erosion of market confidence. On the other hand, strength in the yen is attributable to the persistent Japanese external surplus. Most recently, faster-than-expected growth in Europe may have played a role. There are some who point to concerns that Federal Reserve action has, at times, lagged behind the need to counter a build-up of inflationary pressures and fears that long-term rates may move sharply higher, as they did in the late 1970s. Others cite the anxieties created by official policy toward the dollar. The perceived Administration policy to reduce the bilateral external deficit with Japan one way or another was translated by market participants into a possible threat to lower the dollar's value if the protracted bilateral trade discussions end in stalemate. This led to official denials and some effort by the authorities to limit the dollar's decline in May and again in June when 17 central banks engaged in concerted intervention, and the Treasury Secretary said clearly that the Administration "sees no advantage in an undervalued currency". But that did not eliminate the pressures in the market which persisted into the summer and resumed in September.

One factor influencing the value of the dollar may be the persistent external deficit. While the deficit has not regained the levels of the mid to late 1980s, especially when normalised as a share of GDP, its financing still requires a continuing increase in foreign holdings of U.S. assets. This requirement, coupled with recent developments in the pattern of capital flows (Table 5), has raised renewed concerns as to the sustainability of the U.S. external position. For example, direct investment flows have shifted from net inflows during much of

Table 5. **Balance of payments**

$ million, seasonally adjusted

	1992	1993	1994 S1
Current balance	–67 886	–103 896	–69 287
Long-term capital	–13 592	–52 693	2 530
of which:			
Direct investment	–31 116	–36 504	–16 701
Inward	9 888	21 366	15 868
Outward	–41 004	–57 870	–32 569
Portfolio	16 635	–18 067	17 900
Inward	61 718	102 435	55 000
Outward	–45 114	–119 983	–37 091
Official	920	1 360	1 332
Basic balance	–81 478	–156 588	–66 750
Non-monetary short-term capital	1 516	37 261	–4 660
of which:			
Private, net	18 624	16 166	13 400
Errors and omissions	–17 108	21 096	–18 057
Monetary short-term capital	37 775	50 690	73 875
Liabilities to foreign official monetary agencies	38 286	70 015	1 015
Change in reserves (+ = decrease)	3 901	–1 379	–3 478

Source: U.S. Department of Commerce, Bureau of Economic Analysis, and OECD.

the decade of the 1980s, to net outflows so far in the 1990s. At the same time, there has been a substantial decline in net inflows resulting from securities transactions, reflecting among other factors, an increased interest by U.S. investors in portfolio diversification and a reported reluctance of Japanese investors to add to dollar positions in light of past currency losses. The counterpart has been an increase in financing flows through official and banking channels. For some observers, these shifts in the pattern of financing flows has reinforced the more basic concern that the continuing build-up of net international indebtedness (which reached $556 billion dollars or 8½ per cent of GDP at the end of 1993[28]) to finance the persistent external deficit makes the U.S. economy increasingly vulnerable to changes in market perceptions.

Some progress in fiscal consolidation but persistent longer-term problems

The 1993 outcome

The fiscal year 1993 (ending 30 September) saw a Federal budgetary outcome which diverged significantly from what had been expected at the time the year's Budget was presented in early 1992. But the main reason was a $100 billion favourable surprise in outlays related to deposit insurance (see footnote 30 below). Excluding deposit insurance, the deficit of $255 billion was slightly higher than had been expected – about $4 billion according to the Administration (Table 6), $20 billion according to the Congressional Budget Office (CBO). The Administration primarily blames economic conditions for carving more off receipts ($24 billion) than off interest payments ($13 billion). While real growth was slightly stronger than projected, inflation was far lower, leaving a smaller tax base, with little impact on outlays. Emergency spending decisions also lifted the deficit by $7 billion, but other policy changes offset nearly $5 billion of this. And residual, officially named "technical" factors (mainly lower Medicaid spending) account for a saving of about $12 billion. The CBO attributes slightly less of the overrun to economic surprises ($9 billion) and more to policy changes broadly defined ($12 billion).

On a national-accounts basis (thereby excluding deposit insurance), the deficit was $4 billion less than expected by the Administration in the fiscal year: a smaller shortfall on receipts and a larger saving on interest payments compared with the budget decomposition provided above are the main factors. For the calendar year 1993 the latest estimates for the deficit show a decline of about $50 billion from 1992 to $241 billion (Table 7). Revenue growth accelerated from 4.4 to 7.4 per cent, once corrected for inflation the highest rate since 1987. Nominal expenditure growth slumped to 3.2 per cent – in real terms one of the lowest rates since 1960 – due to continuing defence cut-backs, a sizeable slowing in domestic transfer payments, an absolute declines in net interest payments and a modest rise in non-defence non-wage purchases. However, the growth of compensation per head, at 4.9 per cent, was much higher than private sector (3.7 per cent), as it had been in 1991 (see below).

The State and local government fiscal position showed another slight improvement in 1993. With little change in their surplus on social insurance

Table 6. **Comparison of 1993 Federal fiscal outcome with budget projection**

$ billion, fiscal year

	Policy changes	Economic conditions	Spending cap adjustments	Other	Total changes
A. Budget basis – allocation by cause					
Receipts					
Individual income tax	0.0	–13.5		4.1	–9.4
Corporation income tax	2.0	1.9		7.7	11.6
Social insurance taxes and contributions	–0.1	–9.8		–6.3	–16.2
Excise taxes	0.0	0.3		–0.3	0.1
Estate and gift taxes	0.0	0.0		–0.3	–0.3
Customs duties	–0.1	1.4		–0.5	0.8
Other	–0.1	–4.8		2.8	–2.1
Total	1.8	–24.4		7.1	–15.5
Outlays					
Discretionary	–8.8		7.4	1.1	–0.3
Defence	–8.4		2.0	2.0	–4.4
Non-defence	–0.4		5.4	–0.9	4.1
Mandatory	6.1	0.9		–107.1	–100.2
Deposit insurance				–103.7	–103.7
Other	6.1	0.9		–3.5	3.5
Net interest	–0.2	–12.7		–2.2	–15.1
Total	–2.9	–11.8	7.4	–108.2	–115.6
Deficit	–4.7	12.5	7.4	–115.3	–100.1
Excluding deposit insurance	–4.7	12.5	7.4	–11.6	3.6
B. National accounts basis					
Receipts					
Personal tax and non-tax receipts					–14.9
Corporate tax accruals					15.6
Indirect business tax and non-tax accruals					2.1
Social insurance contributions					–5.9
Total					–3.1
Expenditures					
Purchases					0.7
Defence					1.4
Non-defence					–0.7
Transfer payments					14.1
Domestic					13.9
Foreign					0.2
Grants-in-aid to State and local governments					–9.9
Net interest paid					–24.1
Subsidies less current surplus of government enterprises					–0.4
Total					–19.6
Deficit					–16.5

Source: Survey of Current Business, March 1992, and Budget of the United States Government; Analytical Perspectives Fiscal Year 1995.

Table 7. **Government receipts and expenditures, 1993**

National accounts basis, $ billion

	Federal		State and local		General government	
	Level	% change	Level	% change	Level	% change
Receipts	1 265.7	7.4	891.1	5.7	1 970.7	6.6
Personal tax and non-tax receipts	520.3	6.3	166.1	4.4	686.4	5.8
Corporate tax accruals	143.0	23.7	30.3	25.5	173.3	24.0
Indirect business tax and non-tax accruals	84.6	4.1	440.8	4.2	525.4	4.2
Social insurance contributions	517.8	5.3	67.8	5.2	585.6	5.3
Federal grants-in-aid			186.1	8.1		
Expenditures	1 507.1	3.2	864.7	5.7	2 185.6	3.7
Purchases	443.6	−1.2	704.7	4.2	1 148.4	2.1
of which:						
National defence	302.7	−3.7	0	−	302.7	−3.7
of which:						
Compensation	135.7	−0.1	0	−	135.7	−0.1
Other	167.0	−6.3	0	−	167.0	−6.3
Non-defence	140.9	4.5	704.7	4.2		
of which:						
Compensation	67.9	6.7	483.0	4.6	550.9	4.9
Other	73.0	2.6	221.7	3.3	294.7	3.1
Transfer payments (net)	658.0	5.2	250.4	9.3	908.4	6.3
of which:						
To persons	642.3	5.5	250.4	9.3	892.7	6.5
To rest of world (net)	15.7	−4.6	0	−	15.7	−4.6
Grants in aid to State and local governments	186.1	8.1				
Net interest paid	183.6	−1.7	−63.7	0.8	119.9	−3.0
Subsidies less current surplus of government enterprises	35.7	29.4	−26.8	11.3	9.0	151.0
Surplus/Deficit	−241.1	−14.6	26.3	6.2	−215.0	−16.6
of which:						
Social insurance funds	n.a.	n.a.	66.3	−0.2	n.a.	n.a.
Other	n.a.	n.a.	−40.0	−3.8	n.a.	n.a.

Source: U.S. Department of Commerce, *Survey of Current Business*, and OECD.

funds (primarily pension funds for their employees), their overall surplus edged up to $26 billion from $25 billion in 1992. However, this is a far cry from the outcomes of the mid-1980s which saw surpluses of around $55 billion. Led by transfer payments, spending increases have continued to be in excess of 3 per cent per year in real terms, about the same as real revenue gains, despite a pickup in the share of State and local expenditures accounted for by Federal grants-in-aid (inter-governmental transfers) from 19 to nearly 22 per cent in the 1990s.[29] The growth in transfer payments dropped below double-digit rates for the first time in five years but remained substantial. Much of this was in health care, a subject which is treated in greater depth in the next chapter. Personal tax cuts lowered tax receipts by $0.4 billion after a boost of $3.1 billion due to legislative changes in 1992 (Sullivan, 1994). Similarly, tax hikes added only $1.0 billion to sales tax revenues, after a corresponding rise of $4.0 billion in 1992. Overall, the general-government sector recorded a deficit of 3.4 per cent of GDP, down from the 1992 record of 4.3 per cent, but otherwise the highest since 1986. About one-third of the *change* in 1993 was caused by a narrowing of the output gap, but virtually all of the remaining deficit at the time could be regarded as structural. The Federal government was responsible for all of the structural improvement; indeed, the cyclically-adjusted budgetary position of the State and local governments deteriorated slightly after two years of improvement (Diagram 11).

Developments in 1994

1994 marks the first fiscal year which is completely governed by the terms of the Omnibus Budget Reconciliation Act of 1993 (OBRA93), described in detail in last year's Survey. Signed in August, this legislation was designed to cut some $500 billion from the baseline Federal budget deficit over the years to 1998, with approximately equal contributions from increased taxation and reduced spending. When OBRA93 was passed, Administration projections were for a fiscal deficit of $259 billion in FY 1994, but stronger-than-expected output growth and an improving outlook for deposit insurance[30] led to an initial downward revision to $235 billion. Even this would seem to be rather conservative: over the first eleven months of the fiscal year, the cumulated deficit was running $60 billion below last year's pace and $80 billion less if deposit insurance is excluded. Annualised revenue growth has been nearly 10 per cent, and outlays have been rising only at a $2\frac{1}{2}$ per cent pace. More recently, the Administration has predicted a figure around $220 billion as being more likely for the deficit, while the CBO has projected a figure around $200 billion. While at this point it is too early to assess whether or not receipts on the individual income tax have met official expectations, it is clear that outlay growth has been surprisingly weak. On a national-accounts basis, the Federal deficit in the fiscal year's first three quarters was running at an annual rate of $8 billion less than projected by the

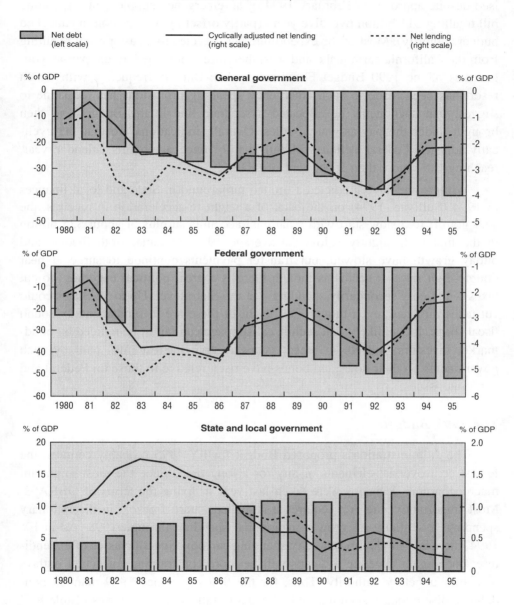

Diagram 11. **GOVERNMENT BUDGET BALANCE AND NET DEBT**
National-accounts basis, % of GDP

Net debt
(left scale)

Cyclically adjusted net lending
(right scale)

Net lending
(right scale)

General government

% of GDP

% of GDP

1980 81 82 83 84 85 86 87 88 89 90 91 92 93 94 95

Federal government

% of GDP

% of GDP

1980 81 82 83 84 85 86 87 88 89 90 91 92 93 94 95

State and local government

% of GDP

% of GDP

1980 81 82 83 84 85 86 87 88 89 90 91 92 93 94 95

Source: OECD.

Administration in its 1995 Budget documentation. This improvement was realised despite approval in February 1994 of an emergency supplemental spending bill totalling $11 billion over five years (partly offset by $3.3 billion in cancelled budget authority). Most of the expenditure was devoted to disaster relief resulting from the California earthquake and was, therefore, not subject to the pay-as-you-go rules of the 1990 Budget Enforcement Act. But the frequency with which resort has been made to such emergency spending provisions has led some to suggest that such items be allocated a separate line in the Budget and then brought under the pay-as-you-go rules. Overall, indications are that the cyclically-adjusted Federal deficit will fall sharply once again this calendar year, reaching little more than 2 per cent of GDP.

While some have predicted a limited turnaround in State and local finances in 1994 (Sullivan, 1994) on the back of a slight re-acceleration in receipts, the year got off to a slow start with a national-accounts surplus of about $25 billion in the first half, slightly below the average 1993 outcome. Both income and outlay growth have slowed, but transfer payments continue to surge at near double-digit rates. It seems as though there is a great political eagerness to cut taxes – and only secondarily spending – at the State level. Up to 18 States could cut taxes this year, even though only eight of these are in fundamentally sound fiscal shape. It is unlikely that such fiscal slippage can fail to be noticed by bond-market investors; indeed, in recent years average interest rates paid by such governments on their notes and bonds have risen relative to those on Federal and corporate issues.

The 1995 Budget

The Administration's proposed Budget for FY 1995 probably contains the fewest controversial elements of any for a long time, since the most important macroeconomic decisions were taken last year in fixing the terms of OBRA93. Most importantly, the Act requires a so-called "hard freeze" in discretionary spending: essentially no growth in nominal spending through 1998. As in FY 1994, there is a single discretionary spending cap covering all classes of expenditure; once again, meeting the caps will be more constraining for actual outlays than for budgetary authority. Thus, for the first time since 1969 planned non-defence discretionary spending would actually fall in nominal terms (Table 8),[31] bringing about a sharp slowdown in overall spending growth from estimated

Table 8. Federal outlays, receipts and deficit summary

$ billion, fiscal year

	1993	% change 1993-94	1994	1995	% change 1994-95	1996	1997	1998	1999	Average % change 1993-99
Outlays										
Discretionary	542.5	1.4	550.1	542.4	-1.4	543.9	544.3	548.1	554.4	0.4
Mandatory	666.9	9.5	730.4	762.9	4.4	814.9	881.4	945.0	1 020.5	7.3
Deposit insurance	-28.0	n.m.[1]	-3.3	-11.1	n.m.[1]	-11.3	-6.1	-4.9	-3.3	n.m.[1]
Other	694.9	5.6	733.7	774.0	5.5	826.1	887.5	949.9	1 023.8	6.7
Net interest	198.8	2.3	203.4	213.1	4.8	224.8	234.6	245.0	255.2	4.3
Total	1 408.2	5.4	1 484.0	1 518.3	2.3	1 583.5	1 660.3	1 738.2	1 830.2	4.5
Receipts	1 153.5	8.3	1 249.2	1 342.2	7.4	1 410.4	1 479.5	1 550.8	1 629.0	5.9
Deficit	254.7	-7.8	234.8	176.1	-25.0	173.1	180.8	187.4	201.2	-3.9
As per cent of GDP										
Outlays	22.4	–	22.3	21.6	–	21.3	21.2	21.0	20.9	–
Receipts	18.3	–	18.8	19.1	–	19.0	18.9	18.7	18.6	–
Deficit	4.0	–	3.5	2.5	–	2.3	2.3	2.3	2.3	–
With health-care reform										
Deficit	254.7	–	234.8	165.1	–	169.6	186.4	190.5	181.1	–
Deficit as per cent of GDP	4.0	–	3.5	2.4	–	2.3	2.4	2.3	2.1	–

1. Not meaningful.
Source: *Budget of the United States Government, Fiscal Year 1995*.

1994 outcomes to 2.3 per cent (1.8 per cent excluding deposit insurance); in volume terms spending would fall sligthly. Outlays are to be nearly $7 billion below current services estimates. With continuing buoyant revenue increases, the deficit is expected to fall sharply to about $176 billion (2.5 per cent of GDP, the lowest since 1979), down by a quarter from the then estimated 1994 outcome. Were the Administration's health-care proposals to be adopted, a further $11 billion in deficit reduction would be achieved in 1995 because of the early introduction of its tobacco tax component. But this would mark the absolute deficit trough for the decade; and the structural deficit would still be one of the largest in the years from 1956 to 1982 (CBO, 1994a).

In its budget resolution, the Congress accepted the broad outlines of the Administration's targets, providing $3.7 billion more in budget authority but $5.3 billion less in outlays. It also cut a further $13 billion from its spending estimates over the next five years, but less than $1 billion of that pertains to FY 1995, and the rest has no binding character. As with last year, it remains to be seen to what extent the Congress will approve the Administration's detailed proposals for new spending appropriations.[32] The President wishes to boost certain spending classified by the Administration as investment by a further 20 per cent (representing $15 billion) in FY 1995 (Table 9), in part by terminating 115 small spending programmes (saving $0.7 billion) and cutting budget authority for more than 300 others (saving $4.8 billion). Major cut-backs are planned in defence ($9 billion), while expenditures for unemployment insurance and agricultural subsidies are expected to fall by $4 billion each. Altogether, spending increases in 60 per cent of all programmatic budget accounts would be held below the rate of inflation. Besides the personnel cuts of 100 000 by 1995 and the 152 000 more called for by 1999 in the National Performance Review, described in the following chapter, the President has also signed an Executive Order to implement a series of cuts in administrative expenses cumulating to 14 per cent by 1997.

The Administration's budget proposals are based on a set of economic assumptions fixed in December 1993 and accordingly subject to risk. Even by the time of its presentation in February, the accompanying text recognised that the deficit projections were over $5 billion too high, as the annualised rate of real GDP growth in the first quarter of the fiscal year was about 3 percentage points greater and the increase in the GDP deflator was less than half the 3 per cent

Table 9. **Proposed Administration-identified investments in the Federal budget**

Budget authority, $ billion

	1993 Enacted	1994 Estimate	1995 Proposed	Change 1993-95		Change 1994-95	
				Dollars	Per cent	Dollars	Per cent
Economic security							
Infrastructure	19.8	22.7	24.0	4.1	21	1.3	6
Education and training	11.9	13.7	17.0	5.1	43	3.3	24
Technology	5.3	6.6	8.0	2.6	50	1.4	22
Environment	5.6	6.0	7.4	1.8	32	1.4	24
Other	11.3	13.4	16.9	5.6	49	3.5	26
Health security	11.7	12.8	14.1	2.3	20	1.3	10
Personal security	0.2	0.0	2.8	2.6	n.m. [1]	2.7	n.m. [1]
Total	65.9	75.2	90.1	24.2	37	14.9	20

1. Not meaningful.
Source: Budget of the United States Government, Fiscal Year 1995.

expected. But the prudence of the short-term assumptions for real activity are balanced by the risks of failing to achieve what amounts to a cycle-free medium-term scenario, with annual economic growth slowing smoothly to its assumed potential rate of 2½ per cent, inflation (as measured by the Consumer Price Index) rising gently to 3.4 per cent and real interest rates remaining extremely modest compared with the 1980s.[33] The unemployment rate in the spring of 1994 was already approaching levels expected for the late 1990s, and as a result both short- and long-term real interest rates are currently much higher than had been assumed. While the impact of this underprediction on the deficit will not be excessive this fiscal year, should it persist, as the OECD Secretariat expects, the extra spending burden will grow quite rapidly over time.

The Budget may also present an unduly favourable picture of spending and/ or deficit trends for a number of other reasons. First, a number of tax provisions are scheduled to expire before the end of the budget planning horizon in 1999 (most prominently the Research and Experimentation tax credit at the end of fiscal 1995), and doubtless there will be strong pressures to extend many or all of them, although such extensions would be subject to the Budget Enforcement Act's "pay-as-you-go" rules (that is they could not be extended unless offsetting savings could be found). The total cost involved would be $17 billion over the next five years. Second, a number of other items were not included in the Budget and will require financing. These include the pay-as-you-go offset to the loss of customs revenues following the GATT agreement (see below), the cost of the welfare-reform proposals presented this spring (see the next chapter) and the cost of the Superfund changes (discussed below). A large share if not all the savings expected from the National Performance Review is being used to finance a substantial increase in crime-related spending (about $30 billion over five years). Third, the official budget assumptions call for Federal pay rises averaging less than 2 per cent per year for the six years 1994 to 1999, a real decline of some 8 per cent. To the extent that such deep cuts are not realised in future annual appropriation rounds, other offsetting savings would have to be found. Further-more, these assumptions are not consistent with the current target calling for the present estimated 26 per cent pay gap between Federal non-defence employees and their private-sector counterparts to be eliminated over the next nine years. In order to reach that target pay rises would have to average about 5¼ per cent per year. Finally, there has been a tendency for longer-term budget deficit projections to be unduly optimistic in recent years. Auerbach (1994) has recently pointed out that official (CBO) deficit forecasts for fiscal 1994 done six years earlier imply a moderate surplus when account of intervening policy changes is taken. The "error" of some $260 billion is attributable to economic errors including under-prediction of real interest rates ($80 billion) and "technical" errors, that is higher health ($40 billion) and other spending ($75 billion, despite the "peace divi-dend") and revenue shortfalls ($65 billion). While this error is unusually large by recent standards, the pattern of excessive optimism is well established.

Some longer-term considerations

Despite the probable success of OBRA93 in preventing deterioration in the Federal deficit over the next few years, there remains cause for longer-term concern about the Federal fiscal position, independent of what may possibly result from any health-care reform. First and foremost, the United States remains at a serious disadvantage with respect to the rest of the world in terms of its lack of investment and especially saving, and there seems little prospect of the private sector providing much relief in this respect. There is, therefore, widespread agreement that the surest way to alleviate the shortage of saving is for the public deficit to be cut.[34] Also growing in popularity is the idea of an overhaul of the tax system to encourage saving and investment more directly by, for example, scrapping the corporate income tax in favour of a consumption-based tax.[35] On the spending side, deficit-reduction advocates call for better controls on entitlement spending. The Administration has proposed to reform health care, but has suggested little thus far on other entitlements other than to set up a bipartisan Entitlement Reform Commission which is due to report by year-end. The trustees of the Social Security system report that the retirement trust fund will probably become insolvent in 2029, seven years earlier than they estimated last year, and that the Medicare hospital trust fund will run out of money in 2001, despite the 1993 tax change removing the ceiling on the contributory wage base. The longer that action is delayed to deal with these solvency problems, the more draconian the solutions will have to be.

The Administration argues that its health-care reform would prevent renewed upward pressure on the deficit over the remainder of the decade. But, even if the Administration's health-care reform were approved, the CBO projects that the Federal deficit would reach a trough by about 1996 and rebound by more than a percentage point of GDP by 2004 (CBO, 1994a and 1994b). This implies upward pressure on the ratio of debt held by the public to GDP which would exceed 57 per cent by 2004; this is 5 percentage points above current figures, more than double early-1980s levels and the highest ratio since 1955 (see Diagram 11 above). After 2004 the picture gets even worse. Auerbach (1994) has argued that the primary deficit will widen by 3 to 6 percentage points of GDP from 2004 to 2030 and by about three-quarters of a percentage point more from 2030 to 2070 because of the impact of population ageing on social security outlays and of increasing public health-care spending. The result is that an immediate permanent reduction of 4 to 6 percentage points of GDP in the primary deficit would be required to prevent a rise in the deficit/GDP from 2004 to 2070. Otherwise, according to Auerbach, the debt/GDP ratio would rise to clearly unsustainable levels.

The worsening historical trend in Federal indebtedness has not been matched by asset acquisition: as best as can be estimated, real Federal investment outlays have been falling as a share of GDP since about 1986, with a particularly sharp decline in 1993-95 (Diagram 12), despite the increases in Administration-identified investments in the 1995 Budget. Even excluding defence-related investment outlays, spending has been much lower in relation to GDP since

Physical Investment (1 + 2 + 3)   Research and Development (4 + 5)   Other
Direct Federal (1 + 2)
  1. National Defence   4. National Defence   6. Education and training
  2. Nondefence   5. Nondefence
3. Grants

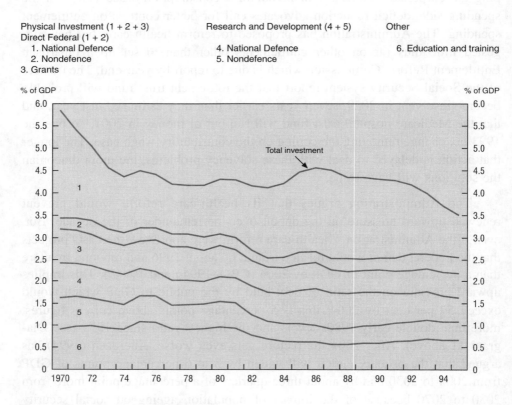

Source: Office of Management and Budget (1994).

1980 then it had been previously. This does not augur well for the Federal contribution to future economic growth. The United States also remains lowest in the OECD in central and total government investment as a share of GDP (Diagram 13). The decline in Federal investment is primarily a result of dwindling defence capital outlays, but even non-defence items are not growing very quickly, and Administration projections call for declining real Federal physical capital spending in the period 1993-99 (Office of Management and Budget, 1994), by no means all of which is the result of defence downsizing. This along

Diagram 13. **GOVERNMENT GROSS FIXED CAPITAL FORMATION**
1986-92 average[1]

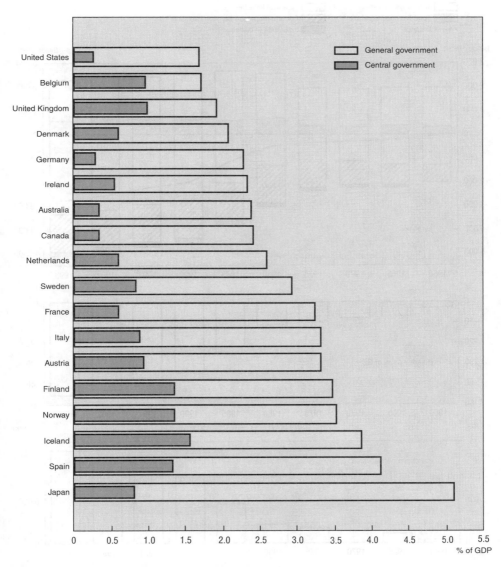

1. Except Ireland, Norway and Spain which are 1986-91 averages.
Source: OECD, *Annual National Accounts.*

Diagram 14. **THE FEDERAL GOVERNMENT BALANCE SHEET**
End fiscal year, in billions of 1993 dollars

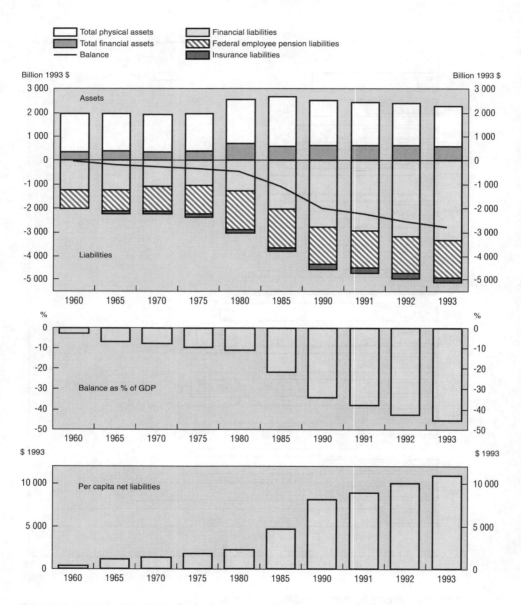

Source: *Budget of the United States Government, Analytical Perspectives; Fiscal Year 1995.*

54

with the declining value of Federal land and mineral rights, has meant that Federal gross assets have been falling slowly in real terms since the mid-1980s (Diagram 14), and net Federal liabilities have surged to over $10 000 per capita in 1993. This represents 5.6 per cent of national wealth, up from 0.4 per cent in 1960 and 1.3 per cent as recently as in 1980.

A "generational accounting" approach – as yet experimental and illustrative – points to the implications of present trends and policies over the long term. While OBRA93 significantly reduced the tax burden for future generations, and health-care reform might make further progress, unchanged policies imply a severe imbalance between the treatment of existing and future generations (Table 10). Although the following estimates rely on a variety of assumptions which together imply wide confidence intervals, it is indicative that, assuming a real annual discount rate of 6 per cent and a productivity growth rate of 0.75 per cent per year, lifetime net tax rates (the present value of taxes less transfers as a share of labour income) might climb from about 36 per cent for those born in 1992 without health-care reform (38 per cent with reform) to 82 per cent (67 per cent) for future generations (Office of Management and Budget, 1994). Further-

Table 10. **Lifetime net tax rates under a generational accounting approach**

In per cent

Generation's year of birth	Before OBRA93	After OBRA93	With health care reform	Health care reform but faster cost growth
1900	23.6	23.6	23.6	23.6
1910	27.2	27.2	27.2	27.2
1920	29.0	29.0	29.1	29.1
1930	30.5	30.6	30.9	30.9
1940	31.6	31.9	32.4	32.2
1950	32.8	33.2	34.0	33.5
1960	34.4	35.0	35.9	35.2
1970	35.7	36.5	37.6	36.6
1980	36.0	36.9	38.2	36.7
1990	35.5	36.5	38.3	36.2
1992	35.4	36.3	38.3	36.0
Future generations	93.7	82.0	66.5	75.2
Percentage point difference: Future generations and generation born in 1992	58.3	45.7	28.2	39.2

Source: Office of Management and Budget (1994).

more, much of the improvement resulting from health reform is attributable to slower cost growth in the sector, and, should it not be realised, tax rate reductions from reform for future generations would be correspondingly smaller.

Structural policies

The Clinton Administration continues its activist approach in a wide range of domains. The health reform is, of course, the most important such subject. Another major reform proposal is the reform of the welfare system, primarily the Aid to Families With Dependent Children (AFDC) programme. Making the Federal government run more efficiently is the goal of the National Performance Review. These three structural reforms are dealt with in detail in the following chapter. Here other structural policy changes will be briefly reviewed. The final chapter focuses on the education system including recent Federal initiatives in that area.

Responding to a steady increase in the share of U.S. employees who feel insecure about their jobs, the Administration introduced the *Re-employment Act of 1994* in March. It would consolidate and expand Federal job-training and retraining programmes[36] and make available income support to dislocated workers in need of long-term retraining (''re-employment insurance''). It would also reform the unemployment insurance system by encouraging States to use their unemployment funds imaginatively for training subsidies or as aid to small-business startups. It would, in addition, create ''one-stop career systems'' for access to employment, education and training information and services and establish a National Labour Market Information System. The total cost would be $13.1 billion for the next five years. Separately, the 10-member Federally-appointed Commission on the Future of Worker-Management Relations produced a preliminary report in May 1994 which called for greater worker involvement in running firms and easier union organising activities in order to reduce hostility in the workplace.

The *banking sector* has been the subject of several pieces of legislation. In one, the Administration proposed to consolidate banking supervision and regulation by merging all four regulators into a new Federal Banking Commission. However, the Federal Reserve Board resisted the loss of its regulatory responsibilities, arguing that all the efficiency benefits could be obtained by merging the

Office of Thrift Supervision and the Office of the Controller of the Currency, leaving the Fed to assume the responsibilities – other than the insurance function – of the Federal Deposit Insurance Corporation. A compromise was nearly reached that would have assigned to the Federal Reserve responsibility for supervision of bank holding companies owning large commercial banks or state member banks and for supervision of state member banks, and joint responsibility (with the new Commission) for supervising some large national banks. But, with insufficient time left on the legislative calendar in 1994, the Administration decided to withdraw the proposal in May. A second bill effectively allows interstate banking and branching. This was often rejected in the past, due to insurance company opposition, but this time the effort was successful. Although it will increase competition, the effect will not be radical, as out-of-state bank holding companies already account for about 30 per cent of commercial-bank assets.

The rapid growth of sophisticated financial instruments has raised questions about the adequacy of current financial regulation. Concern has focused on complex derivative securities, especially those that are traded over the counter rather than on organised exchanges. A report by the General Accounting Office of the Congress recommended that all currently-unregulated major over-the-counter dealers in derivatives be subject to Federal safety and soundness regulation. The intention is to safeguard the stability of the nation's financial markets and to protect the soundness of the securities firms and insurance companies which deal in them but are largely exempt from relevant regulation and capital requirements and thereby to prevent any call on taxpayers for a bailout in the event of a financial panic. Widely publicised losses by several large non-financial firms have pointed to a lack of understanding of the risks involved on the part of some corporate treasurers. But in October 1993 the Office of the Controller of the Currency issued guidelines to banks on the suitability of such products for corporate customers. And both the Administration and the Federal Reserve have gone on record opposing new regulation in this area. Such regulation might have the effect of shifting the market abroad to be handled by lightly regulated foreign firms. The challenge is to improve transparency and public disclosure of derivatives activities without reducing innovation. The Federal Reserve is already very active in strengthening its supervision and regulation of banks' involvement, and market forces may already have succeeded in restraining risk-taking by non-banks involved.

Regulatory reform was proposed for the *telecommunications industry*. Its main impacts would have been to allow the telephone and cable companies to compete with one another and to allow the regional telephone companies to provide long-distance service and to make telephone equipment. The relevant legislation passed the House of Representatives, but was unable to pass the Senate before the end of the session. This spring the Senate also approved an overhaul of the 1978 *Bankruptcy Code* which would deal with overloading of the system by streamlining administration and expediting the process.

In June 1994 the U.S. Supreme Court finally ruled on the earlier California law allowing *"unitary taxation"* – global formulary apportionment methods of taxing corporate profits. The Court ruled that such State taxation was not in violation of the U.S. Constitution. The main alternative approach is based on the arm's length principle. Draft OECD guidelines on how tax authorities should deal with such transfer pricing issues, as well as new U.S. Federal regulations, were issued in July. The U.S. regulations are generally consistent with the OECD draft which contains a strong condemnation of unitary taxation.

There have been quite a number of noteworthy developments on the *environmental front*. First, the market for air pollution rights in Southern California opened this year. Second, in September 1993 the Administration proposed a national action plan on greenhouse gas emissions which called for objectives to be met on a voluntary basis. Third, the overhaul of the 1872 mining law is now in conference, awaiting final Administration proposals on grazing fees and range-land management. The Senate version of the bill calls for a 2 per cent royalty net of production costs, while the House stipulates a 8 per cent gross royalty. The Administration had originally suggested a 12.5 per cent royalty but has proposed an 8 per cent rate in the 1995 Budget. Fourth, the re-authorisation of the 1974 Safe Drinking Water Act and Amendments are also before the Congress. The bills would establish a State drinking water revolving loan fund, provide initiatives for source water protection, establish technology-based standards appropriate for small water treatment systems and improve the process for select-ing contaminants for regulation. Fifth, the 1972 Water Pollution Control Act and its subsequent Amendments are also up for re-authorisation. The key objectives of the bill being considered in Congress are to reduce non-point source pollution through establishment of performance objectives, to slash unfunded mandates to states and localities in their provision of infrastructure for wastewater and stormwater control while setting cost-effective cleanup standards, and to establish more current and comprehensive water quality standards.

Another re-authorisation being debated in the Congress is that of the 1980 Comprehensive Environmental Response Compensation and Liability Act, the so-called "superfund" which deals with cleaning up toxic waste sites. The law requires "potentially responsible parties (PRPs)" to pay the full costs of clean-up even though their activities may have been legal at the time and even though there may be other polluters of the site who are out of business or have not been found. This "joint, several, and retroactive" standard has led to delay of cleanup and excessive litigation. Because firms have preferred to engage in lengthy litigation, 30 per cent of all costs have gone to legal fees. Only 56 of 1 345 identified priority sites have thus far been cleaned up, and new sites may push the number up to 4 500. The cost has already been some $13 billion and may amount to another $75 billion (or even $463 billion, depending on assumptions) over the next 75 years. The new law is designed to make polluters pay only their fair share of costs through a non-binding arbitration process that incorporates incentives for settling and disincentives for taking the case to court. The re-authorisation bills contain provisions for setting national risk goals, permitting the degree of cleanup to vary with the intended land use, and making cleanup costs a more important determinant of remedy selection. Further, the bills call for the establishment of a fund, paid for by the insurance industry, to compensate PRPs for their cleanup costs in return for an end to the host of lawsuits such firms have brought against their insurers.

In the area of *external trade*, NAFTA legislation was signed on 8 December 1993, but a number of serious trade disputes with Canada have erupted, most notably on grains. In August 1994 a preliminary settlement was reached in the dispute regarding Canadian wheat exports to the United States. The agreement involves import restrictions for a year, but NAFTA-consistent policies thereafter, including the setting up of a Commission to examine wheat-trading issues. Other trade disputes, often pertaining to anti-dumping or countervailing duty findings and decisions, involve steel imported from a variety of countries, textile imports from China and synthetic fibre and colour film paper from Europe; the 1986 semiconductor deal with Japan still caused frictions over the latter's failure to attain a market share for total imports of 20 per cent during the first three quarters of 1993, but the 20 per cent threshold has been attained more recently.

The GATT agreement signed this spring in Morocco brings intellectual property rights and trade in services and farm commodities into the GATT purview for the first time, cuts tariffs on 85 per cent of world trade over a five- to ten-year horizon, phases out the Multi-Fiber Arrangement over 10 years and establishes a new World Trade Organisation. It also includes an agreement reached at the last minute between the European Union and the United States opening up their public procurement to each other. Congressional approval of the GATT agreement by the United States will be complicated by the fact that the customs duty loss of some $12 billion over five years must be recouped under budgetary pay-as-you-go requirements. An initial attempt to supplement the legislation with additional "fast-track" authority had to be abandoned for lack of support.

President Clinton renewed for two years the so-called "Super 301" section of the 1988 Trade Act by executive order in March 1994. Since then, Japan has cited for its trade policy in a preliminary report called the National Trade Estimate and in July trade-sanction proceedings were launched in response to alleged discrimination against U.S. telecommunication and medical equipment producers, but a final determination under the clause will only be made in September. Most recently, China and Japan were cited for lack of respect for intellectual property and closed public procurement markets, respectively. It is unclear to what extent the GATT agreement would limit the U.S. ability to resort to this and other trade remedies. The U.S. Administration believes that it would not do so at all: for example, in June it released a report saying that food imports could still be refused as unsafe even if they met lower international standards. Also controversial in the agreement is the clause allowing 75 per cent of research costs and 50 per cent of development costs to escape new rules restricting industrial subsidies. The Administration has also proposed a reform of export licensing procedures and an easing of controls on computers. In addition, it has been much more aggressive in getting involved in individual business deals such as telecommunications equipment and aircraft sales to Saudi Arabia. The latter sector is to benefit as well from a $1.5 billion research contract from NASA to develop a High Speed Civil Transport (a supersonic aircraft).

The U.S. relationship with Japan continues to evolve. Japan's voluntary export restraints on automobiles, first instituted in 1981, expired at the end of March 1994. It will be recalled that a Framework Agreement between the two countries was reached in July 1993. Since then, little in the way of concrete progress has been achieved on the trade front, despite talks which began in earnest in September 1993.[37] Those talks broke down in February 1994, leading to the threatened imposition of "Super 301". They were restarted in May in order to bridge the gap in divergent views of how to measure improvement in market access. In that context, the American side points to the need for "quantitative criteria" in order to assure measurable progress towards the goal of improved market access, while the Japanese side is concerned lest this imply the establishment of *de facto* numerical targets or a commitment to certain results in the future, which could lead to managed trade. In June Framework discussions were restarted in the areas of banking and other financial services and intellectual property rights, in addition to the priority areas automobiles and auto parts, government procurement of medical technology and telecommunications products and insurance. Over the summer an agreement was reached in the area of patents: for its part the United States agreed to extend patent terms to 20 years from the date of application as compared with 17 years from the date of grant; to ease the process of protesting the granting of a patent; and to make patent applications open for public inspection 18 months after submission.

A so-called *National Competitiveness Act* is also being debated in the Congress. Its latest version provides $1.9 billion for forging closer ties between the government and industry. A venture capital provision provides $100 million for government participation of up to five years duration in joint ventures where the grant recipients pay at least half of all costs. Nearly $600 million of the total would go to flat-panel displays, a test case for the new, more activist technology policy. In a related matter, rather than expiring by 1997, subsidies paid to the owners of 80 shipping vessels of about $3 million per year each would be extended at a moderately reduced rate under the latest proposals; the National Performance Review had recommended that they be slashed. The 1995 Budget also calls for a cut in farm subsidies of 30 per cent ($3.6 billion), in line with GATT provisions.

III.   Selected structural reforms

National Performance Review

Introduction

Over the past year and a half, the Administration has begun an ambitious project intended to reform government operations, lower government's cost and increase its effectiveness. The first step in this effort was last year's report issued by the National Performance Review (NPR), following a six-month effort to diagnose the weaknesses of government operating procedures and recommend improvements (Gore, 1993). The report noted a variety of shortcomings of the Federal government: red tape, neglect of the needs of "customers", lack of employee accountability and empowerment, and excess cost. The report made nearly 400 recommendations for action to address these problems. Most of the recommendations were directed at the heads of various government agencies; a number were directed at the President, who has issued 22 directives to begin their phased implementation (National Performance Review, 1994). About one-third of the recommendations required Congressional action; most of those recommendations are currently included in various pieces of legislation wending their way through Congress.

If all of the NPR recommendations were implemented, the savings could be significant over the coming five years – the NPR report estimates a total improvement of $108 billion (Table 11).[38] Nearly three-quarters of this improvement reflects cuts in programmes of Federal agencies and a 13 per cent reduction in Federal civilian employment (excluding the postal service). The remainder comes from procurement reform, improved information technology, and reductions in cost of administering grants to state and local governments.[39] The promise of these additional savings may have swayed some conservatives toward supporting OBRA93, but it would be incorrect to view the NPR reforms mainly as a vehicle for further cost cutting and deficit reduction. Vice-President Gore emphasised

Table 11. **Administration estimates for budget savings from the NPR reforms**

Aggregate savings for fiscal years 1995-1999, $ billion

Reforms and cuts to individual federal agencies	36.4
Streamlining the bureaucracy through re-engineering (primarily a cut of 252 000 in the federal workforce)	40.4
Procurement reform (assuming 5 per cent annual saving in procurement costs)	22.5
Improved information technology	5.4
Intergovernmental efficiency gains (from offering fee-for-service option in lieu of existing administrative costs)	3.3
Total projected savings	108.0

Source: Gore (1993), p. iii.

this point: "The National Performance Review can reduce the deficit further, but it is not just about cutting spending ... {It} is about change ... in the way the government works." (Gore, 1993, p.i) Key NPR reforms are designed to improve the quality of government services – though the gains will often be difficult to measure in dollars and cents.

The most important of the NPR recommendations are described in the rest of this section. The great majority of the reforms appear worthwhile, and some are likely to improve noticeably the efficiency of government operations. But many of these reforms have been attempted by earlier administrations without success.[40] Nagging questions remain: will political pressure prevent legislative passage of the most important recommendations, and will the nature of the Federal government itself prevent some of the reforms from yielding major efficiency improvements? To answer this requires more than a description of proposed changes: one must understand why the government's problems have arisen. Many Federal performance problems are traceable to very basic issues, including:

- the difficulty of measuring government performance;
- short-termism; and
- the disproportionate influence of special-interest groups.

The rest of this section examines how these factors have given rise to many of the problems pointed out by the NPR, and how they bear on the likely fate of NPR reforms.

The difficulty of measuring government performance

It is harder to measure government success (improvements in citizens' well-being) than business success (higher profits). This obvious statement lies at the root of several problems addressed by the NPR – notably the relative lack of financial accountability of Federal employees compared with private employees. If civil servants' incentives were in general targeted solely at their measurable output, important unmeasurable goals could suffer (Tirole, 1994). Partly for this reason, compensation of government employees has traditionally not been closely tied to measured output. Since pay is not closely tied to performance, and procedures for firing are extremely drawn-out, Federal employees often have little incentive to achieve public policy goals – especially those employees whose output is difficult to measure.[41] This has increased the appeal of monitoring and regulation of Federal employee behaviour as a means of implementing Congress' will, to the point where micromanagement and over-regulation sometimes cripple initiative and sharply increase procurement costs (Gore, 1993). Thus, the NPR outlines a systematic programme to deregulate personnel management – reforming recruitment, hiring, classification and promotion. At the start of 1994, the Administration replaced the 10 000-page Federal Personnel Manual with a much slimmed-down set of personnel management rules, decentralising hiring decisions and drastically simplifying the Federal job-classification system. But the overall success of these and other management reforms discussed in the NPR will depend critically on measuring performance more extensively, rewarding good performers and giving managers sufficient flexibility to accomplish their tasks effectively.

Financial incentives can be very powerful tools, and they clearly could play a greater role for the many Federal agencies and employees whose performance is essentially fully measurable. But the ability to measure performance is an obvious prerequisite to such a pay-for-performance scheme. Thus, Congress and the President have taken steps to state formally the goals and measure the output of agencies and employees. In August 1993, the President signed the Government Performance and Results Act requiring agencies to:

– prepare annual performance plans with specific goals;
– prepare annual reports comparing performance with targets; and
– give managers more flexibility and discretion in achieving goals, with easier waivers from regulation.[42]

For its first three years, this programme will affect agencies which employ about one-fifth of all Federal workers – typically agencies for which goals and outcomes are easiest to define.[43] A greater challenge will come in 1997, when the law mandates an extension of this performance planning to all Federal agencies. For many of them, switching from input measurement to performance management will be a non-trivial problem. It is thus difficult to judge the likely overall effectiveness of the Federal government's switch to performance measurement, although the past experience of other government bodies may give some indication. For the State governments, results have been mixed, but some states (Florida and Oregon, for example) claim major improvements from the change (CBO, 1993c). The jury is still out regarding performance budgeting in other industrialised countries (CBO, 1993c and Schick, 1990).

Short-termism

The structure of the U.S. political system, like that of many other OECD countries, can give rise to an excessively short-term policy focus – for the most basic and obvious reasons. Members of Congress and first-term Presidents usually seek to be re-elected: similarly, political appointees typically aim for reappointment in the President's second term. Re-election depends primarily on economic and social conditions up to the time of the election, since it can be quite difficult for a voter to see the link between politicians' actions and the voter's *future* well-being. This leads many politicians to focus on the short-term effects of their actions, sometimes at the expense of constituents' long-term welfare.[44] The classic example is the difficulty in controlling government deficits, since the near-term employment and income gains from overspending are typically much more obvious than the long-term problems created when government purchases eventually "crowd out" private spending or cause debt to balloon relative to national income. Such "short-termism" is also at the root of several problems addressed in the NPR, as described below.

Efforts to make large-scale efficiency improvements in government typically take several years and can involve significant upheaval; they therefore tend to have low pay-off in terms of improved chances for re-election or re-appointment. Budgeting reforms were attempted under Presidents Johnson and Carter, but they ultimately failed – in large part from lack of wholehearted support from Congress and the Federal bureaucracy (CBO, 1993c).[45] For similar reasons, medium-term planning has typically been assigned very low priority in previous administrations. More recently, voter discontent with government inefficiency has become severe: the NPR cites a survey showing that four people out of five do not trust the government to do what is right most of the time. This discontent increases the pressure on Congress to act on the proposed reforms. Even if all the NPR proposals were passed this year, however, some of the reforms would not be fully operative until the next century (Gore, 1993). The lag between legislation and improved efficiency means that appearances count for a lot; bills skirting the more important but difficult reforms may be just as effective in achieving re-election as bills containing all the NPR's proposed reforms. For example, Congress had no trouble last year requiring agencies to carry out strategic medium-term planning – but fundamental procedural reforms needed to counter micromanagement and pork-barrel politics[46] lie buried in committee.

Micromanagement and the disproportionate influence of special interests

Most of those serving in Congress work hard to serve their constituents and the country as a whole – many have given up higher-paying jobs in the private sector. Occasionally, however, incentives exist for those in Congress to engage in behaviour that greatly benefits small groups of constituents but has small adverse effects on much larger numbers. Such pork-barrel politics is often associated with "log-rolling" (vote-trading) and earmarking funds for special purposes within broader pieces of legislation. The NPR pointed out that such earmarks hamper government agencies that seek to manage programmes efficiently (Gore, 1993):[47] log-rolling and earmarks may tend to reduce the country's overall welfare for other reasons, as well.[48] The NPR report thus urged Congress to keep earmarks to a minimum, but unfortunately it could offer no incentive to members of Congress to forego such micromanagement. This lack of incentive may eventually kill two legislative proposals which offer great promise in reducing the extent of earmarks. First, in 1993 the House passed a bill allowing the President to require a second vote on any line item in a bill which passes Congress – without vetoing the entire bill. This "enhanced rescission power" has the potential to reduce significantly Congress' ability to engage in pork-barrel politics.[49] However, the bill would reduce the political power of the Senate Appropriations Committee, whose Chairman opposes the bill and has indefinitely postponed its consideration.[50] A second bill was introduced in the House in early 1994, with the endorsement of over half of its members. This bill would allow seven days each year during which any House member could propose reduced spending on any programme and demand a roll-call vote. However, procedural delays on this bill are quite possible, given the loss of power it would entail for Congressional leadership.

Outdated programmes and overstaffing

A great deal of Federal spending is wasted each year on obsolete pro- grammes: projects that have already achieved their goals, or projects no longer needed because circumstances have changed since they were first authorised. These programmes are sometimes re-authorised even though they serve a much smaller constituency than they did originally: it is very hard to eliminate a programme that still benefits a few people a great deal, even if it no longer serves society as a whole. The NPR thus urges Congress to incorporate sunset clauses into legislation to a much greater extent. It also recommends ending outdated programmes that are still on the books. Many programmes of the Agriculture Department fit this description: the NPR cited the example of subsidies to wool and honey producers, which were finally terminated in fiscal 1994. The number of active farmers has declined dramatically in recent decades, to the point where many Agriculture Department field offices serve only a few farmers. Thus, the NPR proposed closing 1 200 of these offices, with substantial cost savings. In fact, most of the Department's planned staff reduction of 7 500 comes from the field offices: the rest from merging the Department's 43 agencies to about 30 and paring the bloated layers of middle management. Members of Congress from the agricultural states fought some of the reductions, but the Administration deflected much of their opposition when it chose to omit from the final draft of the NPR its preliminary recommendation to cut back on crop support payments.[51] The NPR's recommendations for the Department appeared in the Agriculture Department Reorganisation Bill, which will probably be passed in the near future (Table 12).

Outmoded programmes and administrative structures exist in a variety of Federal agencies. The NPR points out that Federal agencies' management struc- tures are very heavily layered, like the bureaucratic structure of many large U.S. corporations 20 years ago – in sharp contrast with today's ''re-engineered'' firms with flatter hierarchies. This vertical structure has allowed Federal agencies to

Table 12. **Status of key reform legislation**

Legislation	Status
Government streamlining	Passed House 11/93, in Senate Committee since 10/93.
Procurement reform	Passed House and Senate and signed 9/94.
Enhanced rescission authority	Passed House 4/93, in Senate Committee for over a year.
Federal worker buyouts	Passed both houses of Congress and signed 3/94.
Agriculture Department reorganisation	Passed Senate 4/94, approved by House Agriculture Committee 6/94.
Congressional reorganisation	Elements passed House and Senate Committees by 8/94.
FY 1995 budget (restructuring is built into most agency budget allocations)	Passed both houses of Congress and signed by 9/94.

Source: Congressional *Quarterly*, various issues.

reward good performers, in spite of inflexible pay structures – by promoting them more frequently. However, this has sometimes put high-performing technical employees in management jobs for which they are less suited and has created overstaffing at the middle-management level. Part of the solution is to increase the ability of managers to reward performance, as noted above. That NPR recommendation is part of the Federal Workforce Restructuring Act, passed in March 1994. Given this reform in compensation policy, major cuts in middle management staffing are proposed by the NPR and incorporated in the bill. Overall, the bill mandates a cut of 279 000 Federal employees over the next few years, 109 000 more than in the FY 1994 budget. The bill anticipates payroll savings of \$32.5 billion over 5 years. It also incorporates a variety of other spending cuts and efficiency improvements listed in the NPR: additional savings of \$4.6 billion are expected from these provisions.

The workforce cuts proposed in the Federal Workforce Restructuring Act are large, amounting to about 12 per cent of overall Federal employment (excluding the postal service). The cuts are especially large in departments like Defence, Agriculture and Housing and Urban Development. Reductions of this size cannot be achieved in five years solely via attrition and a hiring freeze: a limited number of layoffs are occurring in some agencies, with accompanying morale problems for both departing and remaining staff. Accordingly, the Administration proposed a programme to allow agencies to "buy out" Federal employees, with cash payments for many of those who leave government service voluntarily. The proposal was held up for a while in Congress, but was finally included in the Federal Workforce Restructuring Act.[52] One possible drawback, though, of buyout programmes like this one is "adverse selection": the government, like many downsizing corporations, may discover that the most productive workers (relative to their salary[53]) are often the first to accept buyouts. This factor may offset some of the productivity benefits of better employee morale resulting from the buyout programme.

Procurement reform

Government contracting and procurement procedures have been shaped by some of the same fundamental problems that affect personnel management, to wit:

- it is difficult for the government to cover every possible contingency in contracts for large government purchases;
- it is difficult for Congress to tell whether government managers have properly balanced cost against benefits of alternative bids; and
- it is difficult for Congress to tell whether cost overruns by contractors were unavoidable or the result of lapses by the contractor.

These uncertainties (more precisely, incomplete contracting and moral hazard) give rise to the potential for mismanagement and/or corruption, as has been painfully demonstrated over the years. Thus, Congress and the executive branch have developed elaborate monitoring and procedural rules to limit occasional graft or embarrassing cost overruns. However, such detailed control has its own drawbacks: slowing procurement, increasing contractor costs and prices paid by the government, and reducing Federal employees' incentives to minimise costs. Gains from regulation and monitoring occur when purchases are large relative to monitoring costs, and no private market exists to provide price and quality standards. In many other cases, however, "we're spending millions to save thousands", as one member of the Senate Armed Services Committee put it (Towell, 1994). Overhead costs absorb about 40 per cent of the Pentagon's acquisition budget compared with 15 per cent of a typical commercial company's (Towell, 1994). The NPR gives a variety of examples of procurement fiascos, to demonstrate that monitoring and procedural rules are now so detailed that costs of control often far exceed the gains. Thus, the NPR proposed removal of almost all restrictions on government purchases under $2 500, simplification of procurement procedures for purchases under $100 000 (under current law, the threshold is $25 000) and similar simplification for purchases of "commercial" products. The Government Procurement Reform Bill contains these elements and also limits earmarks for small and minority business in subcontracting.[54] The bill has passed the congress and is likely to be enacted, resulting in substantial cost savings; however, with reduced regulation and monitoring a small increase in cost overruns and/or graft is quite possible. The large overall cost savings from this reform may be much less visible to the press and the public than the occasional lapse. This might force Congress to reimpose greater regulatory control on procurement in the future.

Congressional reform

A variety of other reforms are built into the 1995 Budget and many smaller pieces of legislation. These reforms deal with less fundamental issues than those discussed above, by and large, but one exception is the Congressional Reorganisation Bill. This bill, though not part of the NPR legislation, would make several important procedural reforms. First, it would slim down Congress' bloated committee structure, thereby limiting jurisdictional battles and reducing conflicting demands on members' time. Another attractive change, so far found only in the House version of the bill, would require that committee earmarks not be melded in overall committee reports, but made public and explicit: perhaps increased visibility will limit any lapses into pork-barrel politics. Finally, the bill establishes a two-year budget and appropriation cycle. This was also proposed by the NPR, on grounds that biennial budgeting saves time for both Congress and the executive branch, and reduces the inefficiencies and oversights which result from the annual end-of-year scramble to meet the budget deadline. A joint Congressional committee studied the issue and likewise favoured a two-year cycle. Others have agreed that biennial budgeting is a good idea, and likewise multi-year spending authorisations – but not multi-year appropriations (Mann and Ornstein, 1994). The existing annual appropriations process may offer a useful opportunity for Congressional oversight and adjustment to changing circumstances. Thus, the procedural reforms should not forego annual appropriations decisions, but rather constrain these decisions within a medium-term budgeting strategy. The point is probably moot, however, since senior members in both houses of Congress oppose any change at all in the current timing of budgeting and appropriations.[55] While biennial budgeting faces tough going in Congress, most reforms suggested by the NPR *are* being implemented, and they offer significant potential for improving the efficiency of the Federal government.

Progress in health-care reform

Two years ago the Committee devoted the structural chapter of its annual survey of the United States to the problems associated with the U.S. health-care system (OECD, 1992*a* and 1992*b*). Briefly, they can be summarised under the headings of inefficiency and inequity. *Prima facie* evidence that the system is inefficient can be found in comparing the extraordinarily high level of expenditure with a relatively modest set of health-outcome indicators, although the system provides a fairly high average level of patient satisfaction, at least to those who can afford to pay. Even correcting for relative income levels, outlays are extraordinarily high by international standards. This is because of a high level of administrative costs,[56] significant incentives to supply and demand unnecessary or inappropriate care,[57] an unusually strong tendency to resort to expensive technology, a particularly violent social context[58] and unusually high relative prices of health care. As elsewhere, costs are boosted by the lack of effective price competition due to the preponderance of third-party payment[59] and the resulting weakness of incentives for consumers to seek and consider information regarding price and quality. Furthermore, with the impetus of rising real incomes, an ageing population, and the influence of what is known as "Baumol's Syndrome" (trend declines in productivity levels relative to economy-wide averages due to the nature of the activity), spending has been increasing steadily relative to GDP, reaching 14 per cent of GDP in 1992. Projections indicate that the trend is likely to persist – with the share rising to 20 per cent in 2004 – without thoroughgoing institutional reform.[60] Indeed, if expenditures continue to increase robustly and if real GDP growth is as low as some – such as the CBO – project, then health-care could represent over three-quarters of all per capita spending increases in the decade ending 1998, up from 10, 11, 20 and 27 per cent in the previous four decades (Steuerle, 1994). The political constituency for cost reduction is rather weak, however, since most Americans are happy with the quality of

71

the services they receive, have strong concerns about "rationing" that may result from attempts to reduce costs and tend to think that their employer pays for their health insurance (see below).

The distribution of provision of health-care services to the non-elderly is highly uneven: about 15 per cent of the population (representing around 38 million individuals) is not covered by health insurance, and they receive only about half as much care as others,[61] while a further share, estimated as anywhere from 8 to 20 per cent, is inadequately covered. Medicaid, the public health-insurance plan for the poor, covers less than half of those whose incomes are below the official poverty line. But two out of every three uncovered people do not belong to families with sub-poverty-line incomes. In 1987 some 77 per cent were workers (or their dependents),[62] mostly employed in small firms[63] which do not offer health insurance to their employees partly because of the high premiums they face, resulting either from burdensome administrative costs or from risk-based insurance-industry pricing practices. In order to mitigate the effects of adverse selection, insurers resort to experience rating and what is known as "cherry picking", that is attempts to eliminate the worst actuarial risks, those who in fact need insurance the most. Larger employers often self-insure mainly in order to avoid premium taxes, benefit provisions mandated by States and marketing-related administrative costs.

But the U.S. health-care system also generates other insidious economic and social effects. Apparently a substantial degree of insecurity is felt by many insured Americans who are concerned with increases in the employee's share of total health-care cost as well as reduced provider choice and fear that a loss of their job means a life without insurance coverage and, with one serious illness, a destruction of life savings (before they become eligible for Medicaid). Polls indicate that the average respondent would be willing to pay $227 per year more in tax to guarantee him- or herself health insurance coverage and a further $169 per year to ensure universal coverage. In addition, employer-provided health care implies the risk that workers will not depart from jobs providing coverage for those without such benefits, even if the total compensation package is attractive, for fear of not being able to purchase reasonably-priced insurance directly. This phenomenon is known as "job lock" and has recently been shown to have reduced the voluntary turnover rate of the relevant population from 16 to 12 per cent per year (Madrian, 1993).[64]

Finally, reform of the health-care system is also called for because of the implications of present spending trends for both Federal and State finances. Outlays as a share of Federal government revenues have already increased from 3½ per cent in 1965 to 20 per cent in 1991, and as a share of State and local revenues from 8 to 21 per cent over the same period. Even under the Administration proposal, the Federal share would exceed 27 per cent of revenues by the year 2000. Furthermore, about $53 billion (0.8 per cent of GDP) in revenues were lost due to favourable Federal income tax treatment of health-care expenditures in 1993.

Against this background the Administration set to work a massive team of experts early in its tenure in order to derive a complete overhaul of the system. The result was the proposed Health Security Act (HSA), presented in the autumn of 1993. The draft legislation covers around 1 300 pages, and its main features are discussed in an annex. The overriding trait of the plan (to be phased in by 1998) would be to provide universal coverage for a standard package of benefits through a system combining an employer mandate to pay for insurance and so-called "alliances" which amount to non-profit insurance-purchasing broker/co-operatives. Insurance companies would be required to adopt risk rating based on the average risk of the local population (so-called "community rating") rather than the current practice based on the estimated risk of the individual ("experience rating"). Cost containment would be achieved through insurers putting increased pressure on providers to practise cost-conscious medicine. But, should this be insufficient, ceilings would be imposed on premiums growth on an alliance-specific basis. Guaranteeing coverage to all would alleviate insecurity, solve the problem of job-lock, improve the health and raise the labour-market participation of the uninsured, ease the welfare caseload, and eliminate free-riding by those who know that in an emergency they can always receive uncompensated care. Since the currently uninsured are generally younger, already receive some treatment, compensated or otherwise, and often wait too long with health problems before seeking what turns out to be more expensive emergency-room care, their coverage will boost national health expenditures less than a *pro rata* calculation would indicate: the Administration projects an increase of about 2 to 3 per cent (CBO, 1994b). The impact of any systemic reform such as the HSA on overall health-care spending is extremely difficult to assess and estimated figures should be taken with large margins of error. The

Administration's estimates are for the saving of some $\frac{1}{2}$ per cent of GDP by the year 2000, whereas the CBO reckons that the HSA would boost spending in the phase-in period and savings would only begin in the year 2000.

The Administration's proposal served as a useful starting point for the legislative process. The five committees of the Congress (three on the House side and two on the Senate side) which have jurisdiction over health-care reform then set to work putting together independent reform packages. None adopted the Administration proposal in its entirety. There were initially two main alternative plans which have been put forward by members of the Congress. The most popular was probably the Cooper-Breaux plan for a Managed Competition Act (MCA). Like the HSA, it would set up what amount to regional alliances, but participation would not be mandatory, and employers would not be required to purchase insurance for their employees. Insurance reforms would move toward community rating, and most exclusions on account of pre-existing conditions would be disallowed. But universal coverage would not be achieved; according to the Congressional Budget Office (1994b) nearly $\frac{2}{3}$ of the currently uninsured (or about 9 per cent of the population) would still lack coverage, although they would account for only a very small share of spending. Another plan which has been considered is the Chafee plan. Its alliances would not be regional monopsonies and like the MCA, they would be voluntary. Universal coverage would be achieved by an individual mandate that all Americans must have health insurance by 2005. Another plan with some support is the McDermott-Conyers plan, called the American Health Security Act (AHSA). It is a single-payer plan, patterned after the Canadian system. According to the CBO, its adoption would boost Federal outlays by over $500 billion per year by 1998 (albeit with large reductions in private outlays), despite global budgets and provider fee schedules, and national health savings would begin around the year 2000. As time went by, it became clear that the HSA did not have sufficient Congressional support for passage. Other efforts to mold a compromise plan have been undertaken. At the time of finalising this Survey, there are four alternative plans (see Annex III). Two of these – the House Leadership plan (HLP hereafter) and Senate Leadership plan (SLP) – are modified versions of the HSA and make the formation of alliances voluntary. They differ from the Administration's plan and from each other in terms of coverage (SLP aims at covering 95 per cent of population by 2000), financing (HLP relies more on savings in Medicare and Medicaid) and cost containment (SLP would introduce a tax on high-cost plan's premium, whereas HLP would put a limit on reimbursement). The proponents of the MCA and the Chafee plan have formed a single group to propose the Chafee-Breaux plan which resembles the original MCA. The fourth, the Republican Leadership plan, relies more heavily on private insurance markets to extend the health coverage. Under this plan, subsidies would be provided to the poorest to purchase insurance. The Congress is expected to resume discussion of health-care reform in 1995.

"Welfare reform": efforts to modify the AFDC programme

The social safety net in the United States is widely acknowledged to be less extensive than in most other OECD countries. Policy-makers and the public alike have, however, taken an increasingly critical view of U.S. "welfare" programmes, defined more narrowly by Americans than by Europeans to exclude broad-based entitlements and include only means-tested programmes, particularly the best-known one, Aid to Families with Dependent Children (AFDC). Support for welfare as it was originally conceived (see below) has eroded as social attitudes (views on the value of work, taxes and transfers) have changed, costs have risen dramatically (at least in the 1960s and 1970s), skill-upgrading efforts have been underfunded and at most modestly successful, and opinions have spread that the availability of welfare may have spawned a culture of dependency and contributed to the breakdown of the nuclear family. Despite successful cost containment in recent years, the political attempts to change the system have not abated: correctly or not, many Americans view welfare as largely providing almost indefinite support to non-aged, able-bodied, non-working individuals. During his election campaign, President Clinton promised "to end welfare as we know it", and, subsequent to the election an interdepartmental group in the Administration was charged with developing a reform bill – the Work and Responsibility Act (WRA) of 1994 – which was sent to the Congress late this spring and, if enacted, would take effect on 1 October 1995.

An overview

In the United States, assistance to the needy (in the form of both cash and in-kind transfers) is provided in order to achieve two objectives which may be competing (at least in the short run) and which receive different emphasis, depending on political philosophy – the alleviation of poverty and the promotion of self-sufficiency. Ideally, policies should be designed to meet these objectives in a least-cost fashion. By international standards a large and rising share of transfers is made in-kind. Some in-kind transfers are non-categorical, such as housing assistance and the Food Stamps programme, while others are directed at a target group, usually children, such as Head Start; Women, Infants and Children; the National School Lunch programme; and the public health insurance plan for the poor, Medicaid.[65] But the focus for welfare reform efforts is AFDC, the programme which has provided cash benefits to needy, single-parent families since the Social Security Act of 1935 (childless adults get no Federal benefits and little in the way of State assistance). The remainder of this section will deal exclusively with AFDC.

Viewed from abroad, AFDC would be a means-tested social assistance supplement to family allowances (which do not exist in the United States). Its original intent was to ensure that the children of single parents, then largely widows, would be protected from destitution. To a large extent that objective still holds, even if important changes in single parenthood have occurred in the interim. The single-parent population represents about one-quarter of all families with children and about half for blacks, some of the highest figures in the OECD, and a significant share are at or near the poverty line.[66] With a lack of adequate and affordable child care as well as other barriers to self-sufficiency, such parents experience severe difficulties due to their dual responsibilities as child-rearers and providers.

The size of this entitlement programme grew modestly in its initial decades. But it ballooned in the decade beginning in the mid-1960s. The ''caseload'' – the number of recipients – tripled, boosted by substantial increases in real monthly benefits per family through the 1960s, liberalisation of eligibility rules (in particular, the advent of the ''unemployed father'' benefit in 1961) increases in divorce and out-of-wedlock births and greater take-up of benefits by the pool of eligibles.[67] But there has been little further expansion in inflation-adjusted terms since then (Table 13), and the costs of AFDC, which had risen from 0.2 per cent of GDP in 1964 to 0.6 per cent in 1975, have since fallen back to below 0.4 per cent. An increase in the caseload in recent years (possibly related to diminished job prospects for the unskilled along with continuing increases in the illegitimacy rate) has been contained by legislative restrictions on eligibility (in 1981) and, in

Table 13. **Welfare at a glance** [1]

$ billion

	1970	1975	1980	1985	1990	1993	1998 [2]
Benefits paid	4.1	8.2	11.5	14.6	18.5	22.3	26.4
in $ 1993	15.5	22.6	20.7	19.6	20.7	22.3	23.1
Federal share (in per cent)	53.6	56.7	55.9	53.6	54.7	55.1	54.9
Administrative costs	0.8	1.1	1.5	1.8	2.7	3.0	3.3
in $ 1993	2.9	3.0	2.7	2.4	3.0	3.0	2.9
Federal share (in per cent)	75.5	51.0	50.7	50.0	51.0	51.4	50.5
Share of sum of benefits paid plus							
administrative costs	15.7	11.7	11.4	10.9	12.6	11.7	11.1
Average monthly numbers (in millions)							
Families	1.9	3.3	3.6	3.7	4.0	5.0	5.2
Recipients	7.4	11.1	10.6	10.8	11.5	14.1	14.7
Children	5.5	7.8	7.2	7.2	7.8	9.5	9.9
Child recipients as per cent of child							
population	8.8	11.8	11.5	11.3	12.3	13.9 [3]	n.a.
Child recipients as per cent of children							
in poverty	58.5	71.6	63.2	54.4	59.0	63.1 [3]	n.a.
Average monthly benefits per family	178	208	269	329	389	373	425
in $ 1993	676	576	483	443	434	373	374
Share of benefits paid under AFDC-							
unemployed parent programme							
(in per cent)	5.7	4.4	6.0	10.7	8.0	9.5 [3]	8.4

1. Aid to Families with Dependent Children (AFDC).
2. Administration projection.
3. 1992.
Source: OECD Secretariat calculations based on U.S. House of Representatives, Committee on Ways and Means (1994), *Overview of Entitlement Programs (1994 Green Book),* Washington, D.C.

any case, fully offset by a continuing, steady reduction in the real value of the average monthly benefit per family, given a lack of any systematic indexation.[68]

The costs of the programme are split by formula with the States, each of which sets its own maximum level of monthly benefits for each family size. In 1993 this maximum varied across states by a factor of around seven, as did the ratio of total AFDC expenditures to gross state product in 1990.[69] In the median state (in terms of generosity) AFDC was worth around 39 per cent of the Federal poverty line, with Food Stamps the equivalent of a further 31 per cent. The Federal share has been a fairly constant 55 per cent of benefit payments (100 per cent for Food Stamps) and is fixed at 50 per cent of administrative costs. These administrative costs represent about 11 per cent of the spending associated with the programme but range from less than 5 per cent in some states to well over a quarter in others. Currently, about 13 per cent of all children receive AFDC benefits, up from less than 9 per cent in 1970; but they represent only 60 per cent of all children in families with incomes below the Federal poverty line, barely more than in 1970. In 1990 nearly 45 per cent of all families with children under 18 maintained solely by the mother had incomes below the poverty threshold (U.S. House of Representatives, 1994). Benefits are reduced for income earned beyond certain minimal threshold levels. The benefit reduction rate (the rate by which AFDC payments are reduced for a marginal increase in other income), which is equivalent to a marginal tax rate, has been switched back and forth between $^2/_3$ and 1; since 1982, it has been effectively one. This implies that recipients will be better off leaving the programme only if their other income is greater than the level of the benefit to which they are entitled – a rather obvious work disincentive.

Impact on work incentives

Critics of AFDC have pointed to the negative effects which they believe it has produced. The principal risk of means-tested programmes of this type is that they can dull work incentives if benefit levels are not set so low as to enforce paid employment even at a wage which may not meet longer-term subsistence requirements. In the case of AFDC, the most serious work disincentive is probably the loss of Medicaid eligibility once AFDC eligibility is lost,[70] indicating that implementation of the Administration's health-care reform would contribute to enhancing work incentives.

Historically, few AFDC recipients have simultaneously combined welfare and work: because of their limited educational attainment, a lack of support services and prohibitive programme rates, there has never been more than 18 per cent of all female heads of household receiving AFDC benefits who work, and over the past decade the share has remained close to 6 per cent. By way of comparison, about 89 per cent of female heads of household with dependent children who do not receive AFDC benefits were employed in 1987, a much greater proportion than any other group of women, despite their child-care responsibilities.[71] Even for the group of all lone mothers in poverty, whether or not in receipt of AFDC, employment propensities are higher than those of AFDC recipients. However, it is quite common for women to cycle back and forth between welfare and work – about half of all spells end when the recipient enters the labour market (Pavetti, 1993). A cursory examination of the aggregate national data leads one to believe that the labour supply of potential AFDC beneficiaries (and other generally low-skilled groups) is not very sensitive to unemployment rates, real wages or AFDC parameters: there appears at first sight to be little direct behavioural association between employment rates and either benefit levels or reduction rates for female heads of household (Moffitt, 1992).[72]

Nevertheless, a fairly substantial literature has shown quite clearly that the AFDC programme entails important work disincentives at the margin (Moffitt, 1992): the midpoint of the existing range of estimates implies on a reduction of 30 per cent in work effort by recipients, although the reduction in the real value of the maximum benefit in recent decades has almost certainly mitigated this effect.[73] As a result, for each dollar transferred, an estimated $0.37 has been lost in the form of reduced earnings. Accordingly, the programme must transfer an average of almost $1.60 to the average recipient for each dollar increase in his/ her income.[74] However, very little of this reduced work effort is accounted for by otherwise-ineligible recipients who lower their labour supply sufficiently to qualify for AFDC (Moffitt, 1983); the bulk is attributable to those whose hypothesised supply in a counter factual simulation representing the absence of AFDC would still be so limited as to leave them in a situation of poverty.

Welfare dependency

Another possible negative effect of AFDC is long-term welfare dependency. Rather than acting as a short-term source of assistance allowing the poor to become self-sufficient again, critics contend that many recipients come to view welfare as a permanent way of life, with spells of exceedingly long duration. The best known studies of AFDC spell durations are those of Ellwood (1986) and Bane and Ellwood (1994). They show that the majority of recipients stay on the welfare rolls for short periods of time. Long-term continuous receipt is rare – 70 per cent of recipients leave within two years and 85 per cent within four years, in many cases when recipients enter the labour force. However, the true situation is more disturbing:[75] there is a significant tendency for recidivism, as those leaving the programme often return for additional spells; 45 per cent return within the first year, two-thirds within three years and more than three-quarters by the end of seven years (Pavetti, 1993). Calculating the total time recipients are likely to spend on AFDC in a 25-year period, they find that nearly one-quarter of all new recipients spend over 10 years in the programme. Furthermore, some 57 per cent of all recipients at a given point in time would be in the midst of a 25-year period during which over 10 would be spent on AFDC.

A related question is whether or not there is evidence of what is called "negative duration dependence": does the probability of exit from AFDC decline with the length of the spell? The literature demonstrates that it does, at least beyond the first few months. This helps explain why there is a long right-hand tail in the distribution of spells by duration. The reasons cited for negative duration dependence include many of those appearing in the unemployment literature: a deterioration in human capital; the demotivation generated by "the dole"; the negative signal to potential employers provided by AFDC receipt; and unobserved heterogeneity in the pool of recipients (those who have greater potential leave more quickly). Exits also appear to be negatively related to the level of the benefit. Furthermore, it should be noted that more exits have been attributable to a change in marital status than to improved economic conditions: less than a fifth are due to increased earnings, and two-thirds of those return to AFDC within five years.

Another potential channel of welfare dependency is inter-generational. Many studies have attempted to discern whether the probability of a woman being on welfare is related to welfare receipt by her mother in earlier years. Such an outcome could be explained either by a reduction in the stigma associated with welfare for such women or a lower level of information costs about the programme. It could alternatively be an indirect result of effects of AFDC receipt on family income or human capital investment through a negative influence on aspirations, for example. The available literature does show some support for the hypothesis of a positive inter-generational effect, but the case for causality is not proven, as there has not been adequate control for the inter-generational transmission of poverty. But it would appear to be the case that daughters of parents who are eligible for AFDC and do in fact receive it are significantly more likely to have an early birth and then receive AFDC than those of eligible parents who do not actually receive AFDC (Gottschalk, 1990).[76]

Effects on illegitimacy, the family and social behaviour

But without doubt the most controversial charge levelled against the U.S. welfare system is that it has contributed to the breakdown of traditional family structures and promotes irresponsible behaviour (Murray, 1993 and 1994).[77] Indeed, given a declining participation rate of eligible women in AFDC over the past two decades, the AFDC caseload has risen primarily as a result of increases in the number and rate of female-headed families. It is, therefore, clear that the possible deleterious effects of welfare on marital status (by delaying marriage and remarriage and by boosting rates of separation and divorce) and on illegitimacy (births out of wedlock) are crucial in assessing the validity of this charge. While the empirical tests for the presence of such effects in the 1970s and early 1980s were inconclusive, there has been a trend toward greater consistency in finding positive coefficients over the past decade (Moffitt, 1992). But the estimated effects are quantitatively rather small and insufficient to explain the sharp increases in female headship and especially in illegitimacy that have occurred in recent decades.[78]

Nevertheless, Murray argues, first, that many of the social restraints on illegitimacy and the stigma associated with it have eroded as out-of-wedlock births have become more common; and, second, that the availability of welfare enables (in a financial sense) poor single women to have babies, that is, it assures them of enough income to look after a baby by themselves if they have to.[79] He explains the continuing rise in illegitimacy over time, despite the flattening out in the real value of the welfare package, by a sort of threshold effect in conjunction with declining social stigma. He also examines the influence of welfare on illegitimacy among blacks in particular.[80] With the enormous decline in the propensity of prime-age black women to be married (beginning in the late 1960s and related to the deteriorating employment prospects of black male youths as well as a greater tendency to cohabit), the number of illegitimate births per thousand black women aged 15-44 rose steadily from 33 in 1960 to 60 in 1990, even as the birth rate for unmarried black women declined. Controlling for the size and density of states' black populations in addition to other factors, Murray finds a significant relationship between states' illegitimacy outcomes for blacks and the generosity of their welfare systems two years earlier. However, this research is extremely controversial and has been challenged by other experts.

Recent and prospective reforms

The welfare reform movement had its first major success with the passage of the Work Incentive (WIN) programme in 1967. It provided the first embodiment of a "reciprocal obligation" for welfare recipients, but failed to make much progress in going beyond the transfer aspect of welfare due to the meagre funding for training and job-search efforts (Gueron, 1990). The Omnibus Budget Reconciliation Act of 1981 allowed the States more flexibility in designing their own programmes to meet certain Federal guidelines but cut the amount of Federal resources available. The Family Support Act of 1988 made a more substantial effort to transform AFDC from a means-tested entitlement to a comprehensive scheme to alleviate the short-term problems of poverty. It stipulated that recipients must engage in job search or education/training or risk losing some of their benefits.

The Administration's proposed welfare-reform package (WRA) has four inter-related goals. First, it seeks to make work more rewarding than welfare by sharpening work incentives, thereby breaking the circle of welfare dependency and mitigating pressures on the family. There are two primary and several other means by which this is to be accomplished. Under the terms of OBRA93 the refundable Earned Income Tax Credit is being significantly expanded at a budgetary cost of some $4 billion per year, bringing its total cost to $22 billion in 1995. This credit is expected to be taken by some 13 million taxpayers that year and to help bring 1.4 million of them over the poverty line (Table 14). As pointed out in last year's Survey, however, the added work incentives for the very poor come at the cost of higher marginal effective tax rates and therefore reduced work incentives for those in the phase-out range of the credit.[81] And there is a risk of a further increase in fraudulent EITC refund claims (based on money said to be earned but in fact fictitious). In addition, the universal health-care coverage promised by the Administration in its reform proposal (see above) will serve to reduce work disincentives, since one of the main factors inhibiting AFDC exit has been the loss of Medicaid coverage. The Council of Economic Advisers (1994) cites estimates that up to one-quarter of AFDC recipients would take a job if health insurance coverage equivalent to that provided by Medicaid were available to them. WRA includes outlays provisionally estimated at $2.7 billion over five years for child care for those in mandatory training programmes. It had also been intended to offer subsidised day care to the working poor, but this proposal has been scaled back substantially for budgetary reasons. There is a risk that this will be insufficient to prevent a new perverse incentive to stay on welfare. WRA also includes a small programme to combat teen pregnancy and allows States the options of limiting benefit increases when a welfare recipient has more children.

Table 14. **The impact of the Earned-Income Tax Credit on after-tax incomes**

Dollars

Hourly wage	Earnings (full-time, year-round)	Taxes	EITC [1]	Food stamps	Total after-tax income	Per cent of poverty line
4.25 [2]	8 840	676	3 370	2 256	13 790	116
6.00	12 480	955	3 058	1 380	15 964	134
8.00	16 640	1 826	2 182	0	16 996	143

1. Assumes that expansion passed in 1993 is fully phased-in.
2. The current value of the minimum wage.
Source: "Work and Responsibility Act of 1994: Detailed Summary".

In addition, States would have the option of easing eligibility requirements for two-parent families.

The caseload is to be reduced and the taxpayer burden alleviated by a second objective, stricter enforcement of child-support (in AFDC and non-AFDC cases alike). Only about 38 per cent of AFDC recipients receives any child support (and the overwhelming majority is only partial), even though some 52 per cent have court-ordered awards. However, even if child-support reform managed to reduce programme costs, the literature indicates that it would probably have very small effects on the caseload and might even reduce the overall labour supply of all female heads. In any case, efforts in this direction have been growing since the passage of the Child Support Enforcement Program (part of the Social Security Act) in 1975. Federal and State enforcement expenditures were already nearly $2 billion in 1992. They have succeeded in establishing an average of nearly a million support obligations per year (more than double 1980 levels) and in bringing about collection of $8 billion in child support in 1992, of which over $2 billion represents payments to AFDC recipients (which, therefore, reduced AFDC outlays by over 11 per cent[82]). Recent official projections call for a 50 per cent increase in such AFDC collections over the five years to 1998, in line with the gradual implementation of recently enacted reforms.[83]

The third aim is to provide beneficiaries (or at least new entrants) with education and training in order to improve their chances of finding employment and getting off welfare (as pointed out above, to this point most exits from AFDC have occurred as a result of a change in marital status rather than for economic reasons). This is closely related to the fourth and final piece of the Administration plan: for those born after 1971, a time limit of two years during which an initial job-search is obligatory and then such human capital investment must be undertaken before a minimum-wage, Federally subsidised job (in the WORK programme) is required for recipients to continue receiving any support.[84] These proposals appear to be popular for moral rather than economic reasons. Workfare already exists for about 1 per cent of all recipients but has not been very successful in either reducing the caseload or boosting the future earnings and employment probabilities of participants. The number of recipients who are likely to hit the two-year limit on eligibility is in serious dispute, with estimates ranging from 10 to 45 per cent of the flow. The Administration estimates WORK will have under 400 000 participants in the year 2000, but others project twice as many. The two-year limit and associated welfare and training requirements will apply only to those born since 1972 in order to limit programme costs. Thus, about one-third of the caseload in 1997 and two-thirds in 2004 would be subject to the new rules.

The principal stumbling blocks to these last two objectives (more education and training in exchange for greater individual responsibility), however, are both fundamental and financial.[85] The 1988 Family Support Act, through the associated Job Opportunities and Basic Skills (JOBS) training programme, already called for increased efforts to upgrade the human capital of welfare recipients but then failed to establish a financial framework with sufficient incentives for States to carry out that plan (although those at school or in training jumped from 2.2 per cent of all recipients in 1988 to 11.2 per cent in 1991).[86] Experience has tended to show that most such efforts yield at best only modest returns in the form of higher wages or lower probabilities of unemployment unless the investment is substantial, long-lasting and therefore costly, especially compared with earlier education.[87] Given the pay-as-you-go requirements of the 1990 Budget Enforcement Act, in conjunction with an evident desire to avoid new taxes, proposed new spending under the WRA is rather modest in size, at a total cost estimated by the Administration to be $9.3 billion over five years, of which $2.8 billion for education, training and job placement assistance.[88] While the availability of high-quality training programmes may itself raise the attractiveness and, therefore, boost the caseload of AFDC, in general such training programmes do result in a reduction in government transfers, but often not of a sufficient magnitude to offset the full costs of their implementation. But their modest scale, both currently and under the Administration plan, means that they will have only a secondary role in slimming the AFDC caseload and eliminating poverty among female heads and their children.

IV. Education in the United States

Background

The publication in 1983 of *A Nation at Risk* – a sombre analysis of U.S. educational achievement and of its consequences for the ongoing prosperity of the nation – moved discussion of the performance of the educational system to the centre of policy debate. After a decade of school reform – involving experimentation on a local or state level with nearly every conceivable aspect of education management – the issue continues to occupy a prominent place on the national agenda. In early 1994, the Federal government enacted two major pieces of legislation relating to primary and secondary education and to school-to-work transition. The ongoing debate and policy interest has been spurred by a number of concerns.

First, a higher standard of performance relative to international academic achievement norms has been deemed necessary if U.S. industry and the U.S. workforce are to remain competitive in the world economy. The United States currently enjoys the highest productivity levels and the highest average standard of living in the world. These outcomes are probably in large part due to its flexible labour markets and competitive product markets. They would also seem to indicate that, in some sense, the institutions charged with human capital accumulation are fairly effective or at least not unduly ineffective. Indeed, the U.S. education system does appear to enjoy considerable strengths, especially at the tertiary level. But by far the weakest link in the chain of human capital-building institutions is the system of primary and secondary education, the main focus of this chapter.

Second, there is growing concern in some circles about the effectiveness of social policy in the United States. In this area, problems in primary and secondary education – involving not just low academic achievement but also pervasive violence and drug use in some school districts – are viewed as being both symptomatic of and important contributors to broader social ills. There are inequities that, over a period of many decades, have been built into the allocation of education resources. These inequities translate into very large performance differentials between different ethnic groups and between students following different educational programmes. Because family support is important for successful education, the pervasive neglect of some segments of the population has lent a durable, inter-generational character to education failure. Widespread education failure then contributes to tenacious problems which require costly intervention in other policy areas, such as welfare and law enforcement.

Third, the combination of a good higher education system and sub-standard primary and secondary education is a source of widening income disparity in the United States. The long-term solution to the problems of so-called working poor, which the present Administration has tried to alleviate by means of the Earned Income Tax Credit (see Chapter III) must be found in improving the skill levels of workers at the lower end of the wage scale. Better primary and secondary education, especially for the non-college bound, has an important role to play.

This chapter seeks to describe the key features of the education system that gave rise to this state of affairs. It will concentrate on the economic and organisational characteristics of the system that are of particular relevance for understanding and assessing the recent legislative initiatives. After providing a brief overview of the education sector, the chapter will address the following issues:

–   Institutional and economic characteristics of the educational system: How is the system financed and controlled? Who are the main actors in the supply of formal educational services? How do households, widely recognised as being as important as schools in shaping educational outcomes, interact with the formal education sector? What are the characteristics of demand in the sector?

–   Achievement and attainment: How well do American students fare in international studies of achievement? What are the regional patterns of educational achievement? How do achievement levels vary for the various socio-economic groups? How does educational attainment in the United States compare with that of other countries?

–   Costs of low performance: What are the economic costs of low achievement and what are the pay-offs to improved performance?

–   Measures for improving performance: What is being done to improve the performance of the system? How effective are recent legislative initiatives likely to be?

Overview of the educational system

In 1990, about 60 million people in the United States, nearly one in four, were enrolled in educational institutions. At the primary and secondary levels, enrolments have followed demographic trends with a lag. They started growing again in the mid-1980s and are expected to continue to grow into the early 2000s (Diagram 15). The enrolment rate for different age cohorts has tended to increase since the early 1970s, with this trend being particularly marked in pre-primary education (Table 15). Post-secondary enrolments have increased throughout the twentieth century, although the rate of growth has varied with demographic trends and, perhaps, with the pay-off to tertiary education.

Diagram 15. **ENROLLMENT IN PRIMARY AND SECONDARY EDUCATION**
Fall 1970-Fall 2002

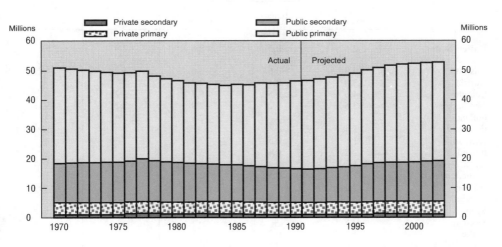

Source: Congressional Budget Office, *The Federal Role in Improving Elementary and Secondary Education,* May 1993.

Table 15. **School enrolment rates by age**

Percentage of population enrolled in school; selected years

October	Age										
	3	4	5	16	17	18	19	20	21	22	23
1972	15.8	34.0	85.7	93.8	85.6	57.5	42.7	37.8	31.2	20.5	16.9
1980	27.6	47.2	93.2	93.9	85.2	54.6	43.0	33.9	30.6	22.3	16.7
1985	29.2	49.5	93.9	94.9	88.6	59.7	45.7	38.3	33.8	22.4	15.7
1990	32.6	56.1	93.2	95.6	89.5	64.4	50.6	42.9	36.4	28.1	19.2

Source: The Condition of Education, National Center for Education Statistics, 1992.

Education is quite a large sector in its own right. With an employment share of 5.6 per cent of the total labour force, it slightly exceeds the OECD average employment share of 5.1 per cent (Table 16). The data show that the share of non-teaching staff employed in the educational sector is rather high – at 2.9 per cent of the labour force[89] – relative to the share of teaching staff in the United

Table 16. **Staff employed in education, 1991**

Teaching and non-teaching staff as a percentage of total labour force

	Teaching staff			Non-teaching staff	All staff
	Primary and secondary	Tertiary	All levels combined		
United States	2.1	0.5	2.6	2.9	5.6
Australia	2.3	0.6	3.0	1.2	4.2
Austria	3.0	0.4	3.7	–	–
Belgium	4.6	0.5	5.3	1.2	6.5
Denmark	2.6	0.2	2.9	2.2	5.1
Finland	–	–	2.8	2.4	5.2
France	2.4	–	–	–	5.9
Germany	1.6	0.5	2.4	–	–
Ireland	2.8	0.4	3.6	–	–
Japan	1.7	0.4	2.4	0.7	3.1
Netherlands	2.1	0.5	2.8	0.7	3.5
Norway	3.4	–	–	–	–
Portugal	3.1	0.3	3.6	–	–
Spain	2.7	0.4	3.4	–	–
Sweden	2.5	–	–	–	–
Turkey	1.9	0.2	2.1	–	–
United Kingdom	2.0	0.3	2.4	–	–

Source: OECD, Centre for Educational Research and Innovation.

States (2.6 per cent) and to the OECD average (1.7 per cent). This may reflect a number of factors. First, American schools may perform functions such as after-school sports, bus transportation, psychological counselling, medical check-ups, after-school day care, provision of meals and driver education that are assigned to other institutions elsewhere. Second, it may reflect other problems of data comparability, such as whether personnel are classified as teachers according to the post occupied or by whether or not they have a teaching degree. Third, it may be a symptom of administrative inefficiency or of high transactions costs associated with attempting to control financing flows through multiple layers of government in a sector where outputs are ill-defined and difficult to measure.

Public and private spending on all levels of education was 4.2 per cent of GDP in 1991. This slightly exceeds the overall OECD average of 4.0 per cent. International comparisons of expenditure per primary and secondary student place the United States – at $5 555 per student in 1991 – well above the OECD mean. Relative to its per capita GDP, however, expenditure per non-tertiary student is at about the OECD norm (Diagram 16). Growth in public spending per

Diagram 16. **EXPENDITURE PER STUDENT BY LEVEL
IN RELATION TO GDP PER CAPITA**

Primary and secondary education

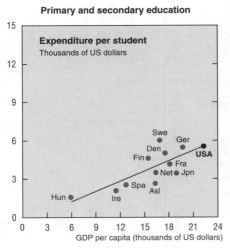

Tertiary education

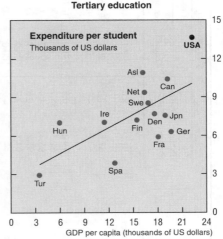

Note: Expenditure from public and private sources.
Source: OECD, *Education at a Glance*, 1993.

89

Table 17. **Sources of funds for education, 1991**

	Primary and secondary education						Tertiary education					
	Public sources	Private sources	Public sources				Public sources	Private sources	Public sources			
			Central	Regional	Local	International			Central	Regional	Local	International
United States	91.6	8.4	7.1	48.2	44.7	0	56.2	43.8	32.1	61.8	6.1	0
Australia	87.8	12.2	20.4	79.6	0	0	79.7	20.3	68.2	31.8	0	0
Belgium	–	–	0	92.9	7.1	0	–	–	0	97.8	2.2	0
Canada	–	–	–	–	–	–	85.6	14.4	–	–	–	–
Denmark	99.2	0.8	31.8	12.0	56.1	0	100.0	0	100.0	0	0	0
Germany	61.3	38.7	–	–	–	–	100.0	0	–	–	–	–
Ireland	95.1	4.9	93.7	0	0.1	6.2	85.7	14.3	67.6	0	0	32.4
Japan	91.2	8.8	24.7	75.3	0	0	39.2	60.8	84.1	15.9	0	0
Netherlands	97.3	2.7	95.9	0	4.1	0	99.8	0.2	100.0	0	0	0
Portugal	–	–	100.0	0	0	0	–	–	100.0	0	0	0
Spain	86.7	13.3	49.8	43.8	6.5	0	81.5	18.5	53.0	45.8	1.2	0
Sweden	100.0	0	53.2	4.3	42.6	0	100.0	0	95.2	3.7	1.1	0
Turkey	–	–	100.0	0	0	0	95.9	4.1	100.0	0	0	0
Country mean	90.0	10.0	52.4	32.4	14.7	–	84.0	16.0	72.7	23.4	1.0	–

Source: Education at a Glance, OECD, Centre for Educational Research and Innovation.

primary and secondary student has been rapid in recent years: there was a 28 per cent real increase over the 1980-91 period. Spending on tertiary education is much higher than in most other Member countries. Public and private expenditure in the United States on tertiary education was 2.4 per cent of GDP in 1991, compared to an OECD average of 1.5 per cent. Per capita expenditure on tertiary education is the highest in the OECD and, relative to per capita GDP, is much higher than the OECD norm (Diagram 16).

The sources of funding for education vary by level. At primary and secondary levels, 8.4 per cent came from private sources in 1991 which was about average for the OECD (Table 17). The United States relies heavily on local funding for schools; local authorities contributed 45 per cent of total financing. In the OECD area only Denmark shows greater reliance on local financing (56 per cent). State governments contributed about 48 per cent of school finance in 1991, and Federal finance stood at approximately 7 per cent of the total. At the tertiary level, 56 per cent of financing came from public sources in 1991, of which 62 per cent was supplied by State governments and 32 per cent by the Federal government.

The organisation of primary and secondary education

The most fundamental organising principles for primary and secondary education in the United States are States' rights and local control. The Supreme Court of the United States has ruled that the right to education is not a "fundamental interest" that warrants "strict scrutiny" under the equal protection clause of the Federal Constitution.[90] Thus, the legal basis of public primary and secondary education is contained in the State constitutions, which require that systems of free public schools be established.[91] In addition to significant school-financing responsibilities (through local property taxes), day-to-day control of public schools and sometimes other decisions (such as choice of curriculum) are delegated to local school districts. These vary in size from only a few hundred students to several hundred thousand. This has resulted in a system – or, more accurately, a diverse collection of systems – in which 83 000 primary and secondary schools are scattered across some 15 000 public school districts.

In practice, the evolution of the public education system has placed heavy emphasis on States' rights and relatively little on their responsibilities. Over a period of many decades, communities with necessary resources and political sophistication have used the flexibility offered by this system to minimise their contribution to the education of less advantaged children. A common strategy has been to create small local school districts that cover only a comparatively affluent community.[92] In this way the local tax base is not ''diluted'' by the need to finance the education of students from less well-off communities. The general pattern of avoiding cross-subsidisation of education systems between poorer and wealthier communities extends to inter-state funding as well. As will be shown below, the distribution of educationally disadvantaged students is far from equal across states. Taken together, these features have created a situation in which some of the best public schools in the country (for example, in Montgomery County, Maryland or in Fairfax County, Virginia) are located only a few miles away from some of the very worst (in downtown Washington, D.C., which has some of the lowest achievement scores in the nation[93]).

The Federal government has always played a limited role in education compared with those of State and local governments. As just noted, the Federal share of funding has in recent years been just over 7 per cent. It has never exceeded 10 per cent. The Federal role has focused mainly on attempting to enhance the equity of the existing system. This role was established in 1965, when the Elementary and Secondary Education Act (ESEA) was enacted as part of President Johnson's War on Poverty. ESEA, through Title I (now known as Chapter I), initiated Federal assistance to school districts for the education of disadvantaged students. In recent years, though, 93 per cent of school districts have received funding under Title I. This has reflected more the need to build political support for the legislation than the actual incidence of disadvantaged students among school districts. Improving education equality continues to be the focus of Federal expenditure on education; in recent years, 70 per cent of Federal aid has gone to programmes whose primary purpose is equal educational opportunity (CBO, 1993a).

The pattern of education expenditure reflects these organisational arrangements: public primary and secondary spending per student is highly uneven, both between and within states. 1988 data (Diagram 17) show public expenditure per primary and secondary student as varying from a high of $6 416 in Alaska to a low of $2 346 in Mississippi. Although international comparisons of school expenditure are hazardous due to data problems, it appears that, even in low-

Diagram 17. **CURRENT PUBLIC EXPENDITURE PER STUDENT ON PREPRIMARY THROUGH SECONDARY EDUCATION, 1988**

1988 US Dollars, thousands

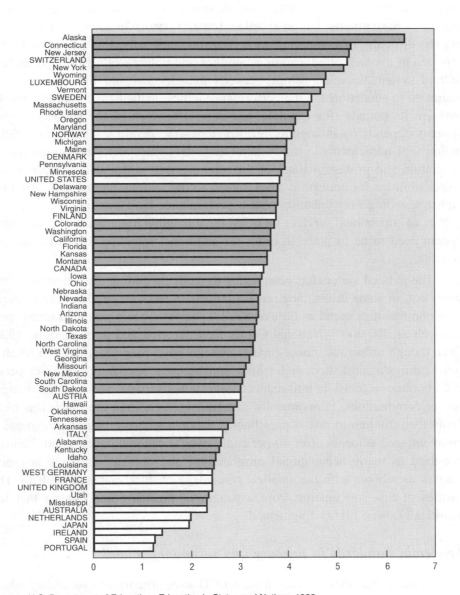

Source: U.S. Department of Education, *Education in States and Nations,* 1988.

93

spending states, expenditure per student is generally high relative to that of countries with very high performance systems. Three states spend more per capita than any OECD country, and all states spend more than Japan (which, judged by most criteria, has an excellent school system). In addition to underscoring the difficulty of comparing such data internationally, this points to another problem in the area of education economics and policy evaluation: it is difficult to find systematic relationships between the physical and financial resources dedicated to education and the performance indicators that are commonly used to measure its outputs (for example, test scores).[94] Much of the success of these systems depends on intangible infrastructure – academic standards to which a majority of participants in the system (students, homes and schools) adhere, the dedication and professionalism of the teaching staff and a shared view of how responsibilities for education are assigned to the various participants. Although higher spending may enhance system performance by expanding the range and quality of educational services on offer, the intangible ingredients of a successful system need to be in place in order for additional spending to yield maximum benefits.

The judicial system has been acting to reduce spending discrepancies within states but, in some states, they remain large.[95] In the state of Ohio, for example, poor communities spend as little as $2 500 per pupil while wealthier areas spend as much as $10 000[96] (National Center for Education and the Economy, 1990). Even though numerous school-finance systems have been modified as a result of court rulings against them under State constitutions, spending disparities persist and continue to translate into reduced educational services for students living in poorer communities. Economically disadvantaged children are much less likely than other children to attend preschool.[97] Schools with the largest percentage of disadvantaged students offer 40 per cent fewer vocational courses and facilities, one-third as many occupational programmes, and one-half as many advanced courses as schools with the smallest percentage of disadvantaged students. Disparities of this sort emerge from a pattern of financing and control that has, historically, been highly fragmented.

Academic standards in primary and secondary school

Unlike most other systems in the OECD area, primary and secondary education in the United States tends not to be organised around established study programmes or curricula. There is no national curriculum, and, frequently, the States leave curriculum design to local school districts as well. This lack of standardisation in study programmes contrasts with the situation in most other OECD countries, where educational programmes are organised into standardised tracks whose content is widely understood by the general public. These may be associated with types of schools (*e.g.* the *Realschule, Hauptschule* and *Gymnasium* in Germany) or with different learning programmes offered in secondary schools (*e.g.* the various *baccalauréats* in France). These well defined tracks are almost entirely absent in the United States. In a related matter, there are few requirements that students demonstrate that a given standard has been achieved: "high stakes" exit tests – which most other countries require young people to pass before obtaining their secondary school diploma – are rare in the United States.

Generally, this lack of well-defined standards and curricula reflects the diversity of beliefs and values in U.S. society. Indeed, forming a political consensus on what such a standard curriculum and associated tests should contain would be a daunting challenge in its own right. This is true for at least two reasons. First, people do not agree on what is important for students to know and, in some areas, they do not even agree on what the facts are.[98] Second, because of the huge spending and service disparities mentioned earlier, the logic of the system requires *de facto* multiple standards (with some of the standards being exceedingly low) in order for students in poorer communities to remain even moderately viable. For this reason, the financial and service disparities inherent in heavy reliance on State and, especially, local funding of schools are a major impediment to reform. Any attempt at reform of standards and curricula without concomitant efforts to reduce disparities in funding and service quality would encounter political resistance from disadvantaged groups.

As a result of the low degree of standardisation and the absence of exit testing, students and their families have a great deal of flexibility in choosing programmes of study. Choices are sometimes made with the help of professional guidance counsellors and, in a limited number of cases, guidelines established by universities are used, but students are relatively free to select their own course of studies. Not surprisingly, relatively few of them opt for the challenging course material that is routinely taken by students in some other countries.[99] Education analysts tend to organise curricula into a typology consisting of: *i)* an academic track for students bound for selective universities; *ii)* a general track consisting primarily of non-vocational classes, but for students not bound for university; and *iii)* vocational studies, putting a heavy emphasis on non-academic subjects.

Ironically (given the absence of exit testing), the U.S. student population may well be one of the most extensively tested in the world, with most of the testing being based on so-called ''standardised tests''. Such tests – usually in multiple-choice format and not closely aligned with any particular curriculum – are used in a number of ways. The Scholastic Aptitude Test (SAT) is taken by some college-bound students and is an important factor in admissions to many universities. The National Assessment of Educational Progress (NAEP) and numerous alternative tests are designed to monitor progress during primary and secondary studies. For some of these tests, results are available to individual students as well as aggregated to a school or district level; they are sometimes published in local newspapers. The tests are statistically rigorous in the sense that their results are calibrated to make them comparable over time, and, in theory at least, individual test items that discriminate unduly against particular ethnic groups are eliminated. Their content, however, is deemed to be too narrow in focus to serve as the basis for an implicit national curriculum.

Competition in primary and secondary education

Running parallel to the public system is a completely independent private education system, consisting of Catholic schools, other religious schools, schools for students with special needs and college preparatory schools. This system enrolled 5.2 million primary and secondary students in 1990 (GAO, 1993). Catholic schools account for a dominant share of private enrolments in non-tertiary education. Inasmuch as they receive no State subsidies, private educators operate at a disadvantage relative to public systems. On the other hand, their relative freedom from regulation confers significant competitive advantages in other areas. For example, because they are allowed to select students, they are able to differentiate themselves more effectively as teaching institutions. This often includes turning away students whose academic prospects are not good or who have behavioural problems. Similarly, public schools – unlike their private counterparts – are required by law to provide expensive special education to disabled students.

Private schools are used extensively (but not exclusively) by middle-and high-income families. Fewer than 80 per cent of relatively well-off families send their children to public schools, while 96 per cent of enrolled poor children attend public schools (GAO, 1993). Because of the availability of private schools in many areas, some families – and especially the affluent – face a wide range of choice in educational services. Choice is further enhanced if the family has the necessary resources to move to communities with more desirable schools. Thus, in some areas, the public schools are subject to a fair amount of competition, both from one another and from private schools.

School choice has occupied an important place in discussions of school reform for some time. The local nature of control of education and the large local disparities in funding and service levels have precluded Federal policy initiatives for choice and have limited even the local scale of such initiatives. Nevertheless, recent years have seen some experimentation with broadening school choice at very local levels. Numerous variations on this theme have evolved – voucher schemes (in Milwaukee Wisconsin[100]); universal enrolment (for example, in Boston and nine other cities in Massachusetts[101]) and magnet schools (schools offering education based on a particular theme; this approach is often adopted as part of a desegregation programme, where the schools' special features are used to attract students so as to obtain the desired racial mix).

The home environment

One of the few incontrovertible empirical findings in the education literature is that the student's home environment is at least as important in explaining educational experience and achievement as the formal educational sector. One study states that the home environment is "the most powerful factor in determining the school learning of students – their level of achievement, their interest in school learning and the number of years of schooling they will receive" (Kellaghn *et al.*, 1993).

The importance of the home stems from its dual role: it encompasses both supply and demand functions. Thus, the formal educational sector maintains two rather separate relationships with the household sector. First, the household sector is a client or consumer of the services provided by the formal sector. Second, households may themselves provide significant education services in the form of tutoring and structuring school-related work undertaken at home.[102] In this respect, they occupy a role (relative to the formal sector) which is similar to that of a partner in a joint venture. The same problems of allocating responsibilities, of communicating and co-ordinating actions are posed. The absence of widely accepted curriculum standards for public schools – already discussed above – may undermine the ability of the public school system to co-ordinate effectively with homes. In addition, the importance of the home in the supply of educational services underscores the inter-generational externalities inherent in the decision to invest in education.

The United States' population features significant ethnic and linguistic diversity. Diversity is relevant to the extent that it gives rise to ''market segmentation'' – or systematic variation – in both the quantity and the type of education services demanded. It may also influence in various ways the propensity to supply education services in the home. In the market for education services a number of crosscutting socio-economic characteristics appear to be relevant: ethnic affiliation; the educational, occupational and marital status of parents; the number of siblings; and place of residence (urban, suburban, rural). These shape the education strategies adopted by individuals or by their families in various ways. First, they influence the external incentives and opportunities presented to individual students. Second, operating through values, beliefs and internal family resources, they influence the way families respond to external incentives and opportunities (Chiswick, 1988 and Steelman and Powell, 1993).

The ethnic composition of elementary and secondary education has been changing more or less in parallel with overall population trends. The proportion of minorities in the school-age population has expanded and is expected to continue to grow (Diagram 18) as a result of their higher fertility rates and of immigration. Minority students are heavily concentrated in the inner cities and, increasingly, in other metropolitan areas. The incidence of ''minority'' enrolment varies markedly by state, ranging from 77.4 per cent in Hawaii to 2.0 per cent in Vermont (Table 18).

By OECD standards, the share of students who are taught in a language different from their mother tongue appears to be relatively low in the United States. In 1991, this share was 6 per cent in both France and the United States, 5 per cent in Scotland, 12 per cent in Canada, 15 per cent in Northern Italy and 20 per cent in Switzerland (Bishop, 1994). It should be noted that such students

Diagram 18. **TRENDS IN THE COMPOSITION OF THE U.S. POPULATION**

Ages 6 to 17 by race or ethnicity

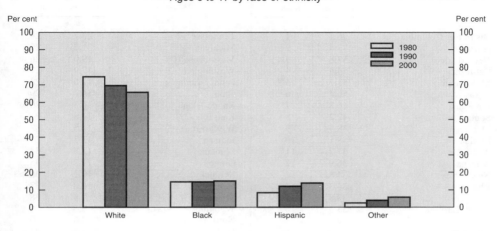

Note: People of Hispanic origin may be of any race.
Source: Congressional Budget Office, *The Federal Role in Improving Elementary and Secondary Education,* May 1993.

are heavily concentrated in the south-western states and, more generally, in urban areas. Thus, some states or school districts face a costly challenge in educating young people whose mother tongue is not English, while others are hardly affected by the problem at all.

The extreme mobility (GAO, 1994*b*) that typifies many American families also presents unusual challenges for education service delivery. One survey shows that 17 per cent of the children in the third grade (that is, of students who are about eight years old) have attended at least three different schools since the beginning of primary school, while 24 per cent had already changed schools once. The study shows this to be a particular problem in the inner cities, where 25 per cent of the eight year-olds had attended at least three schools since the beginning of primary school. This compares with about 15 per cent in the suburbs, small cities and rural areas. Obviously the absence of curriculum standards just discussed exacerbates the difficulty of coping with highly mobile students.

Table 18. **Minority students' share of primary and secondary enrolment by State, 1990**[1]

	Per cent	Rank		Per cent	Rank
District of Columbia	96.1	1	Tennessee	23.7	24
Hawaii	77.4	2	Michigan	21.7	25
New Mexico	57.8	3	Massachusetts	19.0	26
California	54.4	4	Washington	17.9	27
Mississippi	51.7	5	Pennsylvania	17.6	28
Texas	50.4	6	Ohio	16.7	29
Louisiana	46.8	7	Rhode Island	16.3	30
South Carolina	42.2	8	Kansas	14.8	31
Maryland	38.9	9	Wisconsin	14.5	32
Florida	38.1	10	Indiana	13.7	33
Alabama	37.2	11	Montana	11.3	34
Arizona	36.9	12	Oregon	11.2	35
New Jersey	34.8	13	Kentucky	10.2	36
Illinois	34.3	14	Nebraska	10.0	37
New York	33.8	15	Minnesota	9.8	38
North Carolina	33.5	16	Wyoming	9.6	39
Alaska	32.5	17	North Dakota	8.6	40
Delaware	32.0	18	Utah	7.4	41
Nevada	25.8	19	Iowa	5.8	42
Oklahoma	25.8	19	West Virginia	4.4	43
Arkansas	25.5	21	New Hampshire	3.0	44
Connecticut	25.1	22	Vermont	2.0	45
Colorado	24.7	23			

1. Not all States are included because some did not report minority enrolments.
Source: Report Card on American Education, American Legislature Exchange Council.

Sources of demand and the pressure for quality

Education is a service sector which, at the primary and secondary levels, features three types of "customer": *i)* households; *ii)* prospective employers of students who do not intend to go on to college; and *iii)* colleges and universities. With the exception of the last, they are not, on the whole, very demanding.

Although they recognise that the public school system as a whole is not doing well, households in the United States are generally satisfied with the quality of educational services their own children receive. A comparative study of primary education in Taiwan, Japan and the United States found that American mothers are much more pleased with the performance of their local schools than are Taiwanese and Japanese mothers. When asked how good a job their school was doing in educating their offspring, 91 per cent of American mothers responded "excellent" or "good" while only 42 per cent of the Taiwanese and

39 per cent of the Japanese parents were this positive (survey cited in Bishop, 1989).

Prospective employers of non college-bound graduates rarely ask for information about the high school (the name given in the United States to secondary school) experiences of job applicants. A 1987 survey of 2 014 small and medium-size employers found that, when someone with 12 or fewer years of schooling was hired, school records had been obtained prior to the selection decision for only 14.2 per cent of the hires. Referrals from teachers who know the applicant were also uncommon. The survey found that new hires had been recommended by vocational teachers in only 5.2 per cent of the cases and referred by someone else in the high school in only 2.7 per cent of the cases (Bishop, 1994).[103] The lack of standardisation in the high-school curriculum may contribute to this situation. In order to use information contained in high-school records, firms have to be able interpret it in light of the school that produced it and, perhaps, even with reference to specific teachers. This is not a very appealing prospect for firms that deal with a large number of high schools.

As will be shown below in the discussion of higher education, the sector is diverse in terms of the range of institutions it contains and the types of students who enrol in it. The tertiary education sector, therefore, exercises variable pressures on the primary and secondary levels. On the one hand, the selective university sector subjects its candidates for admission to a fairly rigorous set of requirements. Generally, these universities ask for a record of high-school grades and for scores on one of several standardised tests. They often place considerable weight on other signs of accomplishment (distinction awards, activity in student government, achievement in sports). Demands from the selective university sector appear to be the only source of reasonably exacting standards to which lower levels of education are held. These are only relevant, however, for a limited number of students. On the other end of the spectrum are institutions of higher education that have low or non-existent standards for admission. Many private and public institutions will admit students on the basis of a high-school diploma alone.

School-to-work transition

Roughly a third of the students in each age cohort do not go on to tertiary education. Unemployment rates are high for such young people throughout the

OECD area, and the United States is no exception. The unemployment rate among 18 to 19 year-olds stood at 19 per cent nationally in mid-1993. Among 20 to 24 year-olds it was 11 per cent, compared to 5.7 per cent among job seekers aged 25 to 54. The National Longitudinal Survey of Youth shows that, between the ages of 18 and 27, the average high-school graduate who did not enrol in post-secondary education held nearly six different jobs and experienced between four and five spells of unemployment. While spending a total of 387 weeks employed during those years, the average high-school graduate also spent almost 35 weeks unemployed. The position of the non-college bound may be further undermined by the relative scarcity of enterprise-based training for such workers, which may, itself, be related to mobility (OECD, 1993a, Chapter 4). Part of this frequent job changing, however, might be due to normal experimentation and job search in a society in which the costs of moving and changing jobs are relatively small.

School-to-work programmes are offered in many secondary schools and vocational institutions. These are often perceived as being designed for non-college bound students, although, in practice, significant numbers end up in higher education of some sort (Stern *et al.*, 1994). There is now a growing trend toward fuller integration of academic and vocational curricula. These pro-grammes include co-operative education, new youth apprenticeships and school-based enterprises. Co-operative education – involving paid work in the student's field of study – has been a feature of secondary schools for more than seventy years. Evaluations indicate that co-operative education is successful in creating a stronger connection between school and work in students' minds and in improv-ing attitudes toward both school and work. However, co-op students have not generally been found to obtain higher earnings after leaving high school, unless they continue working for the co-op employer. One possible reason for this may be that co-operative programmes do not provide certification that is widely recognised by employers. Therefore, co-op graduates who are not offered perma-nent jobs by their co-op employers may not obtain much advantage in the labour market from their co-op experience.

Other formal school-to-work programmes are of more recent origin. High schools are just becoming involved in new youth apprenticeship initiatives. Like co-operative education, these link high school with a structured work experience, but they are also trying to create a clearer path to post-secondary education in addition to providing occupational certification. For the most part, these are at the demonstration stage. More widespread than youth apprenticeship is school-based enterprise, which involves students in producing goods or services.[104]

Finally, the so-called "Tech Prep" programmes straddle secondary and post-secondary education for the vocationally-minded student. These programmes involve agreements on course co-ordination between community colleges and local high schools and lead to a two-year associate degree or certificate in applied fields such as health, mechanics or agriculture. These programmes attempt to optimise the sequencing of courses for occupational preparation (National Education Association, 1993). The 1990 amendment to the Perkins Vocational Education Act provides Federal support for Tech Prep programmes. Many States, however, were involved in developing Tech Prep programmes prior to the Federal legislation.

Higher education

The number and diversity of institutions found in the U.S. system of higher education is impressive. A leading education economist has observed that one of the system's strengths is that it is "very much driven by individual initiative, and a person who wants to change careers or gain new skills can find numerous ways to do so ... early choices are not binding and the system provides chances (for those with the resources) to start over or to change direction" (cited in National Research Council, 1994). This section covers two main sub-sectors: *i)* four-year colleges and universities; and *ii)* community and technical colleges offering one- or two-year certificates and other adult education programmes.

The four-year university sector in the United States provides a wide range of educational programmes and research services to a diverse array of customers. On the whole, the sector's performance is impressive. It offers graduate and undergraduate teaching that attracts students from many countries. Judged on the basis of scientific awards, its research universities and scholars are very successful.[105] The numerous world-class universities co-exist with a dense network of regional and specialist institutions that includes liberal arts, engineering and design colleges, colleges for women or for ethnic groups and colleges with religious affiliations. Institutions offering four-year degrees include some 3 400 separately governed colleges and universities, which enrolled 14.2 million students in 1990. Aside from purchasing research services from the university sector, Federal involvement consists mainly of guaranteeing loans and extending financial aid to students. Most four-year institutions are either private (usually not-for-profit) or are operated by State governments. A notable development has been the very rapid pace of tuition growth: private four-year universities saw their constant-dollar tuition rise by 50 per cent over the 1977 to 1990 period, while constant-dollar tuition at public four-year universities rose by a more modest 28 per cent (Table 19). In the academic year ending in 1991 average annual tuition for a full-time student was $11 379 for a private four-year college and $2 159 for a public college.

The four-year system is, however, only the most visible component of a much larger system. The lesser known, more local dimension of higher education also plays an essential role by addressing the diverse educational needs of the neighbouring adult population. Indeed, the most noticeable change in tertiary education over the past 30 years has been the very rapid growth and increasingly

Table 19. **Index of average undergraduate tuition charges** [1]

1981 = 100

Academic year ending:	Public institutions			Private institutions		
	University	Other 4-year	2-year	University	Other 4-year	2-year
1977	105	109	101	100	97	92
1978	105	108	103	99	97	93
1979	103	105	102	99	100	92
1980	102	102	101	99	99	95
1981	100	100	100	100	100	100
1982	104	102	101	104	103	98
1983	109	111	103	112	109	107
1984	114	118	110	118	113	104
1985	116	119	114	123	116	111
1986	123	118	121	127	122	112
1987	128	122	119	134	129	108
1988	128	133	123	140	132	117
1989	130	135	120	142	136	128
1990	134	139	119	149	141	135

Note: Tuition charges (tuition and fees) are in constant dollars, adjusted by the Consumer Price Index for the academic year (July 1-June 30). They are for the entire academic year and are average charges paid by students. They were calculated on the basis of full-time-equivalent undergraduates. Tuition at public institutions is the charge to in-state students. The amount at private institutions includes charges at both non-profit and proprietary schools.

1.   At institutions of higher education, by type and control of institution. Academic years ending 1977-1990

Source: U.S. Department of Education, National Center for Education Statistics, *Digest of Education Statistics, 1991*, Tables 36 and 291 (based on IPEDS Institutional Characteristics and Fall Enrolment Surveys).

vocational orientation of publicly funded two-year community and technical[106] colleges, which are funded and run by State and local governments. Enrolment in these colleges has expanded more quickly than at any other level of tertiary education, student numbers having grown from 740 000 (full- and part-time) in the autumn of 1963 to 4.9 million in the autumn of 1990. There are approximately 1 000 community or technical colleges in the United States, spread fairly evenly across the country. The growth of these colleges attests to their success in identifying and addressing adult-education and training needs in their communities. It may also reflect a shift in relative tuitions in their favour, as compared with those of four-year institutions (Table 19).

The community colleges provide a wide range of educational services. Their original purpose was to provide a low-cost entry point into the four-year college system by offering inexpensive college credits. In recent years, though, they have increasingly focused on vocational training, often in connection with large employers. It is estimated, for example, that General Motors, Ford, Chrysler, Nissan, Toyota and Honda now operate over 500 apprenticeship programmes in conjunction with two-year colleges (Stern *et al.*, 1994). Vocational training has in recent years accounted for 65 per cent of these institutions' enrolments. In addition and in response to local conditions, community colleges provide remedial education for adults, classes in English as a second language, retraining for displaced workers and recreation and community service programmes. The average tuition for such institutions is about $900 for a full-time academic year.

Achievement and attainment: how well does the system perform?

While the higher-education sector is effective in meeting the varied educational needs of the adult population, the performance of the primary and secondary systems is much more mixed. These yield achievement results (indicators of how much has been learned) that are low by international standards, notably in mathematics. For certain segments of the population, including some ethnic minorities and the non-college bound, average achievement levels are very low indeed. Attainment levels (years spent in school and diplomas received) for some ethnic minorities are also low. The present section examines data on achievement and attainment outcomes with a particular focus on how scores vary by region and by ethnic minority.

National achievement results: mathematics, science and reading[107]

Achievement scores of primary and secondary students[108] have been stable or have shown slight improvement since 1980. By the early 1990s, then, American students were performing at about 1970 levels, having made up for the gradual deterioration that took place during the 1970s. There is thus little evi-

Diagram 19. **INTERNATIONAL COMPARISON OF MATHEMATICS PROFICIENCY**
Students at age 13 (1991)

▼ Mean significantly lower than comparison country	● No statistically significant difference from comparison country	▲ Mean significantly higher than comparison country

	Mean	Standard error	Switzerland	France	Em.-Rom. (Italy)	Canada	Scotland	England	Ireland	Spain (ex. Catalonia)	United States	Portugal
Switzerland	70.8	1.3		▲	▲	▲	▲	▲	▲	▲	▲	▲
France	64.2	0.8	▼		●	●	●	●	●	▲	▲	▲
Emilia-Romagna (Italy)	64.0	0.9	▼	●		●	●	●	●	▲	▲	▲
Canada	62.0	0.6	▼	●	●		●	●	●	▲	▲	▲
Scotland	60.6	0.9	▼	●	●	●		●	●	▲	▲	▲
England	60.6	2.2	▼	●	●	●	●		●	●	●	▲
Ireland	60.5	0.9	▼	●	●	●	●	●		▲	▲	▲
Spain (ex. Catalonia)	55.4	0.8	▼	▼	▼	▼	▼	●	▼		●	▲
United States	55.3	1.0	▼	▼	▼	▼	▼	●	▼	●		▲
Portugal	48.3	0.8	▼	▼	▼	▼	▼	▼	▼	▼	▼	

Source: OECD.

dence of a long-term deterioration in overall education quality. Viewed in an international perspective, however, the average achievement scores of American children range from mediocre to poor, depending on the subject matter.

The mathematical competence of American students is widely recognised to be low by international standards, and, indeed, OECD data shows this to be the one area where U.S. achievement results are notably poor. Diagram 19 places the mathematics proficiency of 13 year-olds in the United States ninth among ten Member countries, with the bulk of the differences in mean performance being statistically significant. These differences are educationally significant as well – for example, the difference between the French score and the U.S. score is about one and a half years of schooling (*i.e.* U.S. grade level equivalents).

International tests of performance in science place American 13 year-olds eighth in a field of ten (Diagram 20). For the most part, however, the differences between the United States and other countries' average scores are not statistically significant: Switzerland is the only country whose 13 year-olds perform significantly better in science than their counterparts in the United States. Again, in addition to being largely insignificant in a statistical sense, these differences represent only a few months of classroom time.

The reading competence of American adolescents places them roughly in the middle of international comparative rankings. Diagram 21 presents the results of comparative testing of 14 year-olds and shows the United States as ranking seventh in a field of nineteen Member countries. It also indicates the extent to which the differences in mean performance are statistically significant and shows that Finland is the only country whose performance is significantly better than that of the United States.

Performance by state

More detailed examination of these data reveals wide variation in average scores between states. Even in American students' weakest area – mathematics – the state data on proficiency for 13 year-olds attending public schools indicate that the best states perform at levels which are very close to those of Taiwan and Korea, the highest achievers in international comparative testing. Indeed, the ranking depicted in Diagram 22 places the states of Iowa and North Dakota second and third after Taiwan, while thirteen states figure in the top twenty places of a ranking that includes a rather competitive field of comparison countries

Diagram 20. INTERNATIONAL COMPARISON OF SCIENCE PROFICIENCY
Students at age 13 (1991)

▼ Mean significantly lower than comparison country	● No statistically significant difference from comparison country	▲ Mean significantly higher than comparison country

	Mean	Standard error	Switzerland	Em.-Rom. (Italy)	Canada	England	France	Scotland	Spain (ex. Catalonia)	United States	Ireland	Portugal
Switzerland	73.7	0.9		▲	▲	▲	▲	▲	▲	▲	▲	▲
Emilia-Romagna (Italy)	69.9	0.7	▼		●	●	●	●	●	●	▲	▲
Canada	68.8	0.4	▼	●			●	●	●	●	▲	▲
England	68.7	1.2	▼	●	●		●	●	●	●	▲	▲
France	68.6	0.6	▼	●	●	●			●	●	▲	▲
Scotland	67.9	0.6	▼	●	●	●	●		●	●	▲	▲
Spain (ex. Catalonia)	67.6	0.8	▼	●	●	●	●	●		●	▲	▲
United States	67.0	1.0	▼	●	●	●	●	●	●		●	▲
Ireland	63.3	0.6	▼	▼	▼	▼	▼	▼	▼	●		●
Portugal	62.6	0.8	▼	▼	▼	▼	▼	▼	▼	▼	●	

Source: OECD.

(Korea, the former Soviet Union, Switzerland, Hungary, France and Israel). The state of Mississippi takes the lowest place in the ranking, just after Jordan.[109]

These results contribute interesting nuances to what might otherwise be an excessively stark view of U.S. education outcomes. First, they show that the state-wide variation in results is high. According to this study, there is as much variation in test scores between states as there is between countries. The top-

▼	Mean significantly lower than comparison country	●	No statistically significant difference from comparison country	▲	Mean significantly higher than comparison country

	Mean	Standard error	Finland	France	Sweden	New Zealand	Switzerland	Iceland	United States	Germany (E)	Denmark	Portugal	Germany (W)	British Columbia	Norway	Italy	Netherlands	Ireland	Greece	Spain	Belgium (French)
Finland	545	2.3		●	▲	●	▲	▲	▲	▲	▲	▲	▲	▲	▲	▲	▲	▲	▲	▲	▲
France	531	4.4	●		●	●	●	▲	●	▲	▲	▲	▲	▲	▲	▲	▲	▲	▲	▲	▲
Sweden	529	2.4	▼	●		●	●	▲	●	▲	▲	▲	▲	▲	▲	▲	▲	▲	▲	▲	▲
New Zealand	528	6.0	●	●	●		●	▲	●	▲	▲	▲	▲	▲	▲	▲	▲	▲	▲	▲	▲
Switzerland	515	3.3	▼	●	●	●		●	●	●	▲	●	▲	▲	▲	▲	▲	▲	▲	▲	▲
Iceland	514	0.1	▼	▼	▼	▼	●		●	▲	▲	▲	▲	▲	▲	▲	▲	▲	▲	▲	▲
United States	514	5.1	▼	●	●	●	●	●		●	●	●	●	●	▲	▲	▲	▲	▲	▲	▲
Germany (E)	501	3.5	▼	▼	▼	▼	●	▼	●		●	●	●	●	●	●	●	●	▲	▲	▲
Denmark	500	2.5	▼	▼	▼	▼	▼	▼	●	●		●	●	●	●	●	●	●	●	▲	▲
Portugal	500	3.6	▼	▼	▼	▼	●	▼	●	●	●		●	●	●	●	●	●	●	▲	▲
Germany (W)	498	2.5	▼	▼	▼	▼	▼	▼	●	●	●	●		●	●	●	●	●	▲	▲	▲
British Columbia	494	3.1	▼	▼	▼	▼	▼	▼	●	●	●	●	●		●	●	●	●	●	▲	▲
Norway	489	2.6	▼	▼	▼	▼	▼	▼	▼	●	●	●	●	●		●	●	●	●	▲	▲
Italy	488	3.3	▼	▼	▼	▼	▼	▼	▼	●	●	●	●	●	●		●	●	●	▲	▲
Netherlands	486	4.6	▼	▼	▼	▼	▼	▼	▼	●	●	●	●	●	●	●		●	●	▲	▲
Ireland	484	5.1	▼	▼	▼	▼	▼	▼	▼	●	●	●	●	●	●	●	●		●	▲	▲
Greece	482	2.2	▼	▼	▼	▼	▼	▼	▼	▼	▼	▼	▼	●	●	●	●	●		▲	▲
Spain	456	3.0	▼	▼	▼	▼	▼	▼	▼	▼	▼	▼	▼	▼	▼	▼	▼	▼	▼		●
Belgium (French)	446	4.3	▼	▼	▼	▼	▼	▼	▼	▼	▼	▼	▼	▼	▼	▼	▼	▼	▼	●	

Source: OECD.

performing state systems – located predominantly in Midwestern agricultural regions and, to a lesser extent, in the North-east – seem to deliver good and sometimes excellent results. Other state systems – mainly in the ''Sunbelt'' and especially in the south-east – appear to be performing at very poor levels indeed. The difference between the mean scores of the top and the bottom performers is

Diagram 22. PROFICIENCY SCORES FOR 13-YEAR-OLDS IN MATHEMATICS[1]

1991 (other countries) 1992 (U.S. and states)

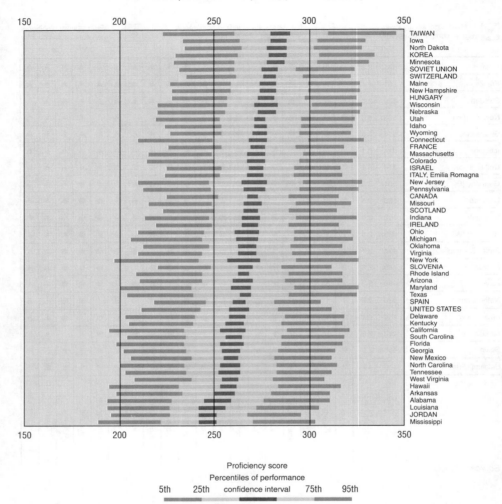

Proficiency score

Percentiles of performance

5th   25th   confidence interval   75th   95th

Note : The center darkest box indicates a confidence interval around the average mathematics proficiency for the country or state calculated as the mean plus or minus two times the standard error. Test scores range from 0 to 500.

1. In countries, proficiency scores are for 13 year olds; in states, they are for 8th-graders (some of whom may be 14) attending public schools.

Source: Educational Testing Service, *IAEP/NAEP Cross-linking Study,* 1993; U.S. Department of Education, *National Center for Education Statistics, NAEP 1992 Mathematics Report Card for the Nation and the States,* 1993.

110

equivalent to 4 grade level equivalents: this means that, on average, 13 year-olds in Mississippi would require about four additional years of schooling in order to catch up with 13 year-olds in Iowa. This difference is clearly very large in relation to the roughly eight years of schooling the pupils had completed at the time they took these tests.

Performance by ethnic-race grouping

Obviously, though, these states face very different problems as they seek to deliver high-quality public education to their young people. Regional differences in poverty rates and minority enrolments are reflected in the state achievement data just discussed. In Iowa, for example, only 12.6 per cent of 5 to 17 year-olds live in poverty compared with a nation-wide average of 17 per cent in 1990. It was already seen above that minority enrolments vary widely by state and they account for only 6 per cent of total enrolments in Iowa (Table 18).[110] The disparities in achievement between various socio-economic groupings – defined by minority affiliation, educational attainment of parents and non-English mother tongue – are large. By the end of high school, black students trail their white counterparts by an average of more than 2 grade levels. Diagram 23 shows that well under 10 per cent of black and Hispanic youths have reached proficiency in mathematics, compared with about 20 per cent for white youths and over 40 per cent for Asian youth by the time they reach the upper grade levels. Achievement statistics also show, however, that there has been some improvement in performance. In many subject areas, minorities partly closed the gaps with white children during the 1980s.

The social dimension of educational failure – or the complex set of factors that influence how the student and his family interact with the external environment in shaping educational outcomes – is widely recognised to be of crucial importance. One study (Ferguson, 1991) examines the relationship between the socio-economic variables and education experience in great detail. It confirms other studies' findings in identifying parents' education as a key factor in explaining students' achievement scores, drop-out rates and likelihood of going on to tertiary studies. Income is found to be important only when parents' education is not included as an explanatory variable. The variable, ''female head of household'' had a statistically significant negative impact on test scores for most grade levels. Ethnic affiliation or race is found to be important, but in rather

Diagram 23. PERCENTAGE OF STUDENTS ACHIEVING PROFICIENCY IN MATH

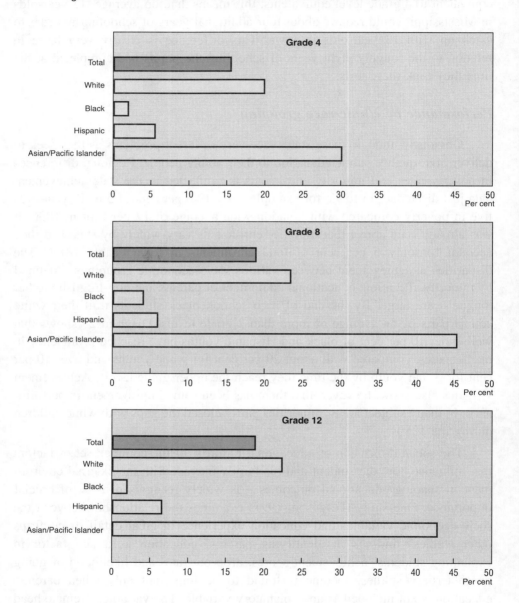

Note: Based on the 1990 National Assessment of Educational Progress, by grade and race or ethnicity.
Source: Congressional Budget Office, The Federal Role in Improving Elementary and Secondary Education, 1993.

subtle ways.[111] This study underscores the fact that both society and individual households face a significant challenge in successfully educating students when their home environment lacks the elements – a tradition of educational attainment and a stable family background – that contribute to educational success. A further problem of particular relevance to minority youths may be that many of them face a moribund local economy. Because job opportunities are relatively limited, the economy in the inner city or in poor rural areas may not transmit wage signals favouring higher educational attainment as effectively as the general economy does.

While it is true that American schools do a particularly poor job of educating blacks and Hispanics, one should not conclude that white students in middle-class suburbs are uniformly well served. In mathematics and science, the nation's top high-school students rank far behind much less elite samples of students in other countries. Substantially larger shares of 17-18 year-old Belgians, Finns, Hungarians, Scots, Swedes and Canadians are studying advanced algebra, pre-calculus and calculus, and their achievement levels are significantly higher than American high-school seniors in such classes. The gap between high-school seniors from middle-class suburbs and their counterparts in many northern European nations and in Japan is often equal to or larger than the two to three grade-level-equivalent gap between whites and blacks in the United States (Bishop, 1994).

Attainment

The graduation rate for upper secondary education in the United States (74 per cent) places it well below such countries as Japan (91 per cent), Austria (86 per cent), Denmark (100 per cent), Finland (124 per cent) and Germany (117 per cent).[112] It is at about the same level as the United Kingdom, France, Canada and Ireland. As shown in Diagram 24, though, this aggregate picture masks considerable underlying variation in the United States. Recent data show that over 10 per cent of black students drop out of secondary school between the eighth and tenth grade (roughly, between the ages of 14 and 16) and another 22 per cent drop out between the tenth and the twelfth grades (between 16 and 18).[113] Hispanics have a 27 per cent drop-out rate between the tenth and twelfth grades. Since students in the United States can graduate without having to

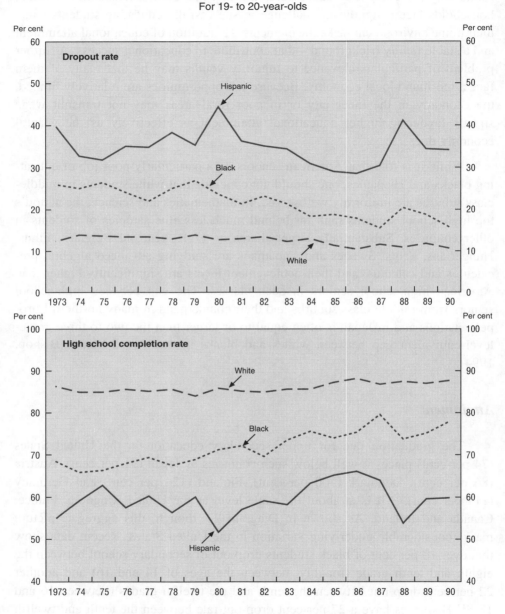

Diagram 24. **HIGH SCHOOL DROPOUT AND COMPLETION RATES**

For 19- to 20-year-olds

Per cent — Dropout rate

Hispanic

Black

White

1973 74 75 76 77 78 79 80 81 82 83 84 85 86 87 88 89 90

Per cent — High school completion rate

White

Black

Hispanic

1973 74 75 76 77 78 79 80 81 82 83 84 85 86 87 88 89 90

Source: U.S. Department of Commerce, Bureau of the Census, October Population Survey.

demonstrate overall academic competence, the fact that the graduation rate is not higher is a particular source of concern.[114]

The U.S. adult population has received on average more years of schooling than those of other large, industrialised nations. A higher percentage of 25 to 64 year-olds have completed secondary school and college than in any of the major seven OECD Member nations. For younger age cohorts, however, these differences have largely disappeared. In Japan, Germany and Canada, 25 to 34 year-olds have completed secondary education at rates similar to their counterparts in the United States. Generally, though, a comparatively high proportion of young people go on to higher education in the United States. In 1991, nearly two-thirds of recent graduates from secondary school were enrolled in higher education of some sort, compared to an OECD average of about 41 per cent (OECD, 1993*b*).

How hard are U.S. students working?

As was just shown, formal attainment levels are fairly high in the United States compared to the OECD average. At the same time, achievement levels are low. This indicates that, although American students spend comparable amounts of time in school (measured as years), they furnish less effort than do their counterparts in other countries, at least in academic areas (National Commission on Time and Learning, 1994). The general impression left by the primary and secondary education system is that, for most students, it is neither demanding nor motivating and that the stakes riding on performance are not high. Standards are vague or non-existent. Students are routinely passed who do not have grade level competences. The diverse system of higher education allows not just second chances, but third and fourth as well.

All of these factors – the structure of formal education; the disciplines, encouragement and inputs supplied by the home; the incentives established by employers and by higher education – combine to induce a pace of learning that is, on the whole, relaxed. While the comparatively small number of students who attend excellent schools or who hope to attend selective universities are required to work fairly hard, pressures on other students – especially those in the vocational and general tracks – are weak.

This can be seen by looking at comparative time-use studies. When homework is added to classroom hours, the total time devoted by secondary students to study, instruction and practice in the U.S. was only 18-20 hours per week on average in 1986 (study cited in Bishop, 1994). By way of comparison, in 1986, the typical student in his last year of secondary school spent nearly 19.6 hours per week watching television.[115] Secondary-school students in other industrialised nations watch much less television: 55 per cent less in Finland, 70 per cent less in Norway and 44 per cent less in Canada (Table 20). Reading, on the other hand, takes up only 1.4 hours of the average American student's time (this compares with 6 hours per week of a Finnish student's non-school time and 4.8 hours for Swiss and Austrian students).[116]

It is worth noting that in 1986 the average student in the last year of secondary school also spent 10 hours a week on a part-time job (Bishop, 1994). Millions of secondary-school students hold paid jobs during the school year. In the National Longitudinal Survey of Youth for 1979 to 1981, 64 per cent of students in their second-last year of high school worked at least one week during the academic year (excluding summer), as did 73 per cent of those in their final year (Stern *et al.*, 1994). The majority of these jobs are not part of the formal school-to-work arrangements described above. Research evidence generally indicates short-term gains in earnings and better access to employment after leaving school for students who work while in school. However, the evidence also suggests that working long hours while in school may interfere with the educational attainment and thus detract from earnings and occupational status in the long run. One study shows that grades at school improved up to 13.5 hours

Table 20.   **Time use by students**

	Watching television		Reading
	Students	Adults	Students
United States	19.6	15.9	1.4
Austria	6.3	10.6	4.9
Canada	10.9	13.3	1.5
Finland	9.0	9.0	6.0
Netherlands	10.6	13.4	4.3
Norway	5.9	7.2	4.3
Switzerland	7.7	9.0	4.8

Source: Hours spent per week on each activity derived from time diary studies. OECD, *Living Conditions in OECD Countries*, 1986, Tables 18.1 and 18.3.

gainfully worked per week and declined for greater numbers of hours. Thus, as the number of hours per week spent working while in school increases, a tradeoff between short-term and long-term gains emerges.[117] A further point worth mentioning is that opportunity for outside work is not evenly distributed among students: for example, young white men and women have better opportunities for paid work than blacks.[118]

In assessing the amount of academic effort furnished by adolescents, it would be inappropriate to draw overly sharp conclusions as to its significance. Little is known about the implications of differences in the timing and pace of education across an individual's life span. Indeed, the relaxed pace may be, to some extent, part of the American "style" of education, according to which education tends to last longer and to be coupled with a broader range of activities. Even from the standpoint of enhancing achievement, it is not obvious that all aspects of the U.S. system are undesirable – for example, the reluctance to fail young students who are not performing at grade level, providing second chances in education for young adults and encouraging upper-secondary students to work in paid jobs. As noted, American parents are generally satisfied with the schools their children attend. It is highly unlikely that most of them would be willing to subject their children to the rigorous requirements prevailing in some other countries. Nevertheless, it would appear that, overall, the incentive balance has tilted too much toward low effort and low achievement for a majority of students.

The costs of low performance

Looked at as a whole, the empirical literature on the relationship between education and economic performance creates a convincing case that the relationship is strong and positive (Bishop, 1994). Despite the broad range of this literature, a full picture of the ways that education affects performance in the work-place has yet to emerge. This is not surprising since the education sector produces so many services that are, at least potentially, inputs to production in other sectors. These include socialisation (which might affect discipline, punctuality or the ability to handle stress), enhancement of general knowledge, reasoning ability, communications skills and the creation of specific knowledge or skills that are relevant for production in particular sectors. Obviously the relevance of each of these education outputs varies by sector and by the type of employee within each sector.

The returns to education: private or public gains?

Analysis of the returns to education is further complicated by the difficult question of who captures the gains from further schooling. In addition to private returns, education may produce services which have positive externalities or which are public goods. Some functions of education – such as preparing young people to participate in society as responsible adults – have obvious public-good characteristics. Likewise, education may give rise to externalities or to quasi-public goods (for example, when the productivity of a team of workers is enhanced by the higher educational achievement of its members). A final complication arises from inter-governmental externalities: for example, while State and local governments account for the bulk of education finance, it is the Federal government – because it collects most income taxes – that is the major public beneficiary of the income generated by higher investment in education. Geographic mobility further complicates the picture, with states or localities in labour-exporting regions providing what amounts to a human-capital subsidy to labour-importing regions.

One thread of the literature circumvents these difficulties by focusing on a rather narrow question: by how much does an additional year of education increase a worker's earnings? Recent contributions to this literature (Box 2) attempt to separate education's earnings effect from those of other determinants of earnings, such as family background and natural ability. The results of these studies confirm earlier findings that the increase in earnings due to an additional year of schooling is, roughly, between 5 and 15 per cent. Although the information contained in these studies does not generally shed light on the pay-offs to different levels of schooling, it is safe to conclude that an additional year of most kinds of education generally pays for itself rather quickly.

Educational achievement and the job performance of the non-college bound

Another stream of literature attempts to assess the effects of higher academic achievement on on-the-job performance. A review of this literature states that: "Over the last 50 years, industrial psychologists have conducted hundreds of studies involving hundreds of thousands of workers, on the relationship between productivity in particular jobs and various predictors of that productivity. They have found that scores on tests measuring competence in reading, arithmetic and

mechanical comprehension are strongly related to productivity in almost all of
the civilian jobs studied'' (Bishop, 1989, p. 57).

A recent study (Bishop, 1989) focuses on the influence of academic achievement on performance in jobs not normally occupied by the university-educated.
In particular, the study examines the influence of mathematics, scientific and
verbal knowledge on job performance in various jobs in the U.S. military. These
jobs involved various technical, clerical and general-service occupations. The

Table 21. **Effects of competencies on hands-on measures of job performance**

Standardised regression coefficients

Military occupational speciality	General science	Math. knowledge	Arithmetic reasoning	Word knowledge	Computer speed	Clerical checking	Electronic information	Shop information	Auto information	Mechanical comprehension	R^2	N
Skilled technical	5.7[1]	12.1[3]	6.2[2]	21.5[3]	3.1	2.4	17.4[3]	13.2[3]	1.7	9.2[3]	0.55	1 324
Skilled electronic	7.2	26.1[3]	-2.1	-0.4	-1.3	8.4[1]	4.5	24.6[3]	9.8	8.6	0.43	349
General maintenance (construction)	13.4[3]	44.1[3]	-10.1[3]	6.6[1]	6.8[2]	4.3[1]	12.1[3]	11.7[3]	8.2[2]	-0.4	0.59	879
Mechanical maintenance	9.6	6.1	-6.3	-0.4	23.5[3]	5.5	-8.9	20.6[1]	31.4[3]	4.2	0.41	131
Missile battery operations and food service workers	7.6[1]	10.6[2]	11.4[3]	6.1	-3.7	5.0	10.0[2]	6.2	17.9[3]	10.9[2]	0.41	814
Unskilled electronic	-2.5	1.8	5.8[1]	-1.0	5.3[1]	3.6	7.7[2]	6.2[1]	2.7	0.4	0.05	2 545
Clerical	6.4	20.6[3]	24.1[3]	11.8[3]	8.5[2]	1.5	6.5	-3.0	8.7[3]	-6.8	0.43	830

R^2 A proportion of the variance as explained by the model.
1.   Significant at the 0.10 level using a two-tailed test.
2.   Significant at the 0.05 level using a two-tailed test.
3.   Significant at the 0.01 level using a two-tailed test.
Source: Bishop (1989). Reanalysis of Maier and Grafton's (1981) data on the ability of ASVAB (6/7 version) to predict skill qualification test scores. Maier and Grafton corrected their correlation matrix for restriction of range so the coefficients measure the effect of a population, standard deviation change in the test score on job performance in standard deviation units multiplied by 100.

120

performance assessments used in the study are job-site evaluations by experts. The regression results relating test scores on a battery of aptitude tests to the job performance measures show that the subtest assessing mathematical reasoning ability had very large positive effects on job performance in five of the seven occupations (Table 21). Computation speed was significant for four out of seven occupations, word knowledge for four occupations and general scientific knowledge for three. Finally, technical literacy (as measured by such variables as electronics information and mechanical comprehension) is also a very important determinant of performance. These results suggest that improved education – especially in mathematics – for the mass of secondary students would improve the productivity of workers involved in fairly routine jobs. Unfortunately, the classes offered in secondary school that develop mathematics reasoning ability are precisely those that non-college bound students tend not to take under the present system.

Academic achievement and the youth labour market

The strong relationship between academic achievement and job performance noted above is not reflected in a similar relationship between achievement and the earnings or wages of high-school graduates. Kang and Bishop (1989) found that, for 1980 high-school graduates not going on to college, those who had taken many academic courses earned substantially less in 1981 than those who had taken vocational courses (Bishop, 1994).

Studies of the relationship between earnings and scores on achievement tests indicate that, for the non-college bound, high-level academic competences do not have positive effects on wage rates and earnings. The weak impact of high-school achievement on earnings as a young adult extends to other aspects of the high school experience as well. The youth labour market fails to reward graduates who develop good work habits in schools, who are seldom absent, who have good study habits, who demonstrate good citizenship and who hold leadership positions in extra-curricular activities. Over time, however, there is a tendency for those with better grades or higher test scores to be promoted more rapidly, to be employed more continuously and to earn more (Bishop, 1994).

What are the reasons for the large apparent gaps between the productivity effects of educational achievement in young people and its immediate effects on wage and earnings? Although the answer to this question is necessarily speculative, a series of factors appears to be at work: the absence of exit testing for high-school graduates, the difficulty of using high-school records for recruitment due to lack of curriculum standardisation and the difficulty of using grades as a reliable indicator of performance point to the possibility of a signalling failure for students who are not on the academic track. Indeed, wage and earnings patterns for high-school graduates would seem to indicate that the system of secondary education produces only a single, reliable signal for the non-college bound: whether or not the student in question has in fact received a diploma. Wage and earnings sanctions for drop-outs are large, immediate and growing. In the late 1980s, the earnings sanction for not finishing high school was about 27 per cent for both white and black males 25-34 years old. For white and black females the differential was larger – 39 and 42 per cent, respectively.

Beyond this binary "diploma-no diploma" signal, however, the educational process culminating in a high-school diploma for the non-college bound appears to generate relatively little information for prospective employers. Since the achievement attributes of recent high-school graduates are not signalled reliably to employers, these and other productivity indicators must be sorted through in other ways: either in an industrial setting, or by paying for alternative sorting mechanisms (such as in-house testing[119]) or by relying on higher education to engage in further sorting.

The wage premium for college graduates

The earnings of college graduates have increased rapidly in recent years. Real starting salaries rose 41 per cent for humanities majors, 30 per cent for education majors and 42 per cent for social science majors between 1976 and 1990 (Bishop, 1994). Diagram 25 shows, furthermore, that the earnings of college graduates rose quite sharply relative to those with less education. Two trends appear to be driving these relative shifts in earnings in favour of college graduates.

First, structural change has resulted in a general upskilling of the qualifications required by employers, accompanied by a loss of high-wage jobs that have traditionally gone to workers with only high-school diplomas. Recent studies suggest that improved technology is complementary with education and human capital (Englander and Gurney, 1994), so that over time the gap between the wages and productivity of high and low educated workers is increasing. Some

Diagram 25. **MEDIAN ANNUAL EARNINGS OF WORKERS 25 TO 34 YEARS OLD**

Ratio to those with 12 years of schooling

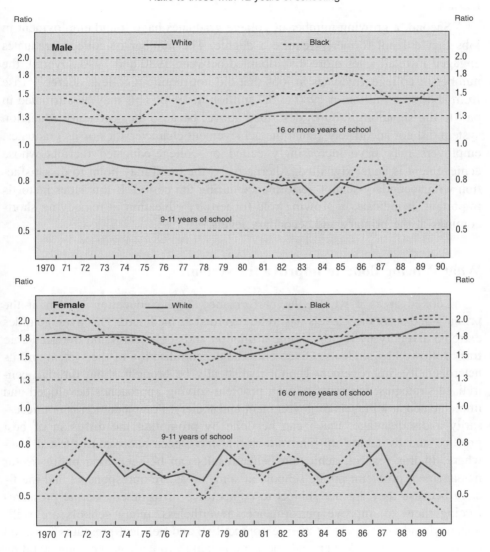

Note: One on the scale represents earnings equal to those with 12 years of school; 2 represents double their earnings; .5 represents half their earnings. The scale makes the distance between 1 and 2, or doubling, the same as betwen 1 and .5, or halving.

Source: U.S. Department of Commerce, Bureau of the Census.

evidence suggests that the premium is being paid, more specifically, for computer literacy.

Second, a growing number of college graduates have found employment in jobs that did not formerly require a degree. The number of college graduates engaged in retail sales more than doubled between 1980 and 1990. Overall, the number of college graduates in jobs that did not require a college degree[120] rose from about 3.5 million in 1980 to 5.7 million in 1990. This may be attributed in part to the signalling failures described above: because the secondary education system did not adequately signal the achievement characteristics of its graduates, employers may have increasingly called on college-educated recruits whose achievement is better signalled. Alternatively, the trend may point to dissatisfaction with secondary-school performance during the period. If this latter factor is important, it indicates a growing role for tertiary education in remedying shortcomings at the primary and secondary levels.[121]

What is being done to improve the system?

Looked at as a whole, the performance of the education system at the primary and secondary levels has to be regarded as mediocre. This average hides extreme diversity by region, ethnic affiliation and social class and the academic track followed by students. Given both the decentralisation of the system and its heterogeneity, improvement cannot realistically be brought about through centralised strategies, but must rely on problem-solving approaches developed and implemented at all levels of government and society. Fragmentation is not necessarily a disadvantage: much can be done by promoting the diffusion of best practice and by taking up innovations that have been successfully tested elsewhere. In this respect, achieving better results can be seen as a public-sector management problem: public schools in some areas are unresponsive and inefficient because they are not subject to competitive or to other external pressures forcing them to improve performance; nevertheless, many schools are well-managed and are subject to intense competitive and political pressures for good performance. But a deeper and more intractable problem is the long-standing social dimension of educational failure in the United States. Progress in this area will depend not only on improvements in the schools, but also the broader areas of social policy which are not delivering adequate service levels for large segments of the population.

State and local governments have been working in various ways to try to improve performance. The search for solutions has ushered in an era of experimentation and innovation. In general, reforms implemented by State and local governments have involved nearly every facet of school policy: management of the teaching staff, programme design, school choice, accountability, contracting out and expenditure levels. These reforms have been associated with some improvements in overall test scores and high-school completion rates[122] and some of the more successful innovations appear to be spreading.[123] Generally, though, much more effort will be required. In an era when employment prospects for poorly-educated individuals are deteriorating rapidly, the American educational system continues to graduate large numbers of young adults whose achievement levels are severely deficient. Education therefore remains a very high priority policy area, one in which equity and efficiency considerations are inextricably bound together.

The Federal role in this process is necessarily a low-profile one. As noted earlier, this is due in part to the constitutional "division of labour" which assigns responsibility for education to the States, who frequently, in turn, assign it to local authorities. In the current fiscal context, this role is further limited by the priority that must be given to Federal budget control. This effectively precludes significant increases in the Federal contribution to education.

Recent Federal initiatives for improving performance

Recent Federal initiatives have accordingly focused on inexpensive ways of improving outcomes. Foremost among these is the Federal government's role in working with school authorities, teachers' associations and others in order to define a mission and a related set of more specific goals for public schools. In relation to academic performance, the initiative seeks to define "voluntary" standards and associated assessment procedures for primary and secondary education. These initiatives date from the Education Summit in September 1989, during which President Bush and the State governors (including then-Governor Clinton of Arkansas) agreed on six national goals for education that were to be met by the year 2000. These were subsequently written into legislation – Goals 2000, signed in April 1994 – in a slightly altered form involving eight goals (Box 3).

Box 3. **National education goals**

In 1989, the nation's governors adopted six National Education Goals, which were incorporated into the "Goals 2000": Educate America Act. The Goals 2000 legislation ultimately defined eight goals:

By the year 2000:

1. **School readiness:** All children in America will start school ready to learn.

2. **School completion:** The high school graduation rate will increase to at least 90 per cent.

3. **Student achievement and citizenship:** American students will leave grades four, eight, and twelve having demonstrated competency in challenging subject matters – including English, Mathematics, Science, Foreign languages, Civics and Government, Economics, Arts, History and Geography – (and leave school) prepared for responsible citizenship, further learning, and productive employment.

4. **Teacher education and professional development:** The nation's teaching force will have access to programmes for the continued improvement of their professional skills and the opportunity to acquire the knowledge and skills needed to prepare students for the next century.

5. **Mathematics and science:** U.S. students will be first in the world in science and mathematics achievement.

6. **Adult literacy and lifelong learning:** Every adult American will be literate and will possess the knowledge and skills necessary to compete in a global economy and exercise the rights and responsibilities of citizenship.

7. **Safe, disciplined and alcohol-and drug-free schools:** Every school in America will be free of drugs, violence and the unauthorised presence of firearms and alcohol and will offer a disciplined environment conducive to learning.

8. **Parental participation:** Every school will promote partnerships that will increase parental involvement and participation in promoting the social, emotional and academic growth of children.

Source: Prisoners of Time, Report of the National Commission on Time and Learning, Washington, April 1994.

Following the Education Summit, a National Educational Goals Panel consisting of governors, Members of Congress and representatives of the Administration was created to report annually on progress toward the goals. In considering how to measure progress in academic content (goals 3 and 4 of Box 3) for its report in 1991, the Panel concluded that national education standards defining what students should know, along with new methods of assessing students' success in meeting the standards, should be considered. In order to assist in this process, Congress created a National Council on Education Standards and Testing (NCEST) in June 1991. In 1992, the Council issued a report advocating voluntary standards for students, for schools and for school systems in the five core areas specified in the national goals (English, mathematics, science, history and geography) and in other areas such as foreign languages and the arts. Earlier, in 1989, the National Council of Teachers of Mathematics had completed a "framework" for mathematics, which is to serve as the starting point for the mathematics standard. The National Academy of Sciences is developing standards for the sciences. The report also concluded that it was both desirable and feasible to develop new methods to assess the progress that U.S. students make toward meeting these standards. Such measures would involve alternative testing techniques so as to reduce reliance on the standardised tests that are now so prevalent in U.S. education.

The Administration plans to use existing funds from Chapter I of the Elementary and Secondary Education Act to promote the adoption of the voluntary standards (by making Federal grants to States contingent on progress in implementing the legislation). Particular emphasis is to be placed on standards development and its translation into related teaching material and assessment techniques.

A second initiative is the School-to-Work Opportunities Act, which was signed in May 1994. This legislation encourages the development of a national system of State-run, local partnerships of employers, educators and others in order to build school-to-work programmes. The goal is to offer young people access to education and training programmes that lead to certificates of competence that are widely recognised by employers, while also increasing their opportunities for further study.[124] In an related effort initiated under Goals 2000, a National Skill Standards Board has been set up to work on industry-recognised standards of skills in various occupational "clusters" (such as health fields, electronics and mechanics). This effort involves representatives of State governments, business and labour. Here, again, the Federal initiatives seek to redress institutional shortcomings in ways that involve relatively few additional outlays.

Assessment of recent initiatives

Although the wording of the goals is sufficiently ambiguous to leave some room for manœuvre, the outlook for meeting many of them is not good. Goal 5, for example, states that American students will be first in the world in mathematics by the year 2000. This would mean that the graduating class of the year 2000 (assuming that the goal is meant to apply to them) would have to have made up what is now a two grade level lag in performance in only six years. Achieving other goals would require improvements in other policy areas that are similarly improbable. In the absence of major overhauls in drug legislation and enforcement and in gun control, it is unlikely that school reform, alone, could eradicate the related problems of drugs and violence in schools (Goal 7). Goal 1 states that all children will start school "ready to learn". This would presumably imply much fuller health care coverage and a more comprehensive Head Start and other early childhood programmes.[125]

Nevertheless, in both Goals 2000 and the School-to-Work Opportunities bills, the emphasis on voluntary standards does seem to embody a pragmatic, first step toward making needed reforms in the system. Inadequate standardisation of educational programmes is clearly a problem: it increases the educational costs of mobility in a society that tends to be highly mobile; it undermines school systems' ability to co-ordinate pedagogical efforts with students' families because no widely-shared view exists of what public schools have a right to expect of students and *vice versa*; it makes it difficult for employers to use records from secondary schools as inputs to recruitment in the youth labour market; the pervasive lack of rigorous curricula encourages students to avoid challenging course material since they have no immediate incentive to do otherwise. In addition to correcting these shortcomings, standards should facilitate nearly every aspect of school management: funding from State or Federal governments can be linked to schools' abilities to adhere to the standards (rather than to control of inputs), and contracting out with private firms for certain services may become easier as course content becomes more standardised.

The impact of the initiatives on the pronounced inequality of educational opportunity in the United States is less clear. The amount of Federal money spent on primary and secondary education hardly changes under the legislation. The pattern of inequitable funding and of related disparities in the quality of education services continues to be one of the major obstacles to the adoption of more meaningful standards. Although there are proposals to alter the formula for allocation of Chapter I funds in order to target them more closely on needy students, minority groups are understandably concerned that the move to enhanced standards will not be accompanied by enhanced "opportunities to learn" for their children. Indeed – in what is undoubtedly an essential feature of any politically feasible reform – the recent initiatives leave State and local control and financing virtually untouched.

Although the legislation makes no major adjustments or concessions to disadvantaged groups, it may nevertheless help them. The greater intellectual investment in the design of school-to-work programmes (which is given additional impetus under the School-to-Work Opportunities Act) and in occupational skills certification will obviously help students who have opted for the vocational track in secondary studies, and these include many disadvantaged students. It is also conceivable that the greater clarity of standards will help minority families (and others as well) to become more effective participants in their children's education. They are especially likely to do this because the growing earnings premium for higher educational attainment is rapidly increasing the private incentives for educational success. More generally, minorities were not big winners under the previous system, which, in practice, gave rise to a set of discriminatory standards that demanded less of them. On the whole, though, the disadvantaged students are not expected to benefit disproportionately from the approach embodied in Goals 2000.

Increased emphasis on their problems is required. The Federal government should encourage the States to find a better balance between rights and responsibilities in the field of education. The States have imposed significant costs on society through their decades-long neglect of the education of children from less advantaged communities (see section on Welfare Reform in Chapter III, for example). U.S. society now finds itself in a situation where whole communities experience massive educational failure at a time when the economic penalties for such failure are growing. Yet, unfortunately, this is not a problem for which ready solutions are available, and trial and error will be a necessary part of the policy approach. A sustained effort will be required on a number of fronts. This will involve, in the first instance, a significant intellectual and institution-building initiative. Closer attention to and experimentation with education innovations designed to address the particular needs of these communities is required. If State and local political processes cannot generate pressures for substantial improvements in these schools, then perhaps an institutional shift allowing the greater play of market-like pressures will succeed in their place. More needs to be learned about the design of such schemes – including "pro-poor" variants of school-choice schemes (Levin, 1991) and greater use of vouchers for the purchase of private auxiliary services such as tutoring and summer programmes for disadvantaged children. At the same time, renewed attempts to make expenditure within states more equitable and better targeting of Federal outlays for disadvantaged students may be required. Although the fiscal situation will constrain the range of options for the forseeable future, ultimately a greater Federal role in the financing of education – accompanied by continued local delivery of education – would seem to be in order.[126]

V. Conclusions

The present economic expansion has now been underway for over three years and has only recently shown any signs of moderating. Led by the interest-sensitive components of demand (consumption of durable goods and all kinds of fixed investment), the underlying momentum of growth actually accelerated to about 4 per cent in late 1993. Other private consumption has also grown robustly, because improved confidence led to a willingness to spend the increased cash flow generated by the interest-rate-induced mortgage refinancing boom. Income growth has been buoyed by a pickup in job creation and in the average work-week, despite an improvement in labour productivity growth. But other categories of spending have been rather weak, preventing any overheating thus far. Public consumption has been held back by successful restraint in Federal discretionary spending, particularly as a result of defence downsizing. Until the spring at least, increases in export sales were modest because of continuing weakness of export market growth due to the lingering recession in many other OECD Member economies. And inventories have been surprisingly lean through most of the recovery, maintaining the downward trend in relation to sales manifest since the early 1980s; the inventory build-up in the second quarter may have only temporarily interrupted that trend. But, with little growth in the labour force this year, unemployment fell sharply until May, reaching levels seen by many as consistent with full employment.

Despite the dwindling slack in both product and labour markets, wage and price inflation trends have manifested little evidence of acceleration for most of the past year. For a long time falling prices for energy and imports in general made important contributions to stability in aggregate price indices, and labour costs have been kept under control primarily by the slowdown in non-wage compensation – reflecting somewhat less rapid growth in the cost of medical insurance, among other factors. Even though the case is by no means air-tight, there is good reason to think that inflation has now reached its trough for this business cycle. Empirical analysis provides little support for the view that there has been any significant structural change in wage-price determination since the late 1980s when unemployment rates equivalent to around $5\frac{1}{2}$ per cent on the new-survey basis seemed to be putting upward pressure on inflation. And more of today's unemployed have been out of work for a long time than at that point, and thus are less effective in competing for new job openings. Consistent evidence that the economy is operating at levels where it is vulnerable to an acceleration in inflation can be found in the recent behaviour of the job-vacancy rate, slower vendor deliveries, spreading capacity constraints and spot shortages in certain sectors and for certain types of high-skilled employees. Upward risks for inflation could also result from a continuation of recent strengthening in commodity prices or further declines in the value of the dollar.

The most immediate macroeconomic question is, therefore, whether the degree of monetary tightening undertaken thus far is sufficient to ease the economy back towards a sustainable growth rate so as not to jeopardise the longer-term trend toward price stability. Some endogenous slowing of GDP growth is expected as pent-up demand for housing and consumer durables, especially cars, is satisfied, disposable income growth falls in response to higher taxes, and the accummulation of business inventory slows from its torrid mid-1994 pace. Given the usual adjustment lags associated with monetary policy, it may be the case that the tightening measures taken to date are sufficient to slow the economy back to a more sustainable rate of growth. However, the Committee believes that the balance of risks is such that the current level of short-term interest rates will not suffice to bring growth down to its potential rate. Reflecting this latter concern, the Secretariat's projections assume that short-term rates will have to rise substantially more by the end of 1995. The impact of that on long-term rates should be relatively benign, as it has already been largely discounted. Indeed, bond markets could begin to strengthen slightly at some point, even in the face of monetary tightening, as they did during the summer of 1984, if they regain confidence that inflation will not surge. With these background assumptions, the underlying rate of growth should decline moderately, falling to sustainable rates of around $2\frac{1}{2}$ per cent by the second half of 1995. But even so, unemployment may continue to decline and could reach a trough of some $5\frac{3}{4}$ per cent by mid-1995.

Such a rate could still lead to an acceleration in the rate of inflation, albeit one which would leave it well below the peak rates of the last cycle. Accordingly, there is a possibility that even more rapid tightening would be needed to prevent any pick-up. Erring on the side of restraint would appear to be the best policy posture at this point in the business cycle. Even if there proves to be more spare capacity at hand than is argued here, such a policy would still be appropriate – given the fundamental strength of activity and the beneficial effects on long-term rates. And it is clearly not worth taking the risk of a marked acceleration of inflation, which would either undo much of what has been gained in terms of eradicating inflation from the economy over more than a decade or require such a vigorous policy response as to elicit a consequent recession. A strategy of additional restraint should comfort financial markets, which have become skittish regarding the likely trends for inflation and interest rates and perceptions of weak political support for a firm anti-inflation policy. Without adequate and timely policy tightening, it is unlikely that any amount of exchange-market intervention or supporting commentary will succeed in satisfying the concerns of private international investors who might be increasingly reluctant to add dollar assets to their portfolios.

The combination of progressive slowing in domestic demand growth and a projected recovery in Europe and Japan should ensure a steady decline in the drag of net exports on real GDP, which could be sufficient to check the widening in the current-account deficit. This is consistent with a rising household saving rate, a declining budget deficit and a slowdown in private investment growth. But a large part of these developments would be cyclical, and with an external deficit in excess of 2 per cent of GDP, there remains a chronic lack of domestic saving. Although such an outcome would still be much smaller than the record deficits of the mid-1980s, the U.S. economy would remain dependent on attracting substantial net capital inflows with a resulting build-up in foreign indebtedness.

Keeping downward pressure on the Federal deficit is therefore vital, not only because of its important contribution to the absorption of scarce domestic savings, but also because of longer-term considerations relating to public debt accumulation and balance-sheet deterioration and the solvency of the Social Security system. Recent outcomes have shown gratifyingly significant deficit reduction. Much of this is probably cyclical rather than structural, however, and another part is accounted for by defence cut-backs which cannot continue indefinitely, so that further gains are likely to prove more difficult, especially if the Administration's medium-term scenario is not realised. The current institutional framework has done a good job in keeping discretionary expenditures under control, but little has been done thus far to limit the much larger and intractable increases in entitlement spending. And health-care reform by itself will by no means be sufficient to solve the long-term deficit problem. Since there is such a strong public distaste for additional taxation, it is in social security that far-sighted policy-makers will have to seek further cuts in order to put the Federal finances on a firmer footing, as the spending pressures of the twenty-first century begin to come into view, and to make room for a needed shift in outlays towards those of a capital nature. A contribution could also be made from a radical overhaul of the tax system to shift taxation from income to a consumption base in order to encourage saving and investment more directly.

The budget deficit is only one of a number of major issues recently addressed by the Administration. The National Performance Review (NPR) has been a laudable attempt to change some of the fundamental ways the government operates: the way procurement is handled; how much responsibility is assigned to individual employees and how they are remunerated; and how legislative proce-dures that work to frustrate efficiency-enhancing reforms can be improved. Implementation of many NPR recommendations that are largely in the domain of the Administration is well underway and should indeed help to make the govern-ment more responsive to the changing demands for its services and possibly even lower the deficit in the process. But Congressional action is also required in relation to some key procedural elements of the NPR, but the incentives are strong for Congress to stick with politics as usual, on occasion excessively influenced by special-interest groups. A failure to reform the system means some inefficient micromanagement of public spending programmes will remain, and short-termism in decision-making more generally will persist. The U.S. political system is known for its admirable checks and balances, but this is a case where there is little counterweight to occasional Congressional excess, and there is therefore a strong argument for granting the President greater power to force Congress to re-examine some of its spending decisions.

But more than any other challenges, the Administration has attached highest priority to alleviating the nation's social problems, in recognition of their interac-tion with economic policy and processes over the long term. This has taken most prominent form in its attempt to overhaul the system of health care with a view to getting better value for the trillion dollars per year spent and to ensuring that all Americans have adequate access to medical services. The Committee has already pointed to the weaknesses of the current system and most particularly to its lack of financial sustainability, and indeed it appears that the U.S. public and policy-makers alike now understand the issues better and may be forming some degree of consensus as to how to undertake this most basic of structural reforms.

The Administration's proposal was a coherent yet complex plan mixing elements of managed competition, a single-payer plan and global budgeting. It guaranteed universal coverage from the start for a generous package of benefits and included mechanisms for enhanced cost containment. Several controversial issues surrounding the Administration proposal – such as whether insurers could effectively provide the countervailing power to providers necessary for cost containment and whether the employer mandate would lead to widespread job losses – have led the Congress to consider a range of alternative proposals which differ in key respects from that of the Administration. But differences of view on the design of health-care reform must not become a stumbling block to the enactment of any significant reform programme. For without a comprehensive overhaul of some sort, spending pressures are likely to remain unabated, while inequality of access to adequate care will continue to increase. Reform has a greater chance of success if it is comprehensive rather than piece-meal and segmented and if it introduces strong incentives for cost containment.

The welfare system is another social domain which has drawn the Administration's attention. Some claim that the availability of benefits for single mothers under the Aid to Families with Dependent Children (AFDC) programme has contributed to the breakdown of traditional family structures and the rising rate of illegitimacy in all sectors of the population and argue that, in the extreme, the programme should be eliminated. But the evidence does not seem sufficiently convincing to justify such a radical approach. Accordingly, the key objective of the Administration's proposed reform is to tilt the balance of incentives for beneficiaries more towards self-sufficiency through work, child care and enforced child support and away from long-term, possibly even inter-genera-tional, welfare dependency. Work incentives have been reinforced by the expan-sion of the refundable Earned Income Tax Credit and would be further strength-ened by any detachment of health coverage from AFDC receipt, such as through the universal coverage included in the Administration's health reform proposal.

But how many AFDC beneficiaries are capable of becoming self-supporting and how hard society should pull and/or push them in this direction are still matters for wide disagreement. The Administration's draft legislation offers a modest boost in resources available to them for engaging in extra education and training and a backstop programme of subsidised employment for those who nevertheless cannot find jobs. But at this point it seems impossible to ascertain whether the former will be effective enough to mitigate the need for a large-scale, deficit-boosting public employment scheme. The best of such training programmes seem indeed to be money well-spent, but only the best and usually only those in which the training is long-lasting and therefore costly. The challenge will be to ensure that the proper lessons in programme design can be learned so that the President's promise to "end welfare as we know it" will not result in just transforming it into dead-end public-sector job creation.

Education is another important area of public spending which presents a mixed picture in terms of performance. The diverse system of higher education – featuring institutions that run the gamut from world-class research universities to local community colleges offering vocational certificates and remedial education programmes – is a major competitive strength for the United States. In contrast, the effectiveness of the primary and secondary education system, while highly variable, can broadly be characterised as mediocre at best: scores are low in international comparative testing and drop-out rates for some ethnic minorities are high, despite the absence of even moderately rigorous exit requirements.

One of the striking characteristics of the U.S. system – compared with most others in the OECD area – is the lack of widely recognised educational standards and programmes of study. The only reasonably exacting standards acting on the primary and secondary sectors stem from the competitive university sector, and these apply only to a narrow range of students. For the non-college bound, this means that there is little incentive to take a challenging academic programme or to be a conscientious student. Much of the difference in international test scores can be attributed to the lax academic programmes followed by most primary and secondary students. The absence of standards complicates other aspects of school management; for example, by raising the costs of mobility in a society that tends to be highly mobile and by making it difficult to send clear signals about an individual's school experience to the system's "customers" (families, prospective employers and tertiary institutions). It should be emphasised, though, that some aspects of the educational system may be beneficial from a social standpoint. For example, while the incentive balance for the vast majority of students promotes low levels of both effort and achievement and must be clearly shifted, the reluctance to fail young children who are not performing at grade level provides a second chance to those who would otherwise probably eventually drop out of school. And the relaxed academic pace also allows secondary-school students to gain valuable experience through extensive participation in the job market and in non-academic activities such as sports and the arts.

The costs of poor performance in the primary and secondary education sectors are, of course, difficult to quantify. Severe failure of some communities' education systems calls into question society's ability to integrate certain population segments into the economy, with attendant costs in the form of crime, drug-use and lack of economic self-sufficiency. In these areas, the education sector is only a part – albeit an important one – of a more general policy failure. In addition, poor performance entails more obvious costs in the form of foregone private incomes and tax revenues. These stem from what are, by now, well documented earnings increases associated with additional years of schooling. Furthermore, numerous studies of the relationship between educational achievement and job performance attest to education's beneficial effects for positions at all skill levels.

Recent initiatives reflect ongoing concern about the failure of the education system for many young people. They have also been shaped by the compelling need for Federal deficit control and by a political environment in which local control of schools is nearly sacrosanct. The Federal government launched two major proposals designed to improve primary and secondary schools. First, legislation entitled ''Goals 2000'' was signed into law in early 1994. It defines eight national goals for the public school system. In working toward these goals, the Federal government has attempted to facilitate States' efforts to define ''voluntary'' national standards for education and associated efforts to develop pedagogical and testing techniques. Second, the recently passed School-to-Work Transition Act and related efforts to establish occupational skills standards attempt to develop programmes and standards for vocational studies. These efforts represent a pragmatic first-step in improving primary and secondary education. They concentrate on making the collective investment – which is more intellectual than financial – needed for society to define its goals in relation to the school system. The Federal government plans to use its political and modest financial leverage to encourage States to make progress on these goals. Even these tentative first steps on the long path to major reform of the system will not be easy to accomplish. For example, the debate over curriculum content – even in what would seem to be straightforward areas such as natural sciences – has a long and strident history in the United States. Arriving at a consensus in many subject areas is going to be difficult and time-consuming. Adding to the political complexity is the extreme and unjustifiable disparity of service quality between affluent and poorer communities, disparities that are largely due to the traditional reliance on local finance and control of schools, and that lead to poorer communities' justifiable fears that the move to enhanced standards will not be accompanied by enhanced opportunities for their children to learn. The Federal government should reinforce its traditional role in reducing such disparities, first by encouraging States to improve service quality in disadvantaged communities and, second, by improving the targeting of existing Federal funds on genuinely needy students.

Indeed, the reforms put in place the first phases of a process that will raise overall achievement levels, but they do little to address the persistent social dimension of educational failure. Federal funding for economically disadvantaged students has been held constant (although some retargetting toward needier students has been attempted). The Federal government needs to encourage the States to find a better balance between rights and responsibilities in the field of education. More attention needs to be paid to the educational needs of poorer communities and of ethnic minorities, who represent a growing proportion of the student population. Experimentation with innovations designed to address these students' needs will be required. If State and local political pressures are not sufficient to bring durable change in this situation, then an institutional shift allowing a greater reliance on market-like mechanisms, including school choice schemes, may be a fruitful area for experimentation.

The U.S. economy, therefore, offers a somewhat contrasting picture: at the macroeconomic level, performance has been remarkably good over the past two years, and the fundamentals seem sound for the immediate future. The expansion has become more firmly established, and job creation has accelerated without the re-emergence of any wage and price pressures thus far. But certain concerns of both macroeconomic and structural nature pertain to 1995 and especially the

138

years beyond. Recognising that there is very little slack remaining in labour and product markets, possibly none at all, policy-makers have acted fairly early by past standards in order to head off a clear acceleration in inflation, with all its painful by-products. But only if such action succeeds in significantly moderating the pace of demand increases will the expansion be sustained for a longer period, avoiding the bust which inevitably follows a boom. Furthermore, over the longer term, the public finances will require further attention, despite last year's successful deficit-reduction package, and additional long-term fiscal consolidation should move back to the top of the agenda again in 1995. But even more, it is worsening social problems that give grounds for concern as one looks further into the future. Many of these problems are related to inequities: between those at the top end of the income distribution – who enjoy some of the finest health and education services in the world – and those at the bottom – who lack access to even minimally adequate social services. Only if these inequities are attended to will the long-term economic future of the nation be secure.

Notes

1. This is not necessarily as favourable for aggregate growth of the capital stock as one might guess, since it reflects in large part a shift in businesses' desired mix of their capital stock, not necessarily a desire for overall capital deepening. Computers constitute a very large fraction of new equipment purchase and depreciate quite rapidly. Thus, as they make up a growing share of the capital stock, gross investment must increase more rapidly just to maintain existing levels of the stock. On a net basis, the share of equipment investment in domestic product is not so unusual.

2. The floods sharply reduced rental income growth for the year, and interest income was held down by low interest rates. This last factor, along with the progressive character of the personal tax increase, reduced the share of total disposable income received by high-income households, thereby increasing slightly the economy-wide average propensity to consume.

3. Also, with the surge in home sales came a sharp increase in investment in existing homes – notably brokers' commissions plus additions and alterations. These totalled 18 per cent in 1992 and 11 per cent in 1993. This increase was nearly as important quantitatively as the rise in single-family construction.

4. The decline in this ratio in recent years goes well beyond the gradual decline that might be expected with the shift in composition of business toward services.

5. Price inflation tends to respond to growth of wages relative to longer-run trends in labour productivity (in effect smoothing through the cyclical pickup and slowdown in productivity growth). Trend growth of output per hour is estimated by the OECD Secretariat to lie in the range of 1.3 to 1.5 per cent per year. This is a bit faster than the measured growth of 0.8 per cent over the past two decades, but actually fairly close to historical experience, after correcting for the shifts in measurement error pointed out by Gordon (1993). Most published econometric estimates of current trend productivity growth lie in the 1 per cent range – but some respected analysts suggest that trend growth in productivity may have picked up a bit in recent years due to lower inflation (Greenspan, 1994. For a detailed analysis, please see Rudebusch and Wilcox, 1994; their results were, however, generally mixed). Others point to business restructuring or the "information revolution" (David, 1989). Gordon (1993) found no clear evidence of such an aggregate improvement in trend productivity growth in the 1990s – indeed, firm conclusions about the trend are not possible as long as the output and employment data for 1992 onward remain subject to annual revision. However, productivity growth since 1989 has been (for all workers in non-farm business) about 0.8 per cent stronger than typical for the 1980s – even after allowing for the normal acceleration in

output per hour that occurs during recoveries. It is noteworthy that such an acceleration in trend productivity is **not** found for the narrower category of "production workers" alone: perhaps business restructuring has instead eased demand for supervisory workers and increased their productivity. The estimated moderate increase in trend productivity growth, combined with the projected wage and price growth, implies little change in the mark-up over unit labour costs over the next year or so, as the effects of tight capacity are offset by the normal lag in price response to wage acceleration.

6. Indexes of non-petroleum commodity prices (as reported, for example, by the Commodity Research Bureau) have picked up significantly in recent months. However, primary commodities make up a relatively small fraction of overall production cost, relative to labour and capital equipment. Prices of storable primary commodities tend to be watched closely because they can embody expectations of future price growth. However, several studies suggest that they offer little extra information to help predict inflation, above and beyond the information contained in current wage growth and the output gap.

7. However, the choice of method for estimating the gap has a great deal to do with one's view on when the gap has disappeared. Diagram 5 shows a simple split-trend estimate of potential GDP, an approach popularised by Perron (1989). Some prefer a more variable measure of potential: for example, using a Hodrick-Prescott filter to smooth actual output. However, this implicitly assumes that potential output actually weakens during recessions – an assumption which some may not find attractive, especially during recoveries. A modified filtering approach, first removing recessions from the data before running the filter, may be preferable. Using this method, the output gap appears to have closed in Q4 1993. Finally, the most conceptually attractive approach may be to estimate potential output from its component parts: working age population, trend labour-force participation, the NAWRU, and lastly trend productivity (whether from a split trend or some filtering method). Using this approach, it appears that the output gap was closed in the second quarter of 1994.

8. The first to suggest demographic adjustment was Perry (1970), who constructed an alternative aggregate unemployment rate with fixed weights for different demographic groups within the overall working-age population. Weiner (1993) used a simpler measure that was just as effective: the unemployment rate for married men, while Englander and Los (1983) used the unemployment rate for prime-age males. The OECD Secretariat's statistical tests found that the unemployment rate for prime-age males was slightly more effective in predicting wage inflation than was unemployment of married males – though even that measure was noticeably more effective than the unadjusted aggregate unemployment rate.

9. Properly specified Phillips curve relationships are very difficult to estimate, since they should incorporate, among other things, both past and expected future rates of inflation and unemployment. Data weaknesses compound the problem. However, estimation of simpler "backward-looking" specifications may nonetheless suggest which indicators are most important in evaluating prospects for wage inflation, and may also contain some information about the NAWRU. The estimates reported below are very suggestive, but should be interpreted with caution.

10. The figure is high whether one defines the long-term unemployed as those without work for more than 14 weeks or more than 26 weeks.

141

11. The relationship was strongest when long-term unemployment was defined as 15 or more weeks, but it was also positive and significant when long-term unemployment was defined as 27 weeks or more.

12. An additional partial explanation might involve the unwinding of past rapid sectoral shifts in the structure of demand. When these shifts are especially severe – *e.g.* in an oil shock, or a defence spending boom in the face of monetary contraction – both structural unemployment and job vacancies will tend to be high. Eventually, though, the Beveridge curve can shift back inward when those laid off in contracting industries find jobs in the expanding industries. Another possible explanation is the availability of new media (electronic billboards, for example) and increased use of personnel supply firms.

13. The index of vendor performance, reported by the National Association of Purchasing Managers, measures the percentage of companies receiving slower deliveries in a given month.

14. The broader aggregate measure – industrial capacity utilisation – also incorporates utilities and the mining sector, where prices often respond more to regulation or international capacity pressures than to domestic utilisation. Thus the narrower measure for the manufacturing sector alone has more power to predict future inflation.

15. The original paper by Hallman *et al.* (1991), for example, presented a "two-gap" equation for inflation acceleration: in this equation, the t-statistic for the output gap was far larger than that for the velocity gap.

16. Given the surge in M2 velocity throughout the 1990s, the corresponding slowdown of two percentage points or so in core consumer prices was mild, relative to what the P-star model would have suggested. The opportunity cost of M2 did increase with the steepened slope of the yield curve in the 1990s, among other things – but this goes only part way toward explaining the apparent shift in equilibrium velocity.

17. Any such estimate of the NAWRU can only be rough: any of the typical published estimates of the aggregate NAWRU (usually in the 5¾ to 6½ per cent range) would not be grossly inconsistent with the estimation results reported in the annex.

18. In 1993, there were 571 initial public offerings of equity in non-financial firms, raising some $25 billion, compared with only 150 for $5.6 billion in 1990. Similarly, $56.4 billion of non-investment-grade bonds were placed, up from $2.9 billion in 1990.

19. By September 1993, 73.3 per cent of all domestic bank assets were in "well-capitalised" institutions and only 8.9 per cent in "under-capitalised" institutions, compared with 30.4 and 31.1 per cent, respectively, at the end of 1990. Parallel to this was the reappearance of premiums of as much as 40 to 50 per cent in the equity price of many banks over their book value.

20. Innovatively, all were announced publicly, rather than being revealed implicitly in Federal Reserve open market operations as had theretofore been the rule, in order to provide as clear a signal as possible to the markets on the occasion of a shift in the direction of policy and to satisfy demands for increased openness.

21. Also, by April, new issuance of bonds and equities fell by half year-on-year to their lowest levels since early 1991; similarly, those of mortgage-backed securities were down by three-quarters to their lowest since end-1990.

22. Such a reaction is not, however, without precedent. In the 13 months from May 1983 to June 1984 three-month Treasury bill rates rose about 170 basis points, as the Fed attempted to brake the surging recovery. And ten-year rates jumped about 320 basis points. However, in the following two months, as short rates rose a further 60 basis points, the bond market began its mid-1980s rally, with long rates falling nearly a full percentage point as credibility was re-established.

23. This argument can be supported by pointing to the continuous narrowing of credit risk premia; spreads of corporate bond rates over Treasuries shrank by more than three-quarters of a percentage point (by about half) in the fourteen months to May 1994.

24. In his Humphrey-Hawkins testimony to Congress in February 1994, Chairman Greenspan said: "A further edging down of the unemployment rate from its January reading (6.7) per cent is viewed as a distinct possibility". By May, the rate was down to 6.0 per cent.

25. Introducing indexed bonds would also reduce uncertainty premiums, thereby saving on interest charges. In particular, it would mitigate the attractiveness of the government trying to inflate its way out of the burden of the public debt. Such securities would also provide a useful vehicle for small, unsophisticated investors to save directly for their retirement.

26. A few observers also claim that uncertainty was given an added boost by the decision to announce the rate changes, interpreting the Federal Reserve's actions as communicating a deeper fear of imminent inflation, but this cannot have had more than a very short-term effect.

27. A final, more technical, explanation relates to the end of the mortgage refinancing boom. As refinancing slowed, the average expected maturity of mortgage-backed securities lengthened, and, in order to maintain the maturity structure of their overall portfolios, holders shortened the maturity of the rest of their portfolios by selling long-term Treasury securities.

28. This figure assumes foreign direct investment is valued at current replacement cost; the corresponding figure when valuation is at market prices is $508 billion.

29. However, such transfers do not cover the cost of unfunded Federal mandates which have become more popular due to Federal budgetary stringencies. According to the National Conference of State Legislators, in 1991-92 alone the Congress passed 15 new laws with unfunded mandates on States, bringing the total to 172. Some claim that covering the cost of Federal mandates also accounts for an average of 12 per cent of city and county budgets.

30. For most of calendar 1993, deposit-insurance outlays were constrained by a lack of spending authority from the Congress. Then, after great difficulty, the RTC Completion Act was passed late in the year. It allows up to $18.3 billion more to be spent to resolve failed savings and loan associations, bringing the total cost of the bailout to about $150 billion in 1990 prices (CBO, 1994a). About 10 per cent of the current slimmed-down industry is still deemed to be troubled. Sometime in the first half of 1995 the RTC is to hand over its responsibilities to the Savings Association Insurance Fund whose reserves provide it with little cushion against negative surprises.

31. Incoming data point to the likelihood that some of that cutback has already occurred in FY 1994 and that 1994 was the first in 25 to experience an absolute decline in discretionary outlays.

32. For FY 1994 Congress appropriated 68.6 per cent of the funds needed for the President's increased spending requests, ranging from about a third for Head Start and various employment and training initiatives and less than half for his education and national service programmes to nearly full funding for environmental programmes and more than 100 per cent for housing and community development programmes. For FY 1995 the prospects are perhaps not as bright, as the CBO scored the Administration Budget as exceeding the BEA discretionary caps by $3½ billion.

33. This latter assumption is particularly surprising, as the Administration had not been nearly so optimistic in its 1994 Budget assumptions: average real long rates were then assumed to be around 4¼ per cent, compared with the 3.0 per cent in the 1995 Budget, and real short rates were assumed to average 2.0 per cent rather than the 1.0 per cent mean in the 1995 document. Each percentage point difference in assumed real interest rates is worth a cumulative $130 billion in extra spending by 1999, of which $41 billion (½ per cent of GDP) is in 1999 alone.

34. Total Federal and Federally-assisted borrowing as a share of total net credit-market borrowing has risen from less than 20 per cent prior to the first energy shock to a peak of 87 per cent in 1992, before falling to 76 per cent in 1993. The majority of this is direct Federal borrowing from the public to cover the deficit. It is, therefore, highly likely that the Federal deficit is pre-empting a substantial share of domestic saving: the national-accounts deficit represented over a quarter of gross private saving in 1992.

35. A move away from income-based taxes might benefit from a reduction of the many tax expenditures contained in those taxes. The sum of all individual revenue losses in 1995 alone from such provisions was $436 billion (this is a maximum figure, since it does not account for interactive or behavioural effects), 59 per cent of the expected revenues from the corporate and individual income tax (Office of Management and Budget, 1994). To put it another way, as much as 37 per cent of the tax base has been eroded. Reversing that erosion would allow the same revenue to be raised with lower statutory rates which presumably would be less distortionary.

36. There are currently six such programmes covering workers displaced most notably for reasons of trade adjustment, defence conversion and pollution controls.

37. However, some progress has been made in other areas under the Common Agenda for Cooperation in Global Perspective.

38. This involves some double counting, since the deficit reduction incorporates the effects of a cut of 143 000 in the Federal workforce that was already included in the 1994 Federal budget. The remainder of the spending cuts contained in the NPR proposals are not contained in OBRA93: thus, if Congress passes the cuts, it has the option of using the additional savings either to increase spending in other ways or simply to keep spending beneath OBRA93 caps. For example, it chose to use most of the savings from the employment cuts to finance the $30 billion crime bill.

39. The NPR proposes to switch most such grants from cost-based reimbursement to fee-for-service, in exchange for granting greater administrative flexibility to the States – simplifying paperwork and reducing the Federal government's cost of administering the grants.

40. See for example Congressional Budget Office (1993c), pp. 23-27.

41. Career concerns can and do substitute for direct financial incentives for many Federal employees whose performance is easy to measure.

42. To assist in this and other management reforms throughout the executive branch, the President has created a Management Council, composed of the chief operating officers of all cabinet-level agencies. The Management Council is charged *inter alia* with overseeing the spread of performance management and new procurement procedures, and "re-engineering" the bureaucracy.

43. As of July 1994, seven agency heads (including five Cabinet Secretaries) have signed "Presidential Performance Agreements" with President Clinton, formulating strategic goals and a corresponding performance plan. The NPR calls for all Cabinet members to sign such performance agreements.

44. Also, re-election often depends heavily on factors in large part independent of performance: changing economic conditions or changing tastes of the electorate, for example. In these circumstances, which can mask the true performance of the politician, performance incentives are lessened: "moral hazard" exists.

45. The study also cites lack of adequate management information systems. For this reason, among others, the 1995 Budget incorporates significant spending increases on computing equipment and software to expedite government financial management. Also, the Government Streamlining Bill creates "franchise funds" to allow agencies the flexibility to increase spending on items such as computers, with the requirement that such spending result in equivalent or greater cost savings later on.

46. A "pork-barrel" project appropriation is a government project yielding rich patronage benefits.

47. The NPR also points out the success of earlier Federal experiments in liberalised financial management – such as the Forest Service's test of reduced line-item restrictions on the budget of an Oregon national park in the late 1980s, as a result of which measured productivity went up 35 per cent within two years. However, the NPR also mentions that Congress chose to reimpose the line-item restrictions on the park a few years later, despite the success of the experiment. A similar experiment in reduced micromanagement was dramatically successful at the China Lake Naval Air Warfare Center during the 1980s. President Reagan proposed to make the China Lake reforms more widespread in 1987 legislation: the bill failed in Congress because it lacked union support and would have involved surrender of Congressional control (Horner, 1993).

48. In principle, programmes which greatly benefit a few may be worthwhile, if the losses to the majority of citizens are small enough. However, several considerations suggest that Congress has an incentive to engage in excessive log-rolling and earmarking. First, each voter tends to focus on a few issues which affect him greatly, without penalising incumbents for the many minor losses to himself which result when the politician accedes to rent-seeking pressure by others (Blinder, 1987). Second, political activism (lobbying, etc.) is too costly and time-consuming to allow attention to the many issues which affect one only marginally – especially since much of the benefit of activism accrues to others. Because one does not capture all the benefits of one's activism, there is a tendency to let others do the work – this "free-rider problem" implies that widely dispersed interest groups often do not exert

political pressure commensurate with their size. Olson (1982) suggests that the cumulative legislative influence of special-interest groups typically makes governments increasingly inefficient over time – unless crisis reduces the effectiveness of their rent-seeking.

49. Opponents of the legislation point out that it involves transfer of power from the Congress to the President, who could conceivably manipulate Congressional opponents by threatening to force another vote on their favoured earmarks. Depending on the character of the President, this mild transfer of power could be good or bad. Others argue that Congress would still retain essentially the same powers it now exercises – but the change would lead Congress to exercise control in a more appropriate manner. Legislation could still specify the results Congress wants for the resources allocated and allow for sanctions if the Administration fails to deliver. In any case the proposed legislation retains one very attractive feature: every time that the enhanced rescission power is successfully exercised, a dubious line item will have been exposed as such and terminated.

50. A key reason why such reform bills tend to pass the House and not the Senate is the procedural difference that Senate rules allow filibuster, while House rules do not. Thus, in effect reform legislation requires more than 60 per cent approval in the Senate, the threshold to shut off filibusters.

51. The draft Federal budget for 1995 nonetheless contains significant reductions in agricultural subsidies relative to 1994.

52. The delay resulted in layoffs in some agencies, but over 13 000 employees signed up for buyouts in the spring.

53. And relative to their years of experience. Workers close to retirement age will naturally find buyouts especially attractive. Kettl (1994, p. 8) discusses these problems in more detail.

54. Small businesses may gain, however, from the bill's provision mandating computer posting of most Federal requests for bids within the next five years.

55. Furthermore, recent action on reform of campaign finance, lobbying and gift rules may have reduced the appetite of members for further reform battles.

56. Administrative costs are high by international standards because there are over 1 500 health insurance firms, each with its own set of procedures to deal with over 6 000 hospitals and 778 000 physicians and dentists. Where some degree of standardisation and centralisation has been achieved, such as the public health programmes, administrative costs are 2 per cent (Medicare) to 4¼ per cent (Medicaid), as compared to 14 per cent in the private insurance sector (Nedde, 1993). The result is that, by some estimates, the United States devotes as much as twice as large a share of its outlays to overhead as does Canada (Consumers Union, 1992). Some overhead costs are indeed necessary to help to control costs by routing out waste, fraud and abuse in billings and claims, and delivery of inappropriate or frivolous services. Some argue that Medicare and Medicaid should make greater efforts to review submitted claims even if that would entail higher administrative costs.

57. The fee-for-service based system induces suppliers to provide the maximum amount of care. Furthermore, "defensive medicine", driven by fears of enormous malpractice awards, adds an estimated 3 per cent to overall costs. Finally, as elsewhere, some procedures are undertaken out of genuine ignorance of a best-practice approach: for example, in a RAND

Corporation survey, nearly one-third of carotid artery surgery was deemed to be inappropriate and a further like amount to be of equivocal value.

58. The Council of Economic Advisers (1994) estimates violent crime to be responsible for about 2 per cent of health spending. Fraud and abuse, also present in other countries, may boost expenditure by 10 per cent.

59. Out-of-pocket expenses have declined from about one-half of health expenditure in 1960 to about one-fifth in 1990.

60. But even discussing a reform of the system seems to have had an effect: recent increases in medical inflation relative to overall price increases have been much lower than in the past, resulting in a much smaller estimated increase in the share of GDP spent on health care in 1993 than in previous years.

61. More exactly, those uninsured all year spend an average of about $1 224 per person per year (36 per cent use no health services whatsoever), while those with any private insurance spend $2 332 (Council of Economic Advisers, 1994). Part of this difference may be attributable to an apparent greater willingness to pay and also to demand extra related services as well as a higher cost structure in hospitals treating privately insured patients. In any case, a large part of the cost of care for the uninsured is shifted onto the insured private sector, since the public programmes have fixed fee schedules which sometimes are insufficient for hospitals to cover their costs. Aaron and Bosworth (1994) argue that Medicare and Medicaid cover less than full hospital costs (Medicare about 95 per cent and Medicaid about 65 per cent), leaving private payers to pay about 130 per cent, a further hidden tax to finance these programmes. An estimated $26 billion was thus shifted in 1991. About half of this was uncompensated care provided by hospitals, representing 6 per cent of total hospital costs, up from 5.1 per cent in 1980 (CBO, 1993b).

62. More is actually known about uninsured workers: according to O'Neill and O'Neill (1994), the uninsured are far more likely to be employed part-time, to work fewer weeks per year, and to be high-school dropouts (and less likely to be college graduates); as a result they earn less than half as much per year as the insured. Young workers have a higher-than-average probability of being uninsured.

63. The smallest firms (with fewer than 10 employees) have more than three times the share of workers who are without coverage as do those with more than 1 000 employees. Scofea (1994) reports that only 69 per cent of workers in small, private establishments participated in employer-provided medical-care plans in 1991. This is well below the 83 per cent share for those employed in medium and large establishments. However, the latter share was as high as 97 per cent as recently as 1984. The author claims that this decline is attributable to declining participation among workers to whom benefits are indeed offered, in part because of the steady rise in the share of employees required to contribute to their own coverage (59 per cent in 1991, up from 28 per cent in 1980). The proportion of workers who decline health benefits that they are offered is undoubtedly related as well to the increasing number of two-worker families. Nearly 80 per cent of eligible workers who decline coverage are covered by another plan (U.S. Department of Labor, 1994).

147

64. This is confirmed by the results of a recent poll which indicated that 20 per cent of respondents or someone in their family had passed up a job change in order to hold on to existing health benefits.

65. A recent summary of these programmes has been provided by Currie (1993).

66. The poverty rate for children in single-parent families is about four times higher than for those in two-parent families.

67. Other factors which have probably increased the caseload include Supreme Court decisions striking down State minimum residency requirements (1969) and rules preventing the presence of a male adult in the household, even if he is providing no financial support (1968). The optional AFDC-UP benefit for two-parent families with either parent unemployed, offered by 26 states in the late-1980s, was made obligatory for all states beginning in fiscal year 1991.

68. To some extent, however, these reductions have been compensated by increases in the real value of other benefits, especially Food Stamps and Medicaid. According to Murray (1993), the real value of the welfare package rebounded during the 1980s almost back to the mid-1970s peak which was twice the 1960 level, primarily due to the surging costs of Medicaid. Most recently, however, states have taken a particularly restrictive stance: in 1991, for example, 31 states left nominal benefit levels unchanged and 9 more proposed deep cuts (Currie and Cole, 1993). By July 1992, the combined value of AFDC and Food Stamps for a three-person family was 26 per cent lower in real terms than it had been 20 years earlier.

69. This ratio ranged from less than 0.09 per cent in Virginia, Alabama and Nevada to around 0.65 per cent in California and Michigan. The coefficient of variation was about 0.5.

70. However, since 1988, one year of transitional Medicaid coverage and childcare has been provided to those leaving AFDC for employment. Nevertheless, as of 1993, a mother of two children with average child-care expenses resident in Pennsylvania, for example, loses both her AFDC and her Medicaid entirely with annual income about equal to earnings from a full-time job at the minimum wage. However, she can earn double the minimum wage before she becomes ineligible for any Food Stamps.

71. Overall, female heads of household with dependent children work as much as other women and generally earn more.

72. While there was a sharp drop in the share of AFDC female heads who were working in 1982 (especially those working full time), precisely the year after the 1981 legislative changes which increased the benefit reduction rate and reduced the maximum allowable income, this effect is entirely attributable to the change in eligibility rules, rather than to any behavioural response.

73. According to Moffitt (1992, Table 5), the impact of a cut of a third in the guarantee or maximum benefit level (such as has occurred since the early 1970s when most of the data used in the literature were generated) in the context of a unit benefit reduction rate would lower the labour-supply impact of AFDC by about 60 per cent. For a summary of the changes in AFDC work incentives which have occurred since 1970, see Burtless (1990). According to Hoynes (1993), participation in the unemployed parent part of AFDC (see footnote 67) is more sensitive to the changing value of benefits than is that in the part

dealing with female heads. AFDC receipt explains about 33 per cent of labour supply differences among male eligibles and 40 per cent among female eligibles. Accordingly, it appears that those entering AFDC are likely to be those less predisposed to labour-market participation in the first place.

74. The 30 per cent reduction in work effort represents a loss of 5.4 hours of work per week. Given data on average wages and average AFDC benefits, Moffitt (1992) calculates a loss fraction of 0.37. The $1.60 figure is derived by taking the inverse of one minus the loss fraction.

75. It should be noted that there is an element of upward bias in these duration data: AFDC receipt is defined as receiving at least one month of benefits in a year, but benefits may be received for only part of the year. Accordingly, others have estimated slightly shorter median durations calculated in months (Moffitt, 1992). For reasons which are not well understood, individual spells have also become noticeably shorter over time: the median has fallen from 31 months in 1975 to 22 months in 1991.

76. However, very recent unpublished work by Zimmerman and Levine, cited in Currie (1993), disputes this conclusion.

77. However, Currie and Cole (1993) have recently shown that birth-weight – a good proxy for child welfare – is *positively* influenced by mother's AFDC receipt (significantly so for whites), so long as the estimation is properly undertaken.

78. This is the conclusion presented by Moffitt in his recent survey. However, an almost simultaneous survey by Murray (1993) cites additional evidence, not mentioned by Moffitt, some of which apparently manages to explain about half of the increase in the non-white illegitimacy ratio from 1963 to 1983 through the growth of AFDC net benefits. Overall, around 30 per cent of all children are now born out of wedlock, up from around 5 per cent as recently as 1960; among blacks, the figure is close to two-thirds.

79. In any case, it is not disputed that welfare allows single mothers to live independently: states with lower benefits tend to have a greater proportion of single mothers living with a parent (Ellwood and Bane, 1985). WRA would require single mothers under 18 to live with a responsible adult, preferably a parent, in order to receive AFDC.

80. Yet it should be noted that, at least superficially, white illegitimacy trends appear similar to those of blacks some 30 years earlier.

81. In the example given in the table, the marginal "tax" rate for someone just beyond the minimum wage is just over 40 per cent. But beyond $6 per hour it rises to over 75 per cent.

82. Beyond $50 per month, child-support receipts are fully offset by lower AFDC payments. There may be a case for reducing the amount withheld by the State in order to sharpen incentives for recipients to seek and for absent fathers to make support payments.

83. For more information, see Lerman (1993).

84. The two-year maximum is seen as a lifetime limit; but there is a possibility of a welfare recipient earning renewed eligibility. Some exemptions are allowed, and time spent on welfare before the age of 18 is not counted. Some 13 states had instituted experimental programmes along these lines by July 1992. Most prominently of late, in 1995 Wisconsin will conduct in two counties a demonstration requiring work or job search. Recipients will

be limited to 24 months of AFDC benefits except under certain conditions such as inability to find employment due to local labour-market conditions.

85. Changing the administrators of the welfare system from cheque-writers into job-placement specialists may be as much of a challenge as any other already described.

86. JOBS requires that any AFDC recipient lacking a high-school diploma or basic literacy be offered relevant education. This usually entails training for the GED examination, whose value has been questioned (Cameron and Heckman, 1993). States are also mandated to provide job-skills training, placement services and two of the following: job-search assistance, on-the-job training or community work experience. JOBS also has a "learn fare" provision whereby States can require teenage AFDC recipients to enrol in school or have their benefits reduced. But, rather than insufficient Federal funding, the problem with this programme has been a lack of State demand: in FY 1992 only $0.56 billion of the $1.0 billion in Federal JOBS funds available was actually spent. In 1991, while 39 per cent of AFDC recipients were subject to JOBS participation requirements, only 15 per cent of them were actually counted as participants. The caps to this entitlement are in the process of rising to $1.5 billion in 1995. In order to avoid a reduction in Federal matching rates, states must have reached Federal targets for JOBS participation rates and for focus on long-term recipients by that year.

87. An evaluation of California's GAIN (workforce) programme showed that it was able to raise participants' income substantially and to get about half of them off welfare after two years. But, another, of the New Chance programme, which involved 1 408 teenage mothers in 10 states, found that after 18 months participants were just as likely to be still on welfare (80 per cent) and jobless as non-participants. In welfare, as in other areas involving education and training, remedial efforts are far less successful than primary learning, suggesting the need for preventive action.

88. Others believe that, once phased in, the programme could ultimately cost $7 billion per year. The financing plan is based on several items including: $3.7 billion over five years in reduced transfers to non-citizens; $1.6 billion in lower aid to States' emergency spending to keep people off welfare; $1.6 billion from the corporate "superfund" tax; $0.8 billion in reduced benefits to drug and alcohol addicts; and $0.5 billion from curbing agricultural subsidies to farmers with more than $100 000 in annual non-farm income.

89. The share of non-teaching staff stabilised during the 1980s after rising in the 1960s and 1970s.

90. This interpretation was handed down by the U.S. Supreme Court in the decision relating to San Antonio School Board versus Rodriguez in 1973. The decision implies that the Federal Constitution does not provide a legal basis for challenging the unequal distribution of education funding.

91. Some of the State constitutions contain language describing the standards that would be applied to public education, but most do not.

92. In many regions, this happened as an integral part of broader shifts in post-war settlement patterns – and especially as part of the tendency for white, relatively affluent populations to move to suburban locations and for poor minorities to become concentrated in the inner cities. These settlement patterns may have been encouraged by the tendency to use local

property taxes to finance some social services. This motivated well-off households to organise themselves into homogeneously affluent communities. See Weir (1992) and Levine and Williams (1992).

93. For example, the state mathematical achievement data for public schools (discussed below) show Washington, D.C. with the nation's lowest score. Its average score of 234 for 1992 means that the typical eighth-grade student (who would normally be either 13 or 14 years old) was unable to do straightforward numerical and did not master beginning problems-solving skills.

94. For a discussion of some of the methodological difficulties see, for example, Hanushek (1986 and 1994) and Hedges *et al.* (1994).

95. Since 1912, 31 states have tested the constitutionality of their public school finance systems, some more than once. Most court challenges have attacked statutory financing schemes using one of three legal foundations: the Federal Constitution, equal opportunity clauses of State constitutions, or State constitutions' education articles. See McUsic (1991). State Supreme courts have, in twelve instances, ruled against the constitutionality of the statutes.

96. This disparity is probably large by U.S. standards, but not unparalleled. Other studies indicate that Ohio is characterised by strong inequality of expenditure, but that it not the least inequitable in this respect. Alaska, Missouri, Montana and Vermont all had higher inequality measures using the Theil coefficient as an indicator (Wyckoff, 1992).

97. In 1990, about 59 per cent of three to four year-olds from families with annual incomes over $40 000 were enrolled in preschool, compared with 30 per cent of similar children from families with less than $20 000 in income.

98. Little can be taken for granted in the debate on curriculum content in the United States. One of the most historically prominent of these debates, for example, concerns the theory of human evolution. For decades, Christian fundamentalists have tried, with varying degrees of success, to block the teaching of this theory or to ensure that the Biblical version of creation is taught at the same time. The long judicial history of this controversy began with a landmark case – commonly known as the "Scopes Monkey Trial" of 1925 – in which the Tennessee court system upheld a law prohibiting the teaching of human evolution. The Tennessee law was repealed in 1967, but in other states, the debate is active to this day.

99. The difficulty of the course material taken by students appears to be very much linked to their mastery of the subject matter. One study, comparing the mathematics proficiency of Japanese and American students, found that the relatively limited number of Americans (14 per cent of the test sample) who had been exposed to the rigorous subject matter had identical scores to the top 20 per cent of students in Japan, where the mathematics programme is more homogeneous and more rigorous for a broad cross-section of students. The study noted further that the performance of the bottom half of the student population is significantly below the equivalent population in Japan. By implication, strengthening curriculum content and obliging many more students to take rigorous courses would improve the test scores of U.S. students relative to those of other countries. See CBO (1993*a*).

100. Since 1990, poor pupils in Milwaukee have been given vouchers to attend private schools. This experiment is limited to non-religious schools and to 1 per cent of the children in the

city's public school system. Despite its limited scope, this experiment is being closely monitored in education policy circles. See OECD (1994).

101.   These arrangements abolished most links between residence and school assignments. All families were obliged to choose at least two schools. Students were assigned to available places according to parents' choice, racial balance and siblings already at the school. The majority of first-choice schools were not within walking distance of the family's residence. One analysis of this experiment (OECD, 1994) indicates that it has helped to stem the flight of white families from Boston schools, with enrolment expected to rise by 5-10 per cent.

102.   The increasing prevalence of "home schooling" – whereby almost 500 000 children are taught at home – underscores the potential scale of educational services provided by the home. In such cases, the home services are in competition with those provided by the formal sector.

103.   The recruitment behaviour of such businesses may reflect a lack of trust in the information coming from high schools or the relative ease of firing a worker with whom one is dissatisfied in the United States.

104.   A survey found that co-operative education was the most common work-study arrangement in 1991, offered in 49 per cent of all high schools and vocational schools (Stern, 1992). School-based enterprise was offered in 19 per cent of the surveyed institutions, apprenticeships in 6 per cent and youth apprenticeship in 2 per cent. Frequently observed activities of high school enterprise are house-building, school stores, restaurants, child care and car repair.

105.   In the 1960 to 1993 period, a disproportionate number of recipients of Nobel prizes were of American nationality or were working at American universities. More specifically, 25 Nobel laureates out of 54 recipients in chemistry were American or did their work at U.S. research institutions. For physics the equivalent number is 37 Nobel laureates out of a total of 68 recipients and, for medicine, 46 laureates out of a total of 80 recipients.

106.   Technical colleges, which are less common than community colleges, focus more on vocational training. They usually offer two-year degree programmes leading to an associate (two-year) degree or a shorter "certificate" programme.

107.   The international comparative data used in this section relies heavily on OECD (1993b).

108.   The achievement scores referred to in this statement are the National Assessment of Educational Progress as reported in National Center for Education Statistics (1992).

109.   These comparisons should be interpreted with caution, since they require "linking" (or establishing equivalences between) two sets of test results using a controversial methodology. The two tests are the National Assessment of Educational Progress (NAEP) which is a widely used achievement test in the United States and the International Assessment of Educational Progress (IAEP). Both of these tests are designed and administered by the Educational Testing Service, a private not-for-profit organisation that does much of the nation-wide educational testing in the United States. The two tests contained a significant number of overlapping questions and groups of students in the United States took both tests. The linking of the test results uses the information on scores from the group that took both tests to map IAEP results into equivalent NAEP results. See Pashley and Phillips (1993).

110. This and the other state data contained in this paragraph are from Iowa Department of Education (1993).

111. For example, being black, once other factors are accounted for, had no effect on test scores in the early grades, but became highly significant in the later grades. The coefficient on ''per cent of Hispanic students'' was always statistically significant and negative, regardless of grade level. This is shown in part to be correlated with English being a second language in the home and with migrant-farm-worker status, though the effects of these variables depend on the grade level under consideration.

112. This figure can be more than 100 per cent because a large number of graduates in countries with apprenticeship programmes complete more than one secondary degree.

113. The compulsory schooling age is 16 in most states and 18 in a few.

114. A General Equivalence Certificate can be earned by adults who do not have a high-school diploma. However, the labour market does not treat this certificate as a close substitute for a high-school diploma (see Chapter III).

115. Numerous studies have found that time spent watching television is negatively correlated with school performance (Bishop, 1994). In addition to watching television, high-school students seem to have ample time for other activities: in 1991, 44 per cent of high-school seniors reported using illegal drugs at least once and 16 per cent reported having taken drugs within the last month (CBO, 1993a).

116. There are some signs that U.S. students have increased the amount of time they spend studying in recent years. According to the NAEP data, the proportion of 13 (17) year-olds reporting they did more than one hour a day of homework rose from 40 (37) in 1983 to 71 (66) per cent in 1990 (NCES, 1993a). In 1991 IAEP survey, 29 per cent of American 13 year-olds said they were doing two or more hours of homework per day. The proportion doing more than two hours of homework was equally low in Canada and Portugal and was even lower in Scotland and Switzerland.

117. These results are reported in Stern et al. (1994). Because of selection bias it is difficult to tell to what extent the observed relationship between work and grades reflects pre-existing differences among students. This study notes that teachers admit holding students who work outside to a easier grading standard than those who do not. Thus, the costs of work for academic achievement may be higher than grades indicate.

118. In October 1992, only 21.2 per cent of 16 to 19 year-old black youth were employed, compared to 45.9 per cent of 16 to 19 year-old white youth (Osterman and Iannozzi, 1993).

119. The use of entry testing for employees is uncommon in the United States because of the threat of litigation under anti-discrimination laws. Since different ethnic minorities exhibit large differences in achievement test scores, these tests could be used as a device for discriminating against minorities. The courts have ruled on the conditions under which such testing is allowable and have ruled that the test must be of demonstrable relevance to tasks performed on the job. In recent years, firms have been given increased flexibility to engage in such testing, but the threat of litigation is still very much present.

120. Material for this section comes from Hecker (1992). This study uses a conservative definition of the jobs that do not require a college degree.

121. This latter explanation is not entirely satisfactory since national testing indicates that performance was declining over the 1970s and improved slightly over the 1980s.

122. These improvements may also be due in part to changes in private behaviour induced by large increases in the private returns to education.

123. An example of an apparently successful innovation is the so-called ''Career Academy''. These are special programmes established in a high school (called a school-within-a-school and usually organised around a vocational theme such as health, finance or electronics) and designed to retain students who are viewed as being likely drop-outs. The first version of this programme was implemented in Philadelphia in 1969. The idea was brought to California in 1981, when two trials programmes where initiated. These were replicated in about ten additional sites. A study of these replications (Stern *et al.*, 1989) estimated that the net benefit from drop-out prevention for a cohort of 327 students was between $1 million and $1.3 million. National networks have been formed to co-ordinate the implementation of such programmes in other states. ''Charter schools'' are another innovation that appears to be spreading. These are public schools that are created and run independently of local school districts. Nine States have enacted legislation permitting such schools since 1991.

124. As inducements for creating State-run systems, the bill includes provisions that would authorise development grants to support State efforts in designing school-to-work transition strategies, implementation grants for States ready to begin operation of their strategies and waivers of certain statutory and regulatory provisions in Federal job training and education programmes that may impede school-to-work transition efforts.

125. The Clinton Administration has been attempting to increase the coverage of Head Start, the programme that provides pre-school services to needy children.

126. This would improve the education system in several ways. First, it would reduce the adverse incentive effects arising from the various inter-governmental externalities identified earlier. For example, the Federal government (because it receives most income tax revenues) is the main public beneficiary of the income-enhancing investments in education made by State and local authorities. Another example is the implicit human-capital subsidy paid by labour-exporting regions of the United States to labour-importing regions. Second, a greater role for Federal financing would allow for greater sharing of the burden of educating economically disadvantaged youth. As shown earlier, the incidence of such students is highly unequal among states.

References

Aaron, Henry and Barry Bosworth (1994), "Health Care Financing and International Competitiveness", paper prepared for the Competitiveness Policy Council, 10 February.

Ando, Albert and Flint Brayton (1993), "Prices, Wages and Employment in the U.S. Economy: A Traditional Model and Tests of Some Alternatives", National Bureau of Economic Research Working Paper 4568, December.

Angrist, Joshua and Alan Krueger (1991), "Estimating the Pay-off to Schooling Using the Vietnam-Era Draft Lottery", Princeton University Industrial Relations Section Working Paper No. 290, August.

Ashenfelter, Orley and Alan Krueger (1992), "Estimates of the Economic Return to Schooling from a New Sample of Twins", Princeton University Industrial Relations Section Working Paper No. 304, forthcoming in *American Economic Review*, July.

Auerbach, Alan J. (1994), "The U.S. Fiscal Problem: Where We Are, How We Got There and Where We're Going", National Bureau of Economic Research Working Paper 4709, April.

Bane, Mary Jo and David T. Ellwood (1994), *Welfare Realities: From Rhetoric to Reform*, Harvard University Press, Cambridge, Massachusetts.

Bishop, John (1989), "Scientific Illiteracy: Causes, Costs and Cures", ILR Reprints No. 641, Cornell University, School of Industrial and Labor Relations.

Bishop, John (1994), unpublished Consultancy Report to the OECD.

Blinder, Alan (1987), *Hard Heads, Soft Hearts*, Addison Wesley Publishing Corporation.

Burtless, Gary (1990), "The Economist's Lament: Public Assistance in America", *Journal of Economic Perspectives*, 4, 1, Winter.

Cameron, Stephen V. and James J. Heckman (1993), "The nonequivalence of high school equivalents", *Journal of Labor Economics*, 11, 1, January.

Card, David (1993), "Using geographic variation in college proximity to estimate the return to schooling", National Bureau of Economic Research Working Paper 4483, October.

Chiswick, Barry (1988), "Differences in Education and Earnings across Racial and Ethnic Groups: Tastes, Discrimination and Investments in Child Quality", *Quarterly Journal of Economics*, August.

Congressional Budget Office (1993a), *The Federal Role in Improving Elementary and Secondary Education*, May.

Congressional Budget Office (1993b), *Trends in Health Spending: An Update*, June.

Congressional Budget Office (1993c), *Using Performance Measures in the Federal Budget Process*, July.

Congressional Budget Office (1994a), *The Economic and Budget Outlook: Fiscal Years 1995-1999*, January.

Congressional Budget Office (1994b), *An Analysis of the Administration's Health Proposal*, February.

Consumers Union (1992), "The Search for Solutions", *Consumer Reports*, September, quoted in Nedde (1993).

Council of Economic Advisers (1994), *Economic Report of the President*, February.

Currie, Janet (1993), "Welfare and the Well-Being of Children: The Relative Effectiveness of Cash and In-Kind Transfers", National Bureau of Economic Research Working Paper 4539, November.

Currie, Janet and Nancy Cole (1993), "Welfare and Child Health: The Link Between AFDC Participation and Birth Weight", *American Economic Review*, 83, 4, September.

Danzon, Patricia M. (1994), "Drug Price Controls, Wrong Prescription", *Wall Street Journal Europe*, 7 February.

David, Paul (1989), "Computer and Dynamo: The Modern Productivity Paradox in a Not-Too-Distant Mirror", OECD International Seminar on Science, Technology and Economic Growth, 5-8 June. Reprinted in Stanford University, Center for Economic Policy Research Publication No. 172.

Ellwood, David T. (1986), "Targeting 'Would-Be' Long-Term Recipients of AFDC", Mathematica Policy Research, Princeton, New Jersey, quoted in Moffitt (1992).

Ellwood, David T. (1988), *Poor Support: Poverty in the American Family*, Basic Books, New York.

Ellwood, David T. and Mary Jo Bane (1985), "The Impact of AFDC on Family Structure and Living Arrangements" in Ronald G. Ehrenberg (ed.), *Research in Labor Economics*, 7, Jai Press, Greenwich, Conn. and London.

Englander, Steven and Cornelis Los (1983), "Recovery without Accelerating Inflation", *Federal Reserve Bank of New York Quarterly Review*, Summer.

Englander, Steven and Andrew Gurney (1994), "Medium-term Determinants of OECD Productivity", *OECD Economic Studies*, 22, Spring.

Galbraith, Karl (1994), "Federal Budget Estimates, Fiscal Year 1995", *Survey of Current Business*, 74, 2, February.

General Accounting Office (1993), *School Age Demographics: Recent Trends Pose New Educational Challenges*, August.

General Accounting Office (1994a), "Prescription Drugs: Companies Typically Charge More in the United States Than in the United Kingdom", GAO/HEHS-94-29, January.

General Accounting Office (1994b), "Elementary School Children: Many Change Schools Frequently, Harming their Education", February.

Gordon, Robert J. (1982), "Inflation, Flexible Exchange Rates, and the Natural Rate of Unemployment" in Baily, Martin (ed.), *Workers, Jobs and Inflation*, Brookings Institution, Washington, D.C.

Gordon, Robert J. (1993), "The Jobless Recovery: Does It Signal a New Era of Productivity-Led Growth?", *Brookings Papers on Economic Activity*, 1.

Gore, Al (1993), *From Red Tape to Results – Creating a Government that Works Better and Costs Less: Report of the National Performance Review*, U.S. Government Printing Office, 10 September.

Gottschalk, Peter (1990), "AFDC Participation Across Generations", *Papers and Proceedings*, American Economics Association, 80, 2, May.

Greenspan, Alan (1994), Testimony before the U.S. Senate Banking Committee hearing on monetary policy, May 27.

Gruber, Jonathan and Brigitte Madrian (1993), "Health Insurance Availability and the Retirement Decision", National Bureau of Economic Research Working Paper 4469, September.

Gruber, Jonathan and Maria Hanratty (1993), "The Labor Market Effects of Introducing National Health Insurance: Evidence from Canada", National Bureau of Economic Research Working Paper 4589, December.

Gueron, Judith M. (1990), "Work and Welfare: Lessons on Employment Programs", *Journal of Economic Perspectives*, 4, 1, Winter.

Hallman, Jeffrey, Richard Porter, and David Small (1991), "Is the Price Level Tied to the M2 Monetary Aggregate in the Long Run?", *American Economic Review*, 81, 4, September.

Hanushek, Eric (1986), "The Economics of Schooling: Production and Efficiency in the Public Schools", *Journal of Economic Literature*, 24, 3, September.

Hanushek, Eric (1994), "Money Might Matter Somewhere: A Response to Hedges, Laine and Greenwald", *Educational Researcher*, 23, 4, May.

Hecker, Daniel (1992), "Reconciling Conflicting Data on Jobs for College Graduates", *Monthly Labour Review*, July.

Hedges, Larry, Richard Laine and Rob Greenwald (1994), "Money Does Matter Somewhere: A Reply to Hanushek", *Educational Researcher*, 23, 4, May.

Horner, Constance (1993), "Deregulating the Federal Service: Is the Time Finally Right?", *The Brookings Review*, Autumn.

Hoynes, Hilary Williamson (1993), "Welfare Transfers in Two-Parent Families: Labor Supply and Welfare Participation Under AFDC-UP", National Bureau of Economic Research Working Paper 4407, July.

Iowa Department of Education (1993), *The Annual Condition of Education Report*.

Kang, Suk and John Bishop (1989), "Vocational and Academic Education in High School: Complements or Substitutes?", *Economics of Education Review*, 8, 2.

Kellaghn, Thomas, Kathryn Sloane, Benjamin Alvarez and Benjamin Bloom (1993), "The Home Environment and School Learning: Promoting Parental Involvement", *Education of Children*, Jossey-Bass Publishers, San Francisco.

Kettl, Donald F. (1994), *Reinventing government? Appraising the National Performance Review*, Brookings Institution Center for Public Management.

Krueger, Alan (1993), "How computers have changed the wage structure: evidence from microdata 1984-89", *Quarterly Journal of Economics*, 111, February.

Layard, Richard and Stephen Nickell (1986), "Unemployment in Britain", *Economica*, 53, unnumbered special issue on unemployment.

Lerman, Robert I. (1993), "Child Support Policies", *Journal of Economic Perspectives*, 7, 1, Winter.

Levin, Henry (1991), "The Economics of Educational Choice", *Economics of Education Review*, 10, 2.

Levine, Robert and Barbara Williams (1992), "Public Policy and the Inner City Across Three Decades", in James Steinberg, David Lyon and Mary Vaiana (eds.), *Urban American*, Rand Corporation.

Lewin-VHI (1994), "The Impact of the Health Security Act on Firms Competing in International Markets", paper prepared for the Competitiveness Policy Council, 12 January.

Madrian, Brigitte (1993), "Employment-Based Health Insurance and Job Mobility: Is There Evidence of Job Lock?", National Bureau of Economic Research Working Paper 4476, September.

Mann, Thomas and Norman Ornstein (1994), "Shipshape? A Progress Report on Congressional Reform", *The Brookings Review*, Spring.

McUsic, Molly (1991), "The Use of Education Clauses in Litigation", *Harvard Journal on Legislation*, 28, 2, Summer.

Medoff, James (1994), "Job Opportunity: The Missing Link Between Unemployment and Inflation", Center for National Policy, May.

Moffitt, Robert (1983), "An Economic Model of Welfare Stigma", *American Economic Review*, 73, 5, December.

Moffitt, Robert (1992), "Incentive Effects of the U.S. Welfare System: A Review", *Journal of Economic Literature*, 30, 1, March.

Murray, Charles (1993), "Welfare and the Family: The U.S. Experience", *Journal of Labor Economics*, 11, 1, Part 2, March.

Murray, Charles (1994), "Does Welfare Bring More Babies?", *American Enterprise*, January-February.

National Center for Education Statistics (1992), *The Condition of Education*.

National Center for Education and the Economy (1990), *America's Choice: High Skills or Low Wages*, June.

National Commission on Time and Learning (1994), *Prisoners of Time*, April.

National Education Association (1993), *Tech Prep Programs*.

National Performance Review (1994), *Creating a government that works better and costs less: Status Report*, September.

National Research Council, "Overview of Post-Secondary Training Institutions and Programs" in Hansen (ed.) (1994), *Preparing for the Workplace: Charting a Course for Federal Postsecondary Training Policy*, National Academy Press.

Nedde, Ellen M. (1993), "U.S. Health Care Reform", International Monetary Fund Working Paper WP/93/93, December.

OECD (1992a), *Economic Survey United States 1992/93*, Paris, November.

OECD (1992b), *U.S. Health Care at the Cross-roads*, Paris, November.

OECD (1993a), "Enterprise Tenure, Labour Turnover and Skill Training", *Employment Outlook*, Paris, Chapter 4.

OECD (1993b), *Education at a Glance*, Centre for Education Research and Innovation, Paris.

OECD (1994), *School: A Matter of Choice*, Centre for Educational Research and Innovation, Paris.

Office of Management and Budget (1994), *Budget of the United States Government Fiscal Year 1995*, Washington.

Olson, Mancur (1982), *The Rise and Decline of Nations: Economic Growth, Stagflation and Social Rigidities*, Yale University Press, New Haven.

O'Neill, June E. and Dave M. O'Neill (1994), "Jobs, Wages and the Clinton Health Care Mandate", *The American Enterprise*, March/April.

Osterman, Paul and Maria Iannozzi (1993), "Youth Apprenticeships and School-to-Work Transition: Current Knowledge and Legislative Strategy", Bureau of Labor Statistics, Working Paper of the National Centre on the Educational Quality of the Workforce.

Pashley, Peter and Gary Phillips (1993), "Toward World-Class Standards: A Research Study Linking International and National Assessments", Educational Testing Service Report, June.

Pavetti, LaDonna (1993), "The Dynamics of Welfare and Work", unpublished Ph.D. dissertation, Harvard University, Cambridge, Massachusetts.

Perron, Pierre (1989), "The Great Crash, the Oil Price Shock, and the Unit Root Hypothesis", *Econometrica*, 57, 6, November.

Perry, George (1970), "Changing Labor Markets and Inflation", *Brookings Papers on Economic Activity*, 3.

Romer, Christina and David Romer (1994), "What ends recessions?", National Bureau of Economic Research Working Paper No. 4765, June.

Rudebusch, Glenn and David Wilcox (1994), "Productivity and Inflation: Evidence and Interpretations", Working Paper, Federal Reserve Board, May.

Schick, Allen (1990), "Budgeting for Results: Recent Developments in Five Industrialised Countries", *Public Administration Review*, 50, 1.

Scofea, Laura A. (1994), "The development and growth of employer-provided health insurance", *Monthly Labor Review*, 117, 3, March.

Steelman, L.C. and B. Powell (1993), "Doing the Right Thing: Race and Parental Locus of Responsibility for Funding College", *Sociology of Education*, 66, October.

Stern, David (1992), "School to work programmes and services in secondary schools and two year public post secondary institutions", Paper prepared for the National Assessment of Vocational Education, University of California, Berkeley.

Stern, David, Charles Dayton, Il-Woo Paik and Alan Weisberg (1989), "Benefits and Costs of Dropout Prevention in a High School Program Combining Academic and Vocational Education: Third-Year Results from Replications of the California Peninsula Academies", *Educational Evaluation and Policy Analysis*, 11, 4, Winter.

Stern, David, Neal Finkelstein, James R. Stone III, John Latting, Carolyn Dornsife (1994), "Research on School to Work Transition Programs in the United States", National Center for Research in Vocational Education, March.

Steuerle, Eugene (1994), "Health Care: But What About Everything Else?", *American Enterprise*, January-February.

Sullivan, David F. (1994), "State and Local Government Fiscal Position in 1993", *Survey of Current Business*, 74, 3, March.

Tirole, Jean (1994), "The Internal Organization of Government", *Oxford Economic Papers*, 46, 1, January.

Towell, Pat (1994), "Pentagon Banking on Plans to Reinvent Procurement", *Congressional Quarterly*, 16 April.

U.S. Department of Labor, Pension and Welfare Benefits Administration, *Pension and Health Benefits of American Workers: New Findings from the April 1993 Current Population Survey*, 1994.

U.S. House of Representatives, Committee on Ways and Means (1994), *Green Book*, July.

Weiner, Stuart (1993), "New Estimates of the Natural Rate of Unemployment", *Federal Reserve Bank of Kansas City Review*, Fourth Quarter.

Weir, Margaret (1992), "Race and Urban Poverty", *The Brookings Review*, Summer.

Wiener, Joshua M. and Laurel Hixon Illston (1994), "How to Share the Burden: Long-Term Care Reform in the 1990s", *The Brookings Review*, Spring.

Wyckoff, James (1992), "The Intrastate Equality of Public Primary and Secondary Education Resources in the U.S. 1980 to 1987", *Economics of Education Review*, 11, 1.

Annex I

Econometric analysis of inflation risks

I. Estimating potential GDP growth

Inflation prospects in coming quarters will depend to a great extent on the level and growth rate of actual relative to potential output. Potential output growth is the sum of several components: growth of working-age population, trend growth of labour-force participation, shifts in the NAWRU (the "natural rate"), trend growth of the workweek, and finally trend growth of productivity (output per hour). Each of these components is estimated below.

Working-age population increased over the course of 1993 at a rate of about 1.0 per cent per year, according to the Bureau of Labor Statistics. The historical revision in January 1994 shifted the level of the working-age population, but the redefinition is assumed not to affect the trend growth of working-age population for 1994-95. The 1.0 per cent rate of working-age population growth is assumed to continue for the near future.

The trend increase in the participation rate of prime-age females is slowing (equation 1), while participation rates for prime-age males (equation 2) and other workers (equation 3) continue to trend downward. Thus, the overall trend labour-force participation rate is estimated to be rising only microscopically – less than 0.1 per cent per year. Over the past year, labour-force participation rates have actually declined, notably so since January.

The workweek's trend decline has slowed considerably since the 1980s (equation 4) – the estimated trend decline for 1993-94 (0.1 per cent per year) is so small that cyclical considerations dominate the recent data.

Long-run average rates of unemployment for prime-age men, prime-age women and other workers rose until 1974 but have not shown much systematic trend movement since then. These rates are assumed not to change much over the next year or so. If the NAWRU does not change, then these trend estimates of population growth, participation and workweek imply trend growth of labour input (in hours) of about 1 per cent per annum.

Hourly labour productivity has increased not quite 1 per cent per year, on average, since 1973. Over the past two years or so, measured productivity growth has been much more rapid, but most of that reflects cyclical factors, rather than trend gains. For production workers, there is little evidence of a pickup in trend growth of productivity. In contrast, productivity growth for all private non-farm workers (including supervisory workers) has been unusually strong since the end of 1989, even after allowing for cyclical effects. For non-farm business, annual trend productivity growth appears to have risen about 0.9 percentage points in the 1989-93 period to roughly 1.7 per cent per annum (equation 5). However, the sharp decline in productivity in the second quarter of 1994 reduces the likelihood that the trend increase in productivity has been quite that dramatic. In any case, economy-wide, the corresponding figure for trend productivity growth is likely to be lower, since productivity growth for government workers is assumed by the Commerce Department to be 0. Overall trend productivity growth is probably in the range of 1.3 to 1.5 per cent.

Labour supply growth of 1 per cent, combined with economy-wide trend productivity growth of 1.3 to 1.5 per cent, would yield potential GDP growth of about 2.3 to 2.5 per cent. Several uncertainties remain, however. It is unclear whether the unusual weakness of labour-force participation by white males in recent months represents a new trend, or whether female labour-force participation has reached a plateau. If so, trend labour supply and GDP growth would be correspondingly slower to increase. On the other hand, data revisions over the next few months may show even stronger productivity growth during the 1990s, and correspondingly faster growth in potential GDP.

The equations which follow were used to generate long-run trend growth rates for labour input and overall potential GDP. Each long-run equation in this section is followed by a second-stage dynamic equation which aims to show that the dependent variable in each long-run equation appears to be trend-stationary. (Equations 1 to 4 use the simple Engle-Granger two-stage specification. But a more detailed second-stage equation was needed in testing equation 5; for productivity, the simple Engle-Granger second-stage specification is inappropriate because the "common-factor" restriction is violated.)

1. *Labour-force participation, prime-age (25-54 year old) females*

PARTF2654 = 1.013 − 124.4/(LINEARTREND + 241.0) + error 1

RBARSQ=.99, S.E.E. = .0053 Jan. 1974-Dec. 1993

Δ(error 1) = −.000102 −.283 Δ(error 1(−1)) −.079 error 1(−2)

     (−0.8)   (−4.5)   (−3.0)

2. *Labour-force participation, prime-age (25-54 year old) males*

PARTM2654 = .948 − .0000683 LINEARTREND + error 2

RBARSQ = .78, S.E.E. = .0025 Jan. 1974-Dec. 1993

Δ(error 2) = −.000043 −.259 Δ(error 2(−1)) −.207 error 2(−2)

     (0.4)   (−4.0)   (−4.9)

3. *Labour-force participation, non-prime-age workers*

PARTOTHER = .486 − .000000969 LINEARTREND**2 + error 3

RBARSQ = .94, S.E.E. = .0041, Jan. 1980-Dec. 1993

Δ(error 3) = −.527 Δ(error 3(−1)) −.278 Δ(error 3(−2)) −.129 error 3(−3)

$$(6.8) \qquad (3.4) \qquad (2.9)$$

RBARSQ = .22, S.E.E. = .0021, Apr. 1980-Dec. 1993

4. Hours per worker, non-farm business sector

WORKWEEK = 38.57 – .749 LN(LINEARTREND) + .045 LN(TREND1082) + error 4

RBARSQ = .92, S.E.E. = .2056 Apr. 1973-Dec. 1993

(TREND1082 = LINEARTREND through 10/82, but = 1 thereafter)

Δ(error 4) = .00328 – .529 Δ(error 4(–1)) – .199 error 4(–2)

$$(0.4) \quad (-8.8) \qquad\qquad (-4.5)$$

5. Output per hour, all workers, non-farm business sector

LN(PRODUCTIVITY) = 7.878 + .002074 LINEARTREND + .001804 TREND89 + error 5

RBARSQ = .93, S.E.E. = .0153, Q2 1973 to Q4 1993

(TREND89 = 0 through Q3 1989, then 1, 2, 3, etc.)

Δ(LN(PRODUCTIVITY)) = .000366 + .494 Δ(LN(NONFARMOUTPUT))

$$(0.6) \qquad (11.5)$$

–.180 Δ(LN(NONFARMOUTPUT(–1))) – .0574 Δ(LN(NONFARMOUTPUT(–2)))

$$(3.8) \qquad\qquad\qquad (1.3)$$

+ .00271 D89Q3ONWARD – .126 error 5(–3)

$$(2.2) \qquad\qquad (3.8)$$

RBARSQ = .67, S.E.E. = .0043, Q1 1974 to Q4 1993

II. Evaluating indicators of future growth of real wages and markups

1. Changes in growth of employee compensation per hour (testing the implications for wage inflation of the prime-age male unemployment rate and the rate of long-run unemployment)

WAGACC = .00437 – .094 WAGACC(–1) – .476 REALWAGEGROWTH(–1)

$$(2.6) \quad (0.9) \qquad\qquad (5.2)$$

–.00156 UNRM2554(–2) + .00221 UNR15WKS(–2)

$$(2.3) \qquad\qquad (1.7)$$

RBARSQ = .32, S.E.E. = .0037, Q1 1974 to Q1 1994

2. **The prime-age male unemployment rate dominates the job vacancy rate as a predictor of wage acceleration:**

$$\text{WAGACC} = .00480 - .512 \text{ REALWAGEGROWTH}(-1) - .00146 \text{ UNRM2554}(-2)$$
    (1.1)   (5.8)   (2.2)
$$+ .00203 \text{ UNR15WKS}(-2) - .00000395 \text{ VACANCYRATE}(-2)$$
    (1.4)   (0.2)

RBARSQ = .31, S.E.E. = .0037, Q1 1974 to Q1 1994

3. **The overall unemployment rate is a poor predictor of wage acceleration** (in contrast to the prime-age male unemployment rate of equation 1 above)

$$\text{WAGACC} = .00682 - .110 \text{ WAGACC}(-1) - .428 \text{ REALWAGEGROWTH}(-1)$$
    (1.6)   (1.0)   (4.2)
$$-.00142 \text{ UNRTOTAL}(-2) + .00185 \text{ UNR15WKS}(-2)$$
    (1.3)   (1.0)

RBARSQ = .29, S.E.E. = .0038, Q1 1974 to Q1 1994

4. **Growth of the markup: business-sector deflator growth minus growth of labour compensation** (this equation tests the explanatory power of manufacturing capacity utilisation)

$$\text{MARKUPGROWTH} = -.0304 - .551 \text{ WAGACC} - .362 \text{ WAGACC}(-1)$$
    (3.2)   (5.4)   (3.6)
$$+.000290 \text{ MANCAPUTIL}(-1) + .00502 \text{ DUMQ273ONWARD}$$
    (2.6)   (4.6)

RBARSQ = .303, S.E.E. = .00463, Q1 1965 to Q1 1991

5. **Growth of the markup** (by comparison with equation 4, this equation shows that vendor performance is as effective as capacity utilisation in explaining the price markup)

$$\text{MARKUPGROWTH} = -.011 - .544 \text{ WAGACC} - .352 \text{ WAGACC}(-1)$$
    (5.0)   (5.4)   (3.5)
$$+.0000985 \text{ VENDORPERF}(-1) + .00407 \text{ DUM73Q2ONWARD}$$
    (2.7)   (4.1)

RBARSQ = .306, S.E.E. = .00462, Q1 1965 to Q1 1991

Annex II

Key features of the Health Security Act

"Health alliances"

Other than the elderly who will continue to receive their coverage through Medicare, most other Americans would, under the HSA, get their insurance from a so-called "health alliance". The role of alliances would be to negotiate the specifications of plans with insurers or even directly with groups of providers,[1] to collect employer and household premiums,[2] as well as government subsidies and then to redistribute them to individual plans. Some alliances would be of a corporate form:[3] firms with over 5 000 employees are to be allowed to offer their workers coverage directly, albeit with a tax of 1 per cent of payroll to help cover the cost of insuring non-workers and of graduate medical education. Corporate alliances would be obligated to offer at least three plans to their workers, of which one must be a traditional fee-for-service plan and two of another kind, such as a health-maintenance organisation (HMO). Otherwise, alliances are to be organised on a geographic basis. There would be only one alliance in a region in order to achieve economies of scale[4] and mitigate problems of adverse selection at the cost of a lack of competition, a loss whose magnitude is difficult to assess. Alliance administrative costs are evaluated at 2.3 per cent of expenditure, with a permitted ceiling of 2.5 per cent. Regional alliances would be required to contract with all plans which meet certain standards and would have to keep average premiums below specified targets. States are to be allowed to opt out of the regional-alliance system in favour of a single-payer system, and several would be expected to do so. Eight others have already passed legislation establishing or allowing equivalent purchasing co-operatives.[5] It should be noted that the system will generate differences in premium levels among regional alliances based on differences in costs as well as in risks, and the lack of uniformity across the States may make administration difficult for multi-state employers.

Reforming insurance markets

One of the principal objectives of the HSA is to reform insurance markets in order to eliminate all insurance-industry efforts at reducing adverse risk. These efforts are costly and constitute one of the main reasons for high administrative outlays. But some observers are sceptical that it will be possible to eliminate all discriminatory factors in any system of competing insurance companies or providers (Aaron and Bosworth, 1994). The Administration expects these costs to drop by about $3\frac{1}{2}$ per cent of claims paid or $7 billion per year. Since plans would have to be open to all those wishing to enrol, the system would be transformed from one based on "experience rating" (the estimated risk of the individual) into one based on "community rating" (the average risk of the local population).[6] Lewin-VHI, a respected firm of health-care consultants, has estimated that in 1998 alone community rating would shift over $37 billion in costs from the government to the private sector by forcing workers to help pay the higher costs of non-workers.[7] Another market response to the adverse-selection problem which the HSA would remove at the same time is the exclusion of coverage for pre-existing conditions.[8] Finally, universal coverage will also overcome another current weakness of private insurance markets: at present, about 80 per cent of conventional policies have ceilings ranging from $250 000 to $1 million on lifetime payouts, thereby leaving major medical risks facing the patient.

The employer mandate

The HSA achieves its aim of universal coverage primarily through an employer mandate to pay for at least 80 per cent of the average cost of insurance in an alliance area, rather than a pure individual mandate or a single-payer type of national-insurance plan. (But it is not a pure employer mandate, since everyone is entitled to insurance, whether they work or not.) This has the advantage of building on the existing system of largely employer-provided insurance.[9] But the risk is that, as with all employer mandates, as labour costs go up, the demand for labour, and, therefore, employment, will fall (see below). Recognising this risk, the HSA proposes that employer costs be capped at no more than 7.9 per cent of payroll and that employees share in the cost of the plan they choose. Federal subsidies or discounts would be provided to the working poor, to those retired people aged 55-64, to non-workers as well as to employers in order to enforce the cap. Smaller, lower-wage firms benefit from even lower caps, ranging down to 3.5 per cent of payroll for firms with fewer than 25 employees and an average annual wage of less than $12 000.[10] Covering the amount above the cap for these firms is estimated by the Administration to cost $29 billion in the year 2000 (Table A1).

Table A.1. **The Administration's health-reform proposal: discounts in the year 2000**

$ billion

Type	Purpose	Amount
Employers	To limit employer costs to a maximum of 7.9 per cent of payroll	29
Household		
Non-retirees	To limit payments for low-wage employees and for time spent not working	47
Retirees	To limit employer payments for low-income retirees	7
Early retirees	To eliminate employer share of payments for those 55-64 years old beginning 1998	5
Other	To help cover out-of-pocket expenses of certain poor families	3
Cushion	To allow for behavioural effects	13
Total		103

Source: Council of Economic Advisers (1994).

The benefits package and cost-sharing

In order to widen the appeal of the HSA, the Administration has proposed a broad set of standardised benefits, one that is probably as comprehensive as the average plan currently provided by a medium- to large-sized firm and, therefore, slightly more generous than the average plan. Importantly, there is coverage for preventive care and long-term care (expected to cost $68 billion over five years) from the outset.[11] By the year 2001 the set is scheduled to expand to cover adult dental benefits and more complete coverage for mental illness and substance abuse. Since the plan includes a prescription-drug benefit, Medicare will be enhanced to include such a provision as well.

In general, the individual is to be liable for the insurance premium above that which is borne by the employer; accordingly, at the margin, (s)he pays all additional costs of more expensive plans. Health plans are to be allowed to offer three options for patient cost-sharing: one fee-for-service and the other two similar to an HMO arrangement and a "preferred provider organisation" (PPO). In any case there would be a ceiling of $1 500 ($3 000 for a family) on all out-of-pocket expenses. Also, if the family's income is less than $1 000 in 1994 prices, it has no financial obligation, as Federal subsidies will be provided. Up to 150 per cent of the poverty line (or about $23 000 for a family of 4 in 1994) its share is the lesser of 20 per cent of the weighted average premium or 3.9 per cent of its income. Federal subsidies to households are estimated by the Administration to reach $59 billion in 2000, of which $12 billion would go to retirees.

Cost containment and premium growth limits

The Administration has recognised the fear that many Americans have that choice would be restricted under its reform proposal and has emphasised that individuals will continue to be able to choose their own doctor, if that is important to them, and they will have a choice of plan (which some do not currently have). Doctors will be able to join the plan or plans they wish or to remain in the traditional fee-for-service sector.[12] Insurers would be expected to put pressure on providers to practise cost-conscious medicine and would compete on the basis of price rather than by cherry-picking. But whether fragmented insurers will succeed in effectively containing costs is a difficult question. In other OECD countries the evidence is that monopsonistic purchasers are needed to hold down costs, especially in the hospital sector.

However, consumers will have incentives to choose cheaper plans, as they are liable for the difference between the price of the plan they select and the employer contribution, and as from 2004 they will no longer get an income tax deduction nor a payroll tax exclusion for directly or indirectly purchasing supplementary coverage either for benefits beyond the guaranteed package or for out-of-pocket expenses. Yet by maintaining the tax break for premiums on the basic package the cost consciousness of consumers and the incentives for efficiency facing providers are weakened significantly. Nevertheless, the Administration[13] expects consumers to shift toward cheaper, HMO-type plans; it cites the case of Minnesota where the State pays a fixed amount for health insurance for its workers and lets them choose the plan they wish: about one-quarter shifted from the highest-cost to the lowest-cost plan. Furthermore, once a year there will be an open period during which consumers may switch plans, based on an enhanced set of information on price and quality of different plans that will have to be made available.

Also, in the wake of a series of studies by the U.S. General Accounting Office (GAO) that show that U.S. name-brand prescription drug prices are much higher than those in Canada or the United Kingdom (GAO, 1994*a*), the HSA includes a provision establishing a Breakthrough Drug Pricing Committee to determine the reasonableness of domestic prices based on those abroad and on costs. But others (for example, Danzon, 1994) have disputed the GAO results, especially for its exclusion from consideration of generics, arguing that the appropriate way to deal with unaffordable out-of-pocket drug costs for the elderly is not to regulate drug prices, which will reduce global supply and harm U.S. pre-eminence in the field, but by recourse to managed drug-benefits programmes.

In order to pay for the additional outlays (the Medicare drug benefit; the subsidies; and the long-term care benefit), the HSA includes, in addition to cost savings, a major increase in excise taxes on tobacco products,[14] expected to yield about $11 billion per year and the corporate alliance tax of 1 per cent of payroll (Table A2). But the biggest offset is found in reduced outlays for Medicare and Medicaid – the details of which are

Table A.2. **Financing the Administration's health-reform proposal**

$ billion

The year 2000			
Source	Amount	Use	Amount
Tobacco tax	11	Discounts: gross spending	103
Corporate alliance assessment	5	*less:* Medicaid and other offsets	−61
Other revenue effects	35	Net	42
Medicare savings	39	Veterans, public health, new	
Medicaid savings	27	administration and other	10
Other Federal savings	11	Medicare drugs benefit	17
Induced reduction in debt service	2	Long-term care benefit	20
		Tax deduction for self-employed	3
Total	130	Total	92
Change in deficit			−38
The years 1995-2000			
Tobacco tax	67	Discounts: gross spending	327
Corporate alliance assessment	24	*less:* Medicaid and other offsets	−176
Other revenue effects	93	Net	151
Medicare savings	118	Veterans, public health, new	
Medicaid savings	61	administration and other	47
Other Federal savings	29	Medicare drugs benefit	69
Induced reduction in debt service	4	Long-term care benefit	62
		Tax deduction for self-employed	9
Total	397	Total	338
Change in deficit			−59

Source: Budget of the United States Government, Fiscal Year 1995.

summarised in CBO (1994a) – and in increased income and payroll taxes resulting from the higher wages expected to be paid and the higher profits earned following the reduction in business health spending which is expected to mount quite rapidly after 1998. As mentioned above, any employer premiums beyond those paying for the standard benefits package will become subject to income and payroll taxation as from 2004.

But, should the reform not generate the expected cost savings, a backstop system of ceilings on premiums would come into play on an alliance-specific basis. For the years up to 2000, premiums may not rise more than the rate of population increase plus the annual rate of overall CPI inflation plus a sliding number of percentage points (1.5 in 1996, 1.0 in 1997, 0.5 in 1998 and 0 thereafter). By the year 2000 premiums could be about 18 per cent below the levels projected in the absence of the premium growth caps. In the next century premium growth would be limited to the rate of CPI inflation plus population growth plus the increase in real GDP per capita. Even if the reform generates substantial savings, if they turn out to be largely of a one-off nature, these controls will eventually begin to bite. A National Health Board would monitor whether a weighted average bid price of all plans accepted by the individual alliances exceeded that alliance's target. If an excess was found, then first voluntary cuts and finally mandatory, across-the-board cuts would be made.[15] The Federal financial exposure to alliances would also be capped through explicit ceilings in the years to 2000 and increases thereafter in line with those on premiums. But in the opinion of the CBO these caps would not be legally binding.

The impact of the reform

To estimate the impact of the HSA is an exceedingly complex task, primarily because the reform is not marginal but systemic and because many of the changes will interact with one another. Furthermore, the impact of the premium growth caps is highly uncertain and might not be politically sustainable. But, with the impetus given to managed care, administrative savings and the cost-containment effects flowing from the elimination of unnecessary care, with or without the discipline of the premium growth caps, the Administration believes that premium growth can be held to an average of about 5 per cent per year in the five years to 2000 with the reform, compared to over 9 per cent in the baseline. For overall health spending the saving by the year 2000 is estimated at $1/2$ per cent of GDP compared with the baseline. The realisation of this ambitious goal is crucial in order to allow the government to pay the promised subsidies without putting upward pressure on the deficit. There is, therefore, a risk either that costs would not be cut to the degree required to maintain access and quality or that the savings will not come fast enough. But, in any case, health spending would still represent about 17 per cent of GDP in 2000 compared with 14.6 per cent in 1994 (Table A3). The CBO (1994b) is less optimistic: it estimates that the HSA would boost spending in the phase-in period and thereafter generate far smaller savings than Administration estimates (Table A4). In its projections, savings would begin only in the year 2000 and would reach 7 per cent of baseline outlays by 2004 (Diagram A1). But the CBO has accepted that premium caps are an effective backstop mechanism in preventing spending overruns.

Table A.3. **The Administration's health-reform proposal: impact of reform over time**

	1995	1996	1997	1998	1999	2000
Health expenditures as per cent of GDP						
Baseline	15.0	15.4	15.9	16.4	16.9	17.4
With reform	15.0	15.6	16.2	16.7	16.7	16.9
Business health expenditures ($ billion)						
Baseline	196	215	235	256	279	303
With reform	197	218	236	253	265	276
New uses of Federal funds	4	24	51	79	89	92
New sources of Federal funds	15	27	45	75	107	130
Change in deficit	−11	−3	7	5	−18	−38
Memorandum items:						
Business health expenditures ($ billion) the Lewin-VHI view						
Baseline	200	217	235	254	274	293
With reform	200	231	262	283	296	309

Source: Council of Economic Advisers (1994) and Lewin-VHI (1994).

As to the Federal finances, the Administration predicts that the HSA would cut the deficit by a cumulative $59 billion in the years to 2000, but the CBO foresees a rise of $74 billion over the same period. The differential impact on the Federal deficit is $48 billion (over ½ per cent of GDP) in 2000 alone. The main reason for this gap is that CBO believes premiums would be higher than does the Administration: every percentage point difference in assumed premiums is worth about $3 billion in extra spending in 2000. Some private-sector estimates go even further in this direction (Table A5). Another cost-increasing effect given greater weight by the CBO is that low-wage workers would tend to migrate to subsidised firms (and conversely high-wage workers would gain by moving to unsubsidised firms), and firms would hive off their low-wage activities in order to take fuller advantage of subsidy availability.[16]

The impact on private employers is similar: initially, reform under the HSA would lift employer costs, as premium subsidies to households and employers net of the corporate alliance payroll tax plus savings on retiree coverage and on premiums for two-worker families would not be sufficient to match the additional cost of covering workers and their dependents who would otherwise be uncovered. The amount of the net shortfall has been estimated to be some $29 billion (11.4 per cent of baseline spending) in 1998.[17] At some point, however, if the spending caps hold, the reform would begin to generate savings relative to baseline projections, and the cost increase could be reversed.[18] The overall results mask important industry- and firm-level considerations because of the adoption of community rating and the employer mandate: employers currently offering insurance are predicted to suffer increased costs only during the phase-in period, with substantial gains in the medium term, while those not otherwise providing insurance would be faced with significant permanent cost increases (an average of nearly

Table A.4. **CBO estimate of the budgetary impact of the Administration's health proposal**

$ billion, fiscal year

	1995	1996	1998	2000	2002	2004
Subsidies	0	9	82	108	142	173
of which:						
To employers	0	5	44	58	81	102
To families	0	6	54	70	83	95
State maintenance-of-effort payments [1]	0	−2	−16	−20	−22	−24
Medicare	0	0	−8	−24	−38	−57
of which:						
Programme savings	0	−7	−19	−37	−54	−77
Drugs benefit	0	6	16	19	23	28
Medicaid	0	−2	−28	−54	−71	−92
of which:						
Discontinued coverage	0	−2	−19	−31	−38	−48
Premium limits and cuts to "disproportionate share" hospitals	0	−1	−14	−24	−33	−45
Long-term care benefit	0	5	12	20	37	40
Other	0	3	−4	−7	−9	−11
Total outlays	0	15	54	43	61	53
Induced income and payroll taxes	0	0	4	12	22	34
Increased excise tax on tobacco	11	11	11	10	10	10
Assessment on employers [2]	0	1	5	6	1	1
Exclusion of health insurance from cafeteria plans [3]	0	0	2	4	6	7
Other	0	2	1	1	1	1
Total revenues	11	14	22	33	40	53
Deficit increase	−10	1	32	10	22	0
Administration's estimate	−11	−3	5	−38	n.a.	n.a.

1. Payments designed to ensure that states continue to pay their share of the costs of jointly-financed programmes.
2. Those forming corporate alliances and those providing subsidies to retirees.
3. Plans which currently allow employees, as part of their compensation package, to choose among a menu of fringe benefits up to an employer-defined ceiling.
Source: Congressional Budget Office (1994*b*).

$2 000 per worker or about 5 per cent). The biggest cost increase would be faced by firms with 10-24 employees and those operating in the retail trade and some primary sectors. Because they are larger and thus tend to offer health insurance to their employees already, companies producing tradeable goods are net beneficiaries, especially those in manufacturing and mining.

Diagram A1. **IMPACT OF THE HEALTH SECURITY ACT ON HEALTH SPENDING**

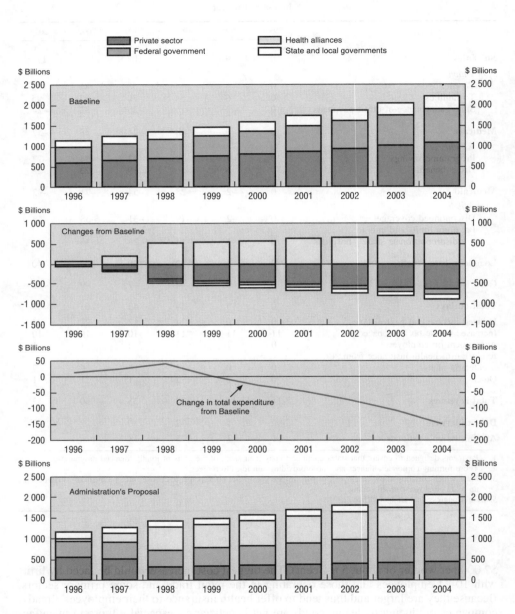

Source: Congressional Budget Office.

Table A.5.   **Estimates of the annual cost of the Administration's proposed benefit package, 1993**

	Administration [1]		Congressional Budget Office [2]		Hewitt Associates		Foster Higgins		Health Insurance Association of America	
	Dollars	Index	Dollars	Index	Dollars	Index	Dollars	Index	Dollars	Index
Single person	1 768	100	1 935	109	2 200	124	2 250	127	2 110	119
Childless couple	3 536	100	3 871	109	4 460	126	4 510	128	4 425	125
Single-parent famille	3 562	100	3 774	106	4 200	118	5 350	150	4 200	118
Dual-parent family	3 989	100	5 129	129	6 300	158	5 970	150	6 300	158

1.   1994 data were reduced by an assumed 8.5 per cent to approximate 1993 levels.
2.   CBO (1994) indicates a total difference of 15 pour cent over administration estimates without specifying figures for each category. it also claims these figures are virtually identical to those estimated by Lewin-VHI, experts in the field.
Source: Secretariat calculations based on data presented in O'Neill and O'Neill (1994) and CBO (1994*b*).

Employers facing initially higher non-wage labour costs will try to pass these costs either forward into higher prices or backward into lower compensation. Either way, real wages would decline until such time as business cost increases were reversed. To the extent that the pass-through is incomplete,[19] labour demand would fall, especially for those whose wage rates are constrained at or near legislated minimum levels. To a lesser extent, the real-wage decline would also reduce labour supply, especially for married women. Second earners would also be worse off, since each worker would have to pay 20 per cent of the cost of coverage for the entire family and each employer slightly more than half the 80 per cent employer share – an implicit marriage tax. Labour supply would probably also fall among those aged 55-64, as universal coverage will remove a cost of early retirement.[20] Such early retirees could rise by around ¹/₂ million (CBO, 1994*b*). But there would be some offsetting effect from increased participation among those currently on welfare and/or Medicaid who refrain from work in order to maintain health coverage; the implicit tax rate on those leaving welfare for employment should fall by up to 10 percentage points (Council of Economic Advisers, 1994). In total, labour supply might be expected to drop anywhere from ¹/₄ to 1 per cent, with a resulting reduction in potential (market) output of about two-thirds as much (CBO, 1994*b*).

But the decline in employment, concentrated on low-wage workers, would probably be much smaller overall – the Administration believes less than ¹/₂ per cent; indeed, recent research has shown that the introduction of national health insurance in Canada led to higher employment and wages (Gruber and Hanratty, 1993). This could be because labour mobility and, therefore, efficiency is improved by the elimination of job lock, and small firms would overcome their current cost disadvantage *vis-à-vis* health-insurance premiums. On the other hand, as mentioned above, reform would provide firms with an incentive to reorganise their operations to exploit the availability of subsidies as fully as possible, with potentially important transitional disruption costs and longer-term inefficiencies. Overall, the CBO (1994*b*) believes that labour-market distortions would probably increase somewhat, but such conclusions must be regarded as extremely tentative.

Notes

1. How aggressive the alliances should be in trying to hold down premiums is a controversial question. Another is how much authority is to be given to States to draw alliance boundaries: there will be pressure from low-cost areas, such as suburbs, to exclude high-cost zones, inner cities for example. Finally, plans are to be paid capitation payments to adjust for the risk composition of their members, but many (Aaron and Bosworth (1994), for example) are doubtful that any such system of risk adjustment can control for selection bias.

2. Within a decade the CBO (1994*b*) expects such payments to reach over $700 billion per year, of which over $500 billion would emanate from non-Federal sources.

3. The firm's decision to join a regional alliance is irrevocable. CBO (1994*b*) estimates that ultimately only 11 per cent of eligible employees would be covered through corporate alliances.

4. That such scale economies exist can be demonstrated by pointing to insurance-industry figures on administrative expenses as a share of claims paid: 5.5 per cent for groups of 10 000 or more, compared to up to 40 per cent for those of less than five.

5. For example, the Health Insurance Plan of California, opened in 1993, has 2 300 small-business clients handled by just 70 employees.

6. In theory, in order to deal with possible moral hazard problems, it would be preferable to apply experience rating to those risks over which the insured has some influence, but it is difficult to isolate these particular risks in practice.

7. Lewin-VHI (1994) estimates that the annual premium in 1998 would be about $1 900 per capita for workers and their dependents, but double that for non-workers. Merging the two groups would, therefore, require a 14 per cent increase in worker premiums.

8. Some 40 states have already limited insurers' ability to raise rates following large claims, a significant step on the road to community rating. Around 30 have legalised "guaranteed issue": the idea that insurers cannot discriminate against firms based on the composition of their staffs.

9. In 1991, 55.6 per cent of all Americans were covered by employment-based insurance (Council of Economic Advisers, 1994). This represents 88 per cent of all private insurance. The mandate would apply to all dependent employees over 18 years old working at least 10 hours per week, except full-time students under the age of 24. In 1992, this represented 111 million workers, of whom 45 million were not insured directly by their employer: 15 million were covered indirectly through a spousal plan, leaving 12 million with other private insurance and 18 million uninsured.

10. The lower caps are to be phased out as the firm's employment approaches 75 or the average annual wage reaches $24 000. The latter threshold is not indexed, implying that eventually all

firms would be subject only to the 7.9 per cent cap. No subsidies are to be provided to firms with 5 000 or more employees until 2003 and then only to those in regional alliances.

11. The current cost of providing nursing-home care averages about $37 000 per annum. The number of users is projected by unofficial sources (Wiener and Illston, 1994) to increase from 2.2 million in 1993 to 3.6 million in 2018. Including home care, total spending on long-term care is expected to rise from $76 billion to $168 billion in 1993 prices. While there has been some significant expansion in private insurance for long-term care, coverage is expensive, mainly because the overwhelming majority of such policies are sold individually and, therefore, subject to high administrative costs and adverse-selection problems. The HSA, therefore, proposes to socialise this risk and to tilt the service delivery system toward care in the home in order to economise on costs. Currently only 18 per cent of paid long-term care is home-delivered, even though the vast majority of the disabled live at home; the implication is that they are being looked after free by their families. Coverage for long-term care will, therefore, bring into the labour market and output statistics all such economic activity which is presently uncompensated. Should long-term care be excluded from the standard benefits package, there is a risk that the long-term care sector could become an escape hatch for spending controls on acute care services (Wiener and Illston, 1994), but its inclusion may render overall spending control difficult.

12. This sector is shrinking: there are already some 50 million people covered by HMOs. In any case, it is likely that fee schedules would be instituted in this market: either maximum or actual prices would eventually have to be dictated, either by the government or by insurance firms, because of the ceilings on premiums described below.

13. But how much cheaper HMO plans will ultimately prove to be and, therefore, how much the reform can hope to save on costs remains an unanswered question.

14. The rise for cigarettes is proposed to be $0.75 per pack (on top of the current level of $0.24).

15. The cuts could be effected through *pro rata* assessments on each plan and its providers. It appears that the incentives to make voluntary cuts are minimal. The major unknown is whether insurers can control costs and simultaneously maintain adequate care.

16. The incentives are substantial: a full-time minimum-wage worker would see his 1998 wage jump 20 per cent if he switched from an unsubsidised firm to one whose payments were capped at $3^1/_2$ per cent and if all the savings were passed on to him.

17. These figures, as well as those which follow, are taken from Lewin-VHI (1994).

18. Lewin-VHI (1994) pegs the reversal point at 2002, but the Administration believes that savings would begin by 1998 and that already by 2000 the average firm would save $230 per worker in health-insurance premiums. CBO (1994b) estimates the saving to be worth about $20 billion per year.

19. Recent empirical work has tended to find that upwards of 80 per cent of the cost of mandated benefits is shifted back onto labour in the form of lower real compensation.

20. Employees of firms with retiree health coverage retire an average of two years earlier than others (Aaron and Bosworth, 1994). Gruber and Madrian (1993) found that mandatory "continuation of coverage" laws boosted early retirement rates by 20 per cent.

Comparision of Health Reform Plans

Bill	Coverage	Benefits	Alliances
Health Security Act (Administration plan)	Guarantees health coverage for all Americans by 1998.	Mandates a package of specific benefits covering routine doctor visits, hospitalisation and emergency services, preventive care and limited coverage for mental illnesses and substance abuse; prescription drugs; rehabilitation services, hospice, home health and extended nursing care services; and lab and diagnos tic services.	Requires that states set up large consumer groups called "health alliances" to collect premiums, bargain with health plans and handle payments. All companies with 5 000 or fewer employees will have to buy coverage through an alliance.
Senate leadership plan	Aims to cover 95 per cent of Americans by 2000.	Requires plans to provide a comprehensive package from preventive care to home health services and prescription drugs. The bill leaves the specific scope of coverage to be determined by a commission.	Allows individuals and businesses of fewer than 500 workers to set up groups to purchase insurance. If no alliances are set up in a state, the Federal government will set one up through the Federal Employees Health Benefits Program.
Republican leadership (Dole) plan	Aims to give all Americans access to insurance but is expected to leave a significant portion of the working poor without coverage. It will provide subsidies to help the poorest, uninsured Americans afford insurance.	Provides no standard package except for the very poor. The plans covering families who receive subsidies have to include comprehensive coverage, preventive care, mental health and substance abuse services and take special account of the needs of children and other vulnerable populations.	Allows but does not require businesses and individuals to form large pools to purchase insurance.
House leadership plan	Aims to cover all Americans by January 1, 1999, by requiring businesses to help pay for workers' insurance and by setting up a new government insurance programme called Medicare Part C.	Requires all insurance plans to cover doctor visits, hospital care, limited skilled-nursing care, laboratory services, preventive care, family planning including abortion, and limited mental health and substance abuse coverage.	Does not require alliances, though they could be formed by groups of businesses and consumers.
Chafee-Breaux plan	Aims to cover 95 per cent of all Americans by 2002. If this goal is not met, a commission will submit recommendations to Congress on expanding coverage in areas that have not reached the target. Early estimates suggest the plan will achieve 92 per cent coverage.	Sets up a commission that will establish a benefits package. The package will include doctor visits, hospital care, preventive-care benefits for high-risk populations, mental illness and substance-abuse care, prescription-drug benefits and pregnancy care.	Does not require alliances, though they could be formed by groups of businesses and consumers.
Health Security Act (Administration plan)	Requires employers to pay at least 80 per cent of the average health insurance plan in their areas for unmarried workers and an average of 55 per cent of the family plan, but no more than 7.9 per cent of payrolls for companies with fewer than 5 000 workers. Companies with 75 or fewer employees and average wages of $24 000 or less are eligible for subsidies.	Raises the current 24-cents-a-pack cigarette tax by 75 cents, to 99 cents. Imposes a 1 per cent payroll tax on companies with 5 000 or more workers that do not join health alliances. Allows alliances to levy an additional 2.5 per cent assessment to help pay their administrative costs.	Limits the annual increase in the price of health insurance premiums after 2000 to the rate of inflation, adjusted for population and other socioeconomic factors. That is less than half the 10 per cent plus annual rate of growth in health care costs in recent years. Government costs will be controlled by a cap on spending for subsidies.

176

Comparision of Health Reform Plans *(continued)*

Bill	Financing	Taxes	Cost Controls
Senate leadership plan	Relies primarily on a combination of cuts in Medicare, a re-targeting of Federal and state spending for Medicaid – the government's insurance programme for the poor – and taxes to provide subsidies for low-income Americans. In addition, if mandated changes in insurance practices and other measures fail to boost coverage to 95 per cent by 2000, employers might have to help pay for workers' insurance in some states.	Imposes an array of new taxes – most are small, but among the larger ones are a 1.75 per cent tax on health plan premiums and an excise tax on gun ammunition. It also raises premiums for high-income elderly people receiving health care through the existing Medicare programme.	Controls private-sector costs primarily through a 25 per cent tax on the amount that a high cost plan's premiums exceeds a target rate. Public-sector cost controls are achieved through reductions in the rate of increase in Medicare costs and a cap on the amount that can be spent annually on all government health care programmes including Medicare and Medicaid. However, the cost controls on Federal programmes can be suspended during a recession.
Republican leadership (Dole) plan	Contains no requirement that employers or individuals buy insurance. Individuals and businesses with two to 50 workers will be able to buy into the Federal Employees Health Benefits Program.	Does not increase any taxes, though the existing 25 per cent deduction for self-employed people rises to 100 per cent by 2000.	Includes no effort to control prices or costs.
House leadership plan	Requires employers to pay at least 80 per cent of their employees' premiums, starting in 1997 for companies with more than 100 workers and in 1999 for smaller firms. Businesses with fewer than 100 employees can enroll in a private plan or in a new government insurance programme called Medicare Part C. If an employer chooses a private plan, its workers can buy coverage through a version of the Federal Employees Health Benefits Program.	Increases the cigarette tax by 45 cents to 69 cents a pack and adds a sales tax of 2 per cent to all insurance premiums.	Controls costs of the new Medicare Part C. programme by limiting the amounts that doctors, hospitals and other providers can be reimbursed for services to patients. For the private sector, cost controls will not occur before 2000, when a commission will determine whether health spending in each state is exceeding a national growth target tied to GDP growth. If so, reimbursement limits similar to those used in Medicare will be applied to providers in the state.
Chafee-Breaux plan	Contains no requirement that employers or individuals buy insurance but subsidises coverage for low-income Americans. If required changes in insurance practices fail to boost coverage sufficiently, a commission will recommend unspecified steps to offer insurance to employees and other measures.	Increases the ability of self-employed people to claim deductions for health insurance costs. The plan limits the deductibility of insurance costs for businesses. The Chafee-Breaux group is still considering how much to increase the tobacco tax.	Limits the deductibility of health insurance costs for employers and encourages marketplace competition through required changes in insurance practices. The plan makes big cuts in Medicare – $255 billion over 10 years – and in Medicaid. If health insurance spending is found to be adding to the Federal budget deficit, subsidies will be delayed for low-income people.

Source: Congressional Quarterly.

Annex IV

Calendar of main economic events

1993

October

The Commodities Futures Trading Commission approves regulations outlawing insider trading, implementing last year's Futures Trading Practices Act.

The Administration introduces a plan to streamline the banking system and uniformly allow U.S. banks from all states to open branches outside their own states.

The Administration follows up on the National Performance Review by sending to Congress a bill to streamline government (mainly *via* cuts in the Federal workforce) and a procurement reform bill.

The United States rejects that part of the Uruguay Round services agreement which would have required equal tax treatment for domestic and foreign companies.

The Administration submits its health care reform plan to Congress, a plan which would boost cigarette taxes, mandate employer contributions, and eventually cap the overall amount of subsidies provided by the government to lower-income families and businesses.

November

Congress approves the North American Free Trade Agreement, which the President signs in December.

The Administration proposes to merge the supervisory duties of the four Federal bank regulators into a new Federal Banking Commission.

Congress approves $18.3 billion in funding for the Resolution Trust Corporation to complete the bailout of U.S. thrift institutions.

December

For the first time, a state (Wisconsin) decides to withdraw from the Federal welfare programme (within five years, and substituting a state welfare plan).

1994

January

The North American Free Trade Agreement comes into force.

An earthquake causes billions of dollars in damage to the state of California, and exceptionally frigid winter weather slows economic activity over much of the country.

The Administration decides to fully fund Federal highway programmes in the fiscal 1995 budget and to increase recommended levels for other transportation programmes.

Under pressure from the United States, Japan agrees to open large public works projects to foreign competitors.

February

The Administration lifts the trade embargo against Vietnam, an embargo first imposed in 1964 against North Vietnam and extended to the whole country in 1975.

The Federal Reserve's Open Market Committee raises the Federal funds rate from 3 to $3^1/_4$ per cent – the first increase in this rate since February 1989.

The United States authorities are to publish within 30 days a list of proposed trade actions against Japan, for public comment, in retaliation for Japan's alleged failure to open up its domestic cellular telephone market per a 1989 agreement.

The Federal Reserve Chairman's semi-annual testimony before Congress confirms previous targets for money growth in 1994, but notes that attention will be paid to a broad spectrum of indicators in determining monetary policy.

March

Voters in the state of Michigan agree to make funding for public school districts less discriminatory by changing its source: from April 1, the state will boost the state sales tax from 4 to 6 per cent, trebling the tobacco tax, and cutting local property taxes by one-third.

The Federal Open Market Committee boosts the Federal funds rate from $3^1/_4$ to $3^1/_2$ per cent.

The House of Representatives passes a telecommunications deregulation act which would allow regional telephone companies to offer long-distance, cable, and electronic publishing services – and allow cable television companies to compete in the telephone business. A similar draft is approved by the Senate Finance Committee in July 1994, but the bill fails to clear the Senate before the end of the session.

The Administration sends its Re-employment Act of 1994 to Congress. It would consolidate and expand Federal job-training programmes and overhaul the unemployment insurance system.

April

The United States joins other countries in signing the Uruguay Round trade liberalisation agreement.

The United States and the European Union agree to allow transatlantic bids on a nondiscriminatory basis on public procurement contracts in the electric utility sector and sub-central government entities.

The Federal Open Market Committee raises the Federal funds rate from 3$^1/_2$ to 3$^3/_4$ per cent.

The Defense Department announces a plan to spend $587 million over the next five years (and eventually a total of $1 billion) to support the development of a domestic industry to produce flat-panel display screens – an industry so far dominated by Japanese producers.

Both houses of Congress approve versions of a bill permitting interstate branching, and allowing banks to merge separate units after 3 years into a unified system, subject to individual states' legal requirements.

May

On 4 May, 17 central banks, led by the Federal Reserve, intervene in support of the dollar. The Treasury Secretary states that "this Administration sees no advantage in an undervalued currency". However, the dollar continues to slide – notably against the Japanese yen – for two more months.

Congress passes a Federal budget resolution for fiscal 1995, with a target deficit of $175 billion (2.5 per cent of GDP).

The Federal Open Market Committee raises the Federal funds rate from 3$^3/_4$ to 4$^1/_4$ per cent, and boosts the discount rate from 3 to 3$^1/_2$ per cent.

Major banks boost their prime lending rates to 7$^1/_4$ per cent.

President Clinton extends most-favoured-nation status to China for another year, without mention of human rights.

June

Both houses of Congress pass versions of a bill to reform government procurement regulations, as recommended in the National Performance Review.

Congressional conferees begin reconciliation of the House- and Senate-passed versions of the ominbus crime bill, which would ban assault weapons and spend between $22 and $28 billion on crime prevention, new police officers, prison construction, etc.

The U.S. Supreme Court rules that California's earlier law allowing "unitary taxation" of corporate profits did not violate the U.S. Constitution.

July

Draft health care bills pass the committee stage and move to the floor of both houses of Congress.

Federal Reserve Chairman Greenspan presents the semi-annual Humphrey-Hawkins testimony to Congress. He anticipates more moderate growth in the second half of 1994, but indicates that if inflation rates deteriorate or if GDP growth does not slow below rates of first-half 1994, additional increases in the Federal funds rate will be called for. He noted that growth of domestic non-financial debt in the first half of 1994 remained near the middle of the target band of 4-8 per cent. The Federal Reserve Board's money growth projection bands for 1995 remain unchanged from 1994, at 1 to 5 per cent for M2, and 0 to 4 per cent for M1. The Board's economic projections (fourth-quarter/fourth-quarter basis) were listed as:

GDP	3 to 3¼ per cent in 1994, and 2½ to 2¾ per cent in 1995
CPI growth	2¾ to 3 per cent in 1994, and 2¾ to 3½ per cent in 1995
Unemployment rate	6 to 6¼ per cent in Q4 1994, and the same for Q4 1995.

August

Preliminary settlement reached with Canada regarding its wheat exports to the United States.

The United States and Japan agree to modify their respective patent laws.

The Federal Reserve's Open Market Committee raises both the Federal funds and discount rates by ½ point, to 4¾ and 4 per cent, respectively.

September

Implementing legislation for the Uruguay Round trade agreement presented to Congress.

A $30 billion crime bill was signed by the President. It boosts spending on prison construction, allows the hiring of 100 000 additional policemen, extends the number of crimes for which capital punishment may be imposed and bans certain kinds of weapons.

Health-care reform efforts abandoned for the year. Likewise, telecommunications regulatory reform fails to clear the Senate and is abandoned.

Interstate banking and branching legislation is passed and signed.

STATISTICAL ANNEX AND STRUCTURAL INDICATORS

Table A. **Selected background statistics**

	Average 1984-93	1984	1985	1986	1987	1988	1989	1990	1991	1992	1993
A. Percentage change from previous year at constant 1987 prices											
Private consumption	2.8	4.8	4.4	3.6	2.8	3.6	1.9	1.5	-0.4	2.7	3.3
Gross fixed capital formation	3.2	15.9	5.0	0.4	-0.5	4.2	0.1	-1.8	-7.6	5.5	11.3
Residential	2.5	14.4	1.3	12.0	-0.4	-1.1	-3.8	-9.2	-12.9	16.2	8.2
Non-residential	3.7	16.5	6.4	-4.1	-0.5	6.6	1.7	1.2	-5.7	2.0	12.5
GDP	2.8	6.2	3.2	2.9	3.1	3.9	2.5	1.2	-0.7	2.3	3.1
GDP price deflator	3.5	4.5	3.6	2.7	3.2	3.9	4.5	4.3	3.8	2.8	2.2
Industrial production	2.7	9.4	1.7	0.9	5.0	4.4	1.5	0.0	-1.9	2.4	4.1
Employment	1.7	4.1	2.0	2.3	2.6	2.3	2.0	0.5	-0.9	0.6	1.5
Compensation of employees (current prices)	6.4	9.7	7.0	5.9	6.9	8.3	6.1	6.4	3.3	5.5	5.3
Productivity (GDP/employment)[1]	0.9	1.8	0.5	1.2	0.4	0.8	0.1	-0.1	0.3	2.6	1.4
Unit labour costs (compensation/GDP)	3.6	3.3	3.7	2.9	3.7	4.2	3.5	5.1	3.9	3.1	2.1
B. Percentage ratios											
Gross fixed capital formation as per cent of GDP at constant prices	15.7	16.6	16.9	16.5	15.9	16.0	15.6	15.1	14.1	14.5	15.7
Stockbuilding as per cent of GDP at constant prices	0.4	1.6	0.5	0.2	0.6	0.4	0.6	0.1	0.0	0.0	0.3
Foreign balance as per cent of GDP at constant prices	-2.0	-2.9	-3.4	-3.5	-3.1	-2.2	-1.5	-1.1	-0.4	-0.6	-1.4
Compensation of employees as per cent of GDP at current prices	59.3	59.0	59.0	59.1	59.4	59.6	59.0	59.5	59.5	59.7	59.6
Direct taxes as per cent of household income	12.0	11.6	12.0	11.8	12.5	11.9	12.5	12.3	11.8	11.6	11.7
Household saving as per cent of disposable income	5.3	8.3	6.6	6.2	4.5	4.5	4.1	4.3	5.1	5.2	4.6
Unemployment as per cent of total labour force	6.5	7.5	7.2	7.0	6.2	5.5	5.3	5.5	6.7	7.4	6.8
C. Other indicator											
Current balance (billion dollars)	-104.6	-99.8	-126.4	-151.2	-167.1	-128.2	-102.8	-91.7	-6.9	-67.9	-103.9

1. Ratio of business sector GDP to business sector employment.
Sources: U.S. Department of Commerce, *Survey of Current Business*, and OECD.

Table B. National product and expenditure

Seasonally adjusted, percentage changes from previous period, annual rates, 1987 prices

	Average 1983-93	1983	1984	1985	1986	1987	1988	1989	1990	1991	1992	1993
Private consumption	3.0	4.6	4.8	4.4	3.6	2.8	3.6	1.9	1.5	-0.4	2.8	3.3
Public expenditure	2.3	2.8	3.1	6.1	5.2	3.0	0.6	2.0	3.1	1.2	-0.7	-0.8
Gross fixed investment	3.6	6.6	15.9	5.0	0.4	-0.5	4.2	0.1	-1.8	-7.6	5.5	11.3
Residential	5.9	40.4	14.4	1.3	12.0	-0.4	-1.1	-3.8	-9.2	-12.9	16.2	8.2
Non-residential	3.1	-3.0	16.5	6.4	-4.1	-0.5	6.6	1.7	1.2	-5.7	2.0	12.5
Final domestic demand	2.9	4.6	6.2	4.8	3.4	2.3	3.1	1.7	1.3	-1.2	2.5	3.7
Stockbuilding[1]	0.1	0.6	1.6	-1.1	-0.3	0.4	-0.1	0.2	-0.5	-0.1	0.1	0.3
Total domestic demand	3.0	5.2	7.8	3.6	3.0	2.7	3.0	1.8	0.8	-1.3	2.5	3.9
Exports of goods and services	6.8	-3.6	6.9	1.2	6.6	10.5	15.8	11.9	8.2	6.3	6.7	4.1
Imports of goods and services	7.7	12.5	25.0	6.3	6.6	4.6	3.7	3.8	3.6	-0.5	8.7	10.7
Foreign balance[1]	-0.2	-1.3	-1.7	-0.6	-0.2	0.3	0.9	0.6	0.4	0.7	-0.3	-0.8
GDP	2.9	3.9	6.2	3.2	2.9	3.1	3.9	2.5	1.2	-0.6	2.3	3.1

	1993 levels (1987 $ billions)	1991 Q4	1992 Q1	1992 Q2	1992 Q3	1992 Q4	1993 Q1	1993 Q2	1993 Q3	1993 Q4	1994 Q1	1994 Q2
Private consumption	3 458.7	-0.5	5.8	1.7	3.9	5.6	1.6	2.6	3.9	4.0	4.7	1.3
Public expenditure	929.8	-2.9	1.5	-3.0	3.4	0.9	-5.9	1.2	1.1	-0.1	-4.9	-1.2
Gross fixed investment	804.7	-0.7	6.4	17.0	3.8	11.7	12.3	8.9	11.4	22.9	10.6	8.6
Residential	213.1	15.6	22.4	22.7	0.8	23.8	5.3	-7.6	9.4	28.2	10.0	7.0
Non-residential	591.6	-5.7	-0.1	15.0	5.0	7.5	15.1	15.6	12.2	21.1	10.9	9.2
Final domestic demand	5 193.1	-1.1	4.9	2.8	3.8	5.6	1.7	3.3	4.5	6.0	3.9	2.0
Stockbuilding[1]	15.3	0.1	-0.4	0.2	0.0	0.0	0.2	0.0	-0.1	0.0	0.3	2.6
Total domestic demand	5 208.4	-0.8	3.2	3.7	3.9	5.7	2.7	3.3	4.0	5.8	5.0	4.6
Exports of goods and services	602.5	13.7	6.1	1.5	5.3	7.2	-1.0	7.7	-3.2	21.7	-3.5	16.6
Imports of goods and services	676.4	5.4	6.6	13.0	8.4	6.5	11.6	14.9	7.4	16.0	9.5	18.9
Foreign balance[1]	-73.9	0.2	0.0	-0.3	-0.1	0.0	-0.4	-0.2	-0.3	0.1	-0.4	-0.6
GDP	5 134.5	0.1	3.1	2.4	3.5	5.7	1.2	2.4	2.7	6.3	3.3	4.1

1. Changes as a percentage of previous period GDP.
Source: U.S. Department of Commerce, Survey of Current Business.

Table C. Labour market

Seasonally adjusted

	1985	1986	1987	1988	1989	1990	1991	1992	1993	1993 Q2	1993 Q3	1993 Q4	1994 Q1	1994 Q2
1. Number of persons, millions														
Population of working age [1,2]	178.2	180.6	182.8	184.6	186.4	188.0	189.8	191.6	193.6	193.3	193.8	194.3	196.1	196.5
Civilian labour force [1]	115.5	117.8	119.9	121.7	123.9	124.8	125.3	127.0	128.0	127.9	128.2	128.7	130.7	130.6
Unemployment [1]	8.3	8.2	7.4	6.7	6.5	6.9	8.4	9.4	8.7	8.9	8.6	8.4	8.6	8.0
Employment [1]	107.2	109.6	112.4	115.0	117.3	117.9	116.9	117.6	119.3	119.0	119.5	120.3	122.1	122.5
Employment [3]	97.4	99.3	102.0	105.2	107.9	109.4	108.3	108.6	110.5	110.3	110.8	111.4	112.0	113.0
Federal government	2.9	2.9	2.9	3.0	3.0	3.1	3.0	3.0	2.9	2.9	2.9	2.9	2.9	2.9
State and local	13.5	13.8	14.1	14.4	14.8	15.2	15.4	15.7	15.9	15.9	15.9	16.0	16.0	16.1
Manufacturing	19.2	18.9	19.0	19.3	19.4	19.1	18.4	18.1	18.0	18.0	18.0	17.9	18.0	18.0
Construction	4.7	4.8	5.0	5.1	5.2	5.1	4.7	4.5	4.6	4.6	4.7	4.7	4.8	4.9
Other	57.1	58.9	61.0	63.4	65.5	66.9	66.8	67.4	69.1	68.8	69.3	69.8	70.3	71.0
2. Percentage change from previous period (s.a.a.r.)														
Population of working age [1,2]	1.0	1.3	1.2	1.0	1.0	0.9	0.9	1.2	1.5	1.0	1.1	1.1	1.1	1.0
Civilian labour force	1.7	2.1	1.7	1.5	1.8	0.8	0.4	1.3	0.8	1.7	0.9	1.7	6.2	-0.3
Employment [1]	2.0	2.3	2.6	2.3	2.0	0.5	-0.9	0.6	1.5	2.0	1.9	2.6	6.0	1.5
Employment [3]	3.1	2.0	2.6	3.2	2.6	1.4	-1.1	0.3	1.8	2.0	1.8	2.2	2.2	3.7
Federal government	2.4	0.8	1.5	0.9	0.6	3.3	-3.8	0.1	-1.8	-3.0	-1.5	0.2	-2.1	-2.6
State and local government	2.3	2.0	2.0	2.5	2.6	2.9	1.4	1.5	1.5	1.7	1.7	1.2	1.1	2.6
Manufacturing	-0.6	-1.5	0.3	1.7	0.4	-1.6	-3.5	-1.6	-0.6	-1.7	-1.6	-0.2	0.7	1.1
Construction	6.5	3.1	3.1	2.8	1.5	-0.9	-9.2	-3.5	3.3	5.7	3.6	5.6	3.5	12.6
Other	4.5	3.2	3.6	4.0	3.4	2.1	-0.2	0.8	2.5	3.0	2.8	2.9	3.0	4.3
3. Unemployment rates														
Total	7.2	7.0	6.2	5.5	5.3	5.5	6.7	7.4	6.8	7.0	6.7	6.5	6.6	6.2
Married men	4.3	4.4	3.9	3.3	3.0	3.4	4.4	5.0	4.4	4.5	4.4	4.1	4.2	3.7
Females	7.4	7.1	6.2	5.6	5.4	5.4	6.3	6.9	6.5	6.6	6.4	6.3	6.5	6.1
Youths	18.6	18.3	16.9	15.3	15.0	15.5	18.6	20.0	19.0	19.8	18.2	18.3	18.0	18.4
4. Activity rate [4]	60.1	60.7	61.5	62.3	62.9	62.7	61.6	61.2	61.2	61.6	61.7	61.9	62.3	62.3

1. Household survey. Data from the household survey for 1994 are not directly comparable to data for 1993 and earlier years because of the implementation in January 1994 of a major redesign of the survey and the introduction of 1990 Census-based population controls, adjusted for the estimated undercount.
2. Non-institutional population aged 16 and over.
3. Non-agricultural payroll.
4. Employment as percentage of population aged from 16 to 64.
Source: U.S. Department of Labor, Monthly Labor Review.

Table D. Costs and prices

Percentage changes from previous period, s.a.a.r.

	1985	1986	1987	1988	1989	1990	1991	1992	1993	1993			1994	
										Q2	Q3	Q4	Q1	Q2
Rates of pay														
Major wage settlements[1]	3.2	2.3	3.1	2.6	3.2	3.5	3.5	3.0	2.9	3.6	3.2	2.8	1.6	3.2
Hourly earnings index[2]	3.0	2.3	2.5	3.3	4.0	3.7	3.1	2.5	2.4	2.1	2.1	3.2	3.1	1.8
Wages and salaries per person	4.6	4.1	4.6	4.8	3.4	4.7	3.4	5.6	1.7	13.5	2.1	1.6	1.7	4.7
Compensation per person	4.9	3.6	4.2	5.9	4.0	5.8	4.2	4.8	3.8	3.2	2.4	2.1	1.8	4.6
Productivity, non-farm business														
Hourly	0.8	2.0	0.8	1.0	-0.9	0.4	1.5	2.7	1.6	0.5	4.1	4.9	2.8	-2.7
Per employee	0.1	0.9	1.4	1.2	-0.6	-0.2	1.0	2.6	2.2	2.7	3.1	5.2	2.7	-0.9
Unit labour cost, non-farm business	3.3	2.9	2.6	3.3	4.3	5.1	3.5	2.4	1.7	2.0	-1.2	-2.4	3.1	3.5
Prices														
GDP deflator	3.6	2.7	3.2	3.9	4.5	4.3	3.9	2.9	2.5	1.7	1.1	1.3	2.7	3.0
Private consumption deflator	3.9	3.1	4.2	4.2	4.9	5.1	4.3	3.3	2.7	2.3	1.1	2.3	1.4	3.3
Consumer price index	3.5	1.9	3.7	4.1	4.8	5.4	4.2	3.0	3.0	3.1	1.6	2.8	2.6	2.6
Food	2.3	3.2	4.2	4.1	5.8	5.8	2.9	1.2	2.1	3.2	1.4	4.5	0.5	1.6
Wholesale prices	-0.5	-2.9	2.6	4.0	5.0	3.6	0.2	0.6	1.5	3.9	-2.1	0.1	1.6	2.3
Crude products	-7.5	-8.4	6.7	2.5	7.4	5.7	-7.0	-0.8	2.0	12.6	-13.8	3.9	4.1	2.9
Intermediate products	-0.4	-3.5	2.4	5.5	4.6	2.2	-0.0	0.2	1.4	2.8	0.9	-1.3	0.8	2.9
Finished products	0.9	-1.4	2.1	2.5	5.1	4.9	2.1	1.2	1.2	3.7	-3.7	-0.1	1.1	1.7

1. Total effective wage adjustment in all industries under collective agreements in non-farm industry covering at least 1 000 workers, not seasonally adjusted.
2. Production or non-supervisory workers on private non-agricultural payrolls.
Source: U.S. Department of Labor, Bureau of Labor Statistics, Monthly Labor Review; U.S. Department of Commerce, Survey of Current Business.

Table E. Monetary indicators

	1985	1986	1987	1988	1989	1990	1991	1992	1993	1993 Q2	1993 Q3	1993 Q4	1994 Q1	1994 Q2
Monetary aggregates (percentage changes from previous period) s.a.a.r														
M1	9.0	13.5	11.6	4.3	1.0	3.6	6.0	12.4	11.6	11.1	12.6	9.7	6.1	1.9
M2	8.9	8.3	6.6	5.2	3.9	5.3	3.2	2.1	1.1	2.2	2.5	2.4	1.9	1.8
M3	9.0	8.2	6.8	6.3	4.5	2.6	1.7	0.6	-0.1	2.1	1.1	2.6	0.2	0.4
Velocity of circulation														
GDP/M1	6.9	6.4	6.1	6.3	6.7	6.8	6.7	6.2	5.9	5.9	5.8	5.8	5.8	5.8
GDP/M2	1.6	1.6	1.6	1.6	1.7	1.7	1.7	1.7	1.8	1.8	1.8	1.8	1.8	1.9
GDP/M3	1.3	1.3	1.3	1.3	1.3	1.4	1.4	1.4	1.5	1.5	1.5	1.5	1.6	1.6
Federal Reserve Bank reserves ($ billion)														
Non-borrowed	27.8	33.6	38.6	37.8	38.7	39.9	42.7	50.0	57.2	56.2	57.8	60.0	60.6	59.8
Borrowed	1.3	0.8	0.8	2.4	1.1	0.9	0.4	0.2	0.2	0.1	0.3	0.2	0.1	0.2
Total	29.1	34.5	39.4	40.1	39.8	40.9	43.1	50.2	57.4	56.4	58.1	60.2	60.7	60.0
Required	28.3	33.5	38.4	39.1	38.9	39.9	41.9	49.1	56.3	55.4	57.1	59.1	59.5	58.9
Excess	0.8	0.9	1.0	1.0	1.0	1.0	1.2	1.1	1.1	1.0	1.0	1.1	1.2	1.1
Free (excess – borrowed)	-0.5	0.1	0.3	-1.3	-0.2	0.0	0.8	0.9	0.9	0.9	0.7	0.9	1.1	0.9
Interest rates (%)														
Federal funds rate	8.1	6.8	6.7	7.6	9.2	8.1	5.7	3.5	3.0	3.0	3.1	3.0	3.2	3.9
Discount rate[1]	7.7	6.3	5.7	6.2	7.0	7.0	5.4	3.3	3.0	3.0	3.0	3.0	3.0	3.3
Prime rate[2]	9.9	8.3	8.2	9.3	10.9	10.0	8.5	6.3	6.0	6.0	6.0	6.0	6.0	6.9
3-month Treasury Bills	7.5	6.0	5.8	6.7	8.1	7.5	5.4	3.4	3.0	3.0	3.0	3.1	3.2	4.0
AAA rate[3]	11.4	9.0	9.4	9.7	9.3	9.3	8.8	8.1	7.2	7.4	6.9	6.8	7.2	7.9
10-year Treasury Notes	10.6	7.7	8.4	8.8	8.5	8.6	7.9	7.0	5.9	6.0	5.6	5.6	6.1	7.1

1. Rate for Federal Reserve Bank of New York.
2. Prime rate on short-term business loans.
3. Corporate Bonds, AAA rating group, quoted by Moody's Investors Services.
Source: Board of the Governors of the Federal Reserve System, Federal Reserve Bulletin.

	1980	1981	1982	1983	1984
Exports, fob [1]	224 250	237 044	211 157	201 799	219 926
Imports, fob [1]	249 750	265 067	247 642	268 901	332 418
Trade balance	−25 500	−28 023	−36 485	−67 102	−112 492
Services, net [2]	36 166	44 755	42 118	40 384	33 330
Balance on goods and services	10 666	16 732	5 633	−26 718	−79 162
Private transfers, net	−1 044	−4 516	−8 738	−9 066	−9 756
Official transfers, net	−7 304	−7 186	−8 338	−8 676	−10 853
Current balance	2 317	5 030	−11 443	−44 460	−99 771
U.S. assets abroad other than official reserves	−78 813	−108 972	−117 370	−57 539	−31 787
U.S. private assets, net [3]	−73 651	−103 875	−111 239	−52 533	−26 298
Reported by U.S. banks	−46 838	−84 175	−111 070	−29 928	−11 127
U.S. government assets [4]	−5 162	−5 097	−6 131	−5 006	−5 489
Foreign assets in the United States					
Liabilities to foreign official monetary agencies [5]	15 497	4 960	3 593	5 845	3 140
Other liabilities to foreign monetary agencies [6]	42 615	78 072	88 826	77 534	110 792
Reported by U.S. banks	10 743	42 128	65 633	50 342	33 849
Allocation of SDR's	1 150	1 090	−	−	−
Errors and omissions	25 386	24 992	41 359	19 815	20 758
Change in reserves (+ = increase)	8 155	5 175	4 965	1 196	3 131
a) Gold	−	−	−	−	−
b) Currency assets	6 471	861	1 040	−3 305	1 156
c) Reserve position in IMF	1 667	2 492	2 552	4 435	995
d) Special drawing rights	16	1 823	1 372	65	979

1. Excluding military goods.
2. Services include reinvested earnings of incorporated affiliates.
3. Including: Direct investment financed by reinvested earnings of incorporated affiliates; foreign securities; U.S. claims on unaffiliated foreigners reported by U.S. nonbanking concerns; and U.S. claims reported by U.S. banks, not included elsewhere.
4. Including: U.S. credits and other long-term assets; repayments on U.S. credits and other long-term assets, U.S. foreign currency holdings and U.S. short-term assets, net.

payments, OECD basis

of dollars

1985	1986	1987	1988	1989	1990	1991	1992	1993
215 915	223 344	250 208	320 230	362 116	389 303	416 913	440 361	456 866
338 088	368 425	409 765	447 189	477 365	498 336	490 981	536 458	589 441
−122 173	−145 081	−159 557	−126 959	−115 249	−109 033	−74 068	−96 097	−132 575
19 751	18 055	15 513	23 742	38 563	50 948	60 429	60 253	60 796
−102 422	−127 026	−144 044	−103 217	−76 686	−58 085	−13 639	−35 844	−71 779
−9 545	−10 112	−10 544	−11 958	−12 700	−13 043	−13 811	−13 297	−13 712
−13 406	−14 064	−12 508	−13 019	−13 434	−20 619	20 498	−18 745	−18 405
−125 373	−151 202	−167 096	−128 194	−102 820	−91 747	−6 952	−67 886	−103 896
−35 368	−105 131	−80 591	−95 447	−143 451	−68 205	−57 275	−65 411	−146 519
−32 547	−103 109	−81 597	−98 414	−144 710	−70 512	−60 175	−63 759	−146 213
−1 323	−59 975	−42 119	53 927	58 160	16 027	4 763	22 314	32 238
−2 821	−2 022	1 006	2 967	1 259	2 307	2 900	−1 652	−306
−1 119	35 648	45 387	39 758	8 503	33 910	17 199	40 858	71 681
142 301	190 463	197 596	200 507	209 987	88 282	80 935	105 646	159 017
41 045	76 737	86 537	63 744	51 780	−3 824	3 994	15 461	18 452
–	–	–	–	–	–	–	–	–
23 415	29 908	−4 443	−12 712	53 075	39 919	−39 670	−17 108	21 096
3 858	−312	−9 149	3 912	25 293	2 158	−5 763	−3 901	1 379
–	–	–	–	–	–	–	–	–
3 869	942	−7 589	5 065	25 229	2 697	−6 307	−4 277	797
−909	−1 501	−2 070	−1 024	−471	−731	367	2 692	44
897	246	509	−127	535	192	177	−2 316	537

5. Including: U.S. Government securities and other U.S. Government liabilities, U.S. liabilities reported by U.S. banks not included elsewhere and other foreign official assets.
6. Including direct investment; U.S. Treasury securities; other U.S. securities; U.S. liabilities to unaffiliated foreigners reported by U.S. non-banking concerns; U.S. liabilities reported by U.S. banks not included elsewhere.
Source: U.S. Department of Commerce, *Survey of Current Business.*

Table G. **Public sector**

	1960	1970	1980	1990	1991	1992	1993
A. Budget indicators:							
General government accounts (% GDP)							
Current receipts	27.7	29.7	30.5	30.8	30.7	30.6	30.9
Non-interest expenditures	25.0	29.6	30.6	31.2	31.8	32.9	32.5
Primary budget balance	2.0	0.1	−0.1	−0.4	−3.4	−4.5	−1.6
Net interest	−1.3	−1.2	−1.2	−2.1	0.0	0.0	−2.0
General government budget balance	0.7	−1.1	−1.3	−2.5	−3.4	−4.5	−3.5
of which:							
Central government	0.7	−1.3	−2.2	−2.9	−3.6	−4.6	−3.6
Excluding Social security [1]			−2.2	−4.0	−4.5	−5.4	−4.3
B. The structure of expenditure and taxation							
(% GDP)							
Government expenditure							
Transfers	5.7	8.3	11.7	12.3	12.6	14.1	14.2
Subsidies	−0.1	0.3	0.2	0.1	0.0	0.0	0.1

	United States			OECD Average		
	1990	1991	1992	1990	1991	1992
Tax receipts (% GDP)						
Income tax	10.5	10.3	10.1	11.5	11.5	11.5
Social security tax	8.7	8.8	8.8	9.4	9.8	9.9
Consumption tax	4.2	4.3	4.4	10.9	11.0	11.2

C. Tax rates (%)						
Top rate				39.6		
Lower rate				15.0		
Social security tax rate						
Employer				7.15		
Employee				7.15		

	1960	1970	1980	1990	1991	1992	1993
D. Government debt (% GDP)							
General government gross debt	60.3	45.4	37.7	55.4	58.9	62.0	63.9
Net debt	46.6	28.5	18.8	32.6	34.2	37.4	39.3

1. OECD estimates derived from fiscal year off-budget items (primarily retirement pension balance), converted to a calendar year basis.

Source: Economic Report of the President, February 1994; Department of Treasury, Office of Tax Analysis; *Revenue Statistics of OECD Member Countries, 1965-1993*, OECD, 1994, and OECD calculations.

Table H. Financial markets

	1970	1975	1980	1989	1990	1991	1992	1993
A. Financial and corporate flows								
Share of private financial institutions' financial assets in national net assets (%)[1]	47.8	43.2	39.9	66.3	68.1	74.6	80.7	86.6
Market value of equities including corporate farm equities (billions of dollars)[1]	0.631	0.635	1.256	3.173	3.011	4.126	4.609	5.127
Debt-to-equity ratio in non-financial corporate business excluding farms (%)[1]	56.5	87.6	70.5	74.6	82.0	59.5	54.2	49.6
Ratio of market value to net worth[1]	77.8	39.0	41.3	76.1	73.3	106.8	126.4	135.6
B. Foreign sector (billions of dollars)								
Net foreign assets outstanding[1,3]	68.7	81.4	278.6	-244.8	-266.9	-346.0	-472.5	-632.6
Changes in net foreign investment[2]	3.0	24.0	25.7	-49.8	-51.8	-46.6	-85.0	-82.8
of which net financial investment of:								
Private sector	17.1	93.3	81.2	186.5	202.3	270.7	306.9	177.3
Public sector	-22.3	-80.1	-63.7	-224.4	-217.6	-306.3	-389.1	-326.7
Foreign purchases of U.S. corporate equities[2]	0.7	3.1	4.2	9.0	-16.0	10.4	-5.8	20.6
U.S. purchases of foreign equities[2]	1.1	-0.9	2.4	17.2	7.4	30.7	30.7	60.6
C. Net worth (billions of dollars)[1]								
Total, all sectors	3.070	5.558	10.666	18.285	18.323	18.459	18.500	19.044
Private, consolidated	3.488	6.203	11.689	20.680	20.941	21.321	21.592	22.325
Household	3.349	5.109	9.666	19.041	19.059	20.900	21.879	23.027
Total owner-occupied real estate	0.867	1.572	3.289	6.059	5.979	6.016	6.484	6.709
Home mortgages as a per cent of owner-occupied real estate	31.5	27.9	27.5	37.2	40.8	40.3	41.6	42.4
D. Debt to net worth ratios, private sector (%)[4]								
Household	13.5	14.3	14.4	17.8	19.0	18.1	18.3	18.6
Non-farm non-corporate business	38.3	46.5	42.5	61.6	64.5	65.5	64.8	63.3
Farm business	18.3	16.8	17.6	17.1	16.9	17.0	16.8	16.5
Non-financial corporate business excluding farms	44.0	34.2	29.1	56.7	60.1	63.7	68.6	67.3
Private financial institutions	65.2	73.9	77.3	114.1	114.7	108.5	109.6	108.4

1. Data are year-end outstandings.
2. Data are annual flows.
3. Net foreign assets exclude U.S. holdings of foreign equities and foreign holdings of U.S. equities.
4. Debt is credit market debt.
Source: Board of Governors of the Federal Reserve System, *Balance Sheets for the U.S. Economy, 1945-93.*

Table I. **Labour market indicators**

A. Evolution

	Peak	Trough	1989	1990	1991	1992	1993
Standardised unemployment rate	1982: 9.6	1969:3.4	5.2	5.4	6.7	7.3	6.7
Unemployment rate							
Total	1982: 9.5	1969:3.4	5.2	5.4	6.6	7.3	6.7
Male	1983: 9.7	1969:2.7	5.1	5.5	6.9	7.6	7.0
Female	1982: 9.4	1969:4.7	5.5	5.4	6.3	6.9	6.5
Youth[1]	1982:17.0	1969:7.4	10.9	11.1	13.4	14.2	13.3
Share of long-term unemployment[2]	1983:13.4	1969:1.9	5.8	5.6	6.3	11.2	11.7
Productivity index, 1987 = 100[3]			102.1	102.9	103.0	105.0	106.6

B. Structural or institutional characteristics

	1970	1980	1989	1990	1991	1992	1993
Participation rate[4]							
Global	60.4	63.8	66.5	66.4	66.0	66.3	66.1
Male	79.7	77.4	76.4	76.1	75.6	75.6	75.2
Female	43.3	51.5	57.4	57.5	57.3	57.8	57.6
Employment/population between 16 and 64 years	57.4	59.2	62.9	62.7	61.6	61.2	61.2
Employment by sector							
Agriculture – per cent of total	4.5	3.6	2.9	2.8	2.9	2.9	2.7
– per cent change	-3.6	0.6	1.4	-0.5	1.0	-0.3	3.5
Industry – per cent of total	34.3	30.5	26.7	26.2	25.3	24.6	24.0
– per cent change	-1.8	-1.9	1.1	-1.2	-4.3	-2.1	-0.9
Services – per cent of total	61.1	65.9	70.5	71.0	71.8	72.5	73.2
– per cent change	3.0	1.7	2.4	1.2	0.3	1.6	2.4
of which:							
Government – per cent of total	0.2	0.2	0.2	0.2	0.2	0.2	0.2
– per cent change	3.0	1.8	2.3	2.9	0.5	1.3	1.0
Voluntary part-time work[5]	13.9	14.2	14.1	13.7	13.7	13.4	13.4
Social insurance as a per cent of compensation	10.8	16.3	16.6	16.8	17.3	17.0	18.3
Government unemployment insurance benefits[6]	12.3	12.6	8.3	9.9	10.9	13.7	12.3
Minimum wage: as a percentage of average wage[7]	49.6	46.6	34.7	36.8	40.1	40.2	39.2

1. People between 16 and 24 years as a percentage of the labour force of the same age group.
2. People looking for a job since one year or more as a percentage of total unemployment.
3. Production as a percentage of employment.
4. Labour force as a percentage of the corresponding population aged between 16 and 64 years.
5. As a percentage of salary workers.
6. Value of the unemployment benefits per unemployed divided by the compensation per employee.
7. Private non-agricultural sector.
Source: U.S. Department of Labor, Bureau of Labor Statistics, Data Resources Incorporated, and OECD.

BASIC STATISTICS

BASIC STATISTICS:

INTERNATIONAL COMPARISONS

	Units	Reference period [1]	Australia	Austria
Population				
Total	Thousands	1991	17 292	7 823
Inhabitants per sq. km	Number	1991	2	93
Net average annual increase over previous 10 years	%	1991	1.5	0.3
Employment				
Total civilian employment (TCE)[2]	Thousands	1991	7 705	3 482
Of which: Agriculture	% of TCE		5.5	7.4
Industry	% of TCE		24.2	36.9
Services	% of TCE		70.4	55.8
Gross domestic product (GDP)				
At current prices and current exchange rates	Bill. US$	1991	297.4	164.7
Per capita	US$		17 200	21 048
At current prices using current PPP's[3]	Bill. US$	1991	280	135.6
Per capita	US$		16 195	17 329
Average annual volume growth over previous 5 years	%	1991	2.8	3.3
Gross fixed capital formation (GFCF)	% of GDP	1991	20.5	25.1
Of which: Machinery and equipment	% of GDP		8.8	10.4
Residential construction	% of GDP		4.6	4.6 (90
Average annual volume growth over previous 5 years	%	1991	0.3	5.2
Gross saving ratio[4]	% of GDP	1991	17.2	25.6
General government				
Current expenditure on goods and services	% of GDP	1991	18.3	18.2
Current disbursements[5]	% of GDP	1991	36.6	45.7
Current receipts	% of GDP	1991	33.7	47.2
Net official development assistance	% of GDP	1991	0.35	0.33
Indicators of living standards				
Private consumption per capita using current PPP's[3]	US$	1991	9 827	9 591
Passenger cars, per 1 000 inhabitants	Number	1990	430	382
Telephones, per 1 000 inhabitants	Number	1990	448 (89)	589
Television sets, per 1 000 inhabitants	Number	1989	484	475
Doctors, per 1 000 inhabitants	Number	1991	2	2.1
Infant mortality per 1 000 live births	Number	1991	7.1	7.4
Wages and prices (average annual increase over previous 5 years)				
Wages (earnings or rates according to availability)	%	1991	5.4	5.2
Consumer prices	%	1991	6.7	2.5
Foreign trade				
Exports of goods, fob*	Mill. US$	1991	39 764	40 985
As % of GDP	%		13.4	24.9
Average annual increase over previous 5 years	%		13.2	12.8
Imports of goods, cif*	Mill. US$	1991	38 844	48 914
As % of GDP	%		13.1	29.7
Average annual increase over previous 5 years	%		10.1	13.7
Total official reserves[6]	Mill. SDR's	1991	11 432	6 591
As ratio of average monthly imports of goods	Ratio		3.5	1.6

*   At current prices and exchange rates.
1.   Unless otherwise stated.
2.   According to the definitions used in OECD *Labour Force Statistics.*
3.   PPP's = Purchasing Power Parities.
4.   Gross saving = Gross national disposable income minus private and government consumption.
5.   Current disbursements = Current expenditure on goods and services plus current transfers and payments of property income.
6.   Gold included in reserves is valued at 35 SDR's per ounce. End of year.
7.   Including Luxembourg.

EMPLOYMENT OPPORTUNITIES

Economics Department, OECD

The Economics Department of the OECD offers challenging and rewarding opportunities to economists interested in applied policy analysis in an international environment. The Department's concerns extend across the entire field of economic policy analysis, both macro-economic and micro-economic. Its main task is to provide, for discussion by committees of senior officials from Member countries, documents and papers dealing with current policy concerns. Within this programme of work, three major responsibilities are:

- to prepare regular surveys of the economies of individual Member countries;
- to issue full twice-yearly reviews of the economic situation and prospects of the OECD countries in the context of world economic trends;
- to analyse specific policy issues in a medium-term context for theOECD as a whole, and to a lesser extent for the non-OECD countries.

The documents prepared for these purposes, together with much of the Department's other economic work, appear in published form in the *OECD Economic Outlook, OECD Economic Surveys, OECD Economic Studies* and the Department's *Working Papers* series.

The Department maintains a world econometric model, INTERLINK, which plays an important role in the preparation of the policy analyses and twice-yearly projections. The availability of extensive cross-country data bases and good computer resources facilitates comparative empirical analysis, much of which is incorporated into the model.

The Department is made up of about 75 professional economists from a variety of backgrounds and Member countries. Most projects are carried out by small teams and last from four to eighteen months. Within the Department, ideas and points of view are widely discussed; there is a lively professional interchange, and all professional staff have the opportunity to contribute actively to the programme of work.

Skills the Economics Department is looking for:

a) Solid competence in using the tools of both micro-economic and macro-economic theory to answer policy questions. Experience indicates that this normally requires the equivalent of a PH.D. in economics or substantial relevant professional experience to compensate for a lower degree.

b) Solid knowledge of economic statistics and quantitative methods; this includes how to identify data, estimate structural relationships, apply basic techniques of time series analysis, and test hypotheses. It is essential to be able to interpret results sensibly in an economic policy context.

c) A keen interest in and knowledge of policy issues, economic developments and their political/social contexts.

d) Interest and experience in analysing questions posed by policy-makers and presenting the results to them effectively and judiciously. Thus, work experience in government agencies or policy research institutions is an advantage.

e) The ability to write clearly, effectively, and to the point. The OECD is a bilingual organisation with French and English as the official languages. Candidates must have excellent knowledge of one of these languages, and some knowledge of the other. Knowledge of other languages might also be an advantage for certain posts.

f) For some posts, expertise in a particular area may be important, but a successful candidate is expected to be able to work on a broader range of topics relevant to the work of the Department. Thus, except in rare cases, the Department does not recruit narrow specialists.

g) The Department works on a tight time schedule and strict deadlines. Moreover, much of the work in the Department is carried out in small groups of economists. Thus, the ability to work with other economists from a variety of cultural and professional backgrounds, to supervise junior staff, and to produce work on time is important.

General Information

The salary for recruits depends on educational and professional background. Positions carry a basic salary from FF 262 512 or FF 323 916 for Administrators (economists) and from FF 375 708 for Principal Administrators (senior economists). This may be supplemented by expatriation and/or family allowances, depending on nationality, residence and family situation. Initial appointments are for a fixed term of two to three years.

Vacancies are open to candidates from OECD Member countries. The Organisation seeks to maintain an appropriate balance between female and male staff and among nationals from Member countries.

For further information on employment opportunities in the Economics Department, contact:

Administrative Unit
Economics Department
OECD
2, rue André-Pascal
75775 PARIS CEDEX 16
FRANCE

Applications citing "ECSUR", together with a detailed *curriculum vitae* in English or French, should be sent to the Head of Personnel at the above address.

MAIN SALES OUTLETS OF OECD PUBLICATIONS
PRINCIPAUX POINTS DE VENTE DES PUBLICATIONS DE L'OCDE

ARGENTINA – ARGENTINE
Carlos Hirsch S.R.L.
Galería Güemes, Florida 165, 4° Piso
1333 Buenos Aires   Tel. (1) 331.1787 y 331.2391
Telefax: (1) 331.1787

AUSTRALIA – AUSTRALIE
D.A. Information Services
648 Whitehorse Road, P.O.B 163
Mitcham, Victoria 3132   Tel. (03) 873.4411
Telefax: (03) 873.5679

AUSTRIA – AUTRICHE
Gerold & Co.
Graben 31
Wien I   Tel. (0222) 533.50.14

BELGIUM – BELGIQUE
Jean De Lannoy
Avenue du Roi 202
B-1060 Bruxelles   Tel. (02) 538.51.69/538.08.41
Telefax: (02) 538.08.41

CANADA
Renouf Publishing Company Ltd.
1294 Algoma Road
Ottawa, ON K1B 3W8   Tel. (613) 741.4333
Telefax: (613) 741.5439
Stores:
61 Sparks Street
Ottawa, ON K1P 5R1   Tel. (613) 238.8985
211 Yonge Street
Toronto, ON M5B 1M4   Tel. (416) 363.3171
Telefax: (416)363.59.63

Les Éditions La Liberté Inc.
3020 Chemin Sainte-Foy
Sainte-Foy, PQ G1X 3V6   Tel. (418) 658.3763
Telefax: (418) 658.3763

Federal Publications Inc.
165 University Avenue, Suite 701
Toronto, ON M5H 3B8   Tel. (416) 860.1611
Telefax: (416) 860.1608

Les Publications Fédérales
1185 Université
Montréal, QC H3B 3A7   Tel. (514) 954.1633
Telefax : (514) 954.1635

CHINA – CHINE
China National Publications Import
Export Corporation (CNPIEC)
16 Gongti E. Road, Chaoyang District
P.O. Box 88 or 50
Beijing 100704 PR   Tel. (01) 506.6688
Telefax: (01) 506.3101

DENMARK – DANEMARK
Munksgaard Book and Subscription Service
35, Nørre Søgade, P.O. Box 2148
DK-1016 København K   Tel. (33) 12.85.70
Telefax: (33) 12.93.87

FINLAND – FINLANDE
Akateeminen Kirjakauppa
Keskuskatu 1, P.O. Box 128
00100 Helsinki
Subscription Services/Agence d'abonnements :
P.O. Box 23
00371 Helsinki   Tel. (358 0) 12141
Telefax: (358 0) 121.4450

FRANCE
OECD/OCDE
Mail Orders/Commandes par correspondance:
2, rue André-Pascal
75775 Paris Cedex 16   Tel. (33-1) 45.24.82.00
Telefax: (33-1) 49.10.42.76
Telex: 640048 OCDE

OECD Bookshop/Librairie de l'OCDE :
33, rue Octave-Feuillet
75016 Paris   Tel. (33-1) 45.24.81.67
(33-1) 45.24.81.81
Documentation Française
29, quai Voltaire
75007 Paris   Tel. 40.15.70.00
Gibert Jeune (Droit-Économie)
6, place Saint-Michel
75006 Paris   Tel. 43.25.91.19
Librairie du Commerce International
10, avenue d'Iéna
75016 Paris   Tel. 40.73.34.60
Librairie Dunod
Université Paris-Dauphine
Place du Maréchal de Lattre de Tassigny
75016 Paris   Tel. (1) 44.05.40.13
Librairie Lavoisier
11, rue Lavoisier
75008 Paris   Tel. 42.65.39.95
Librairie L.G.D.J. - Montchrestien
20, rue Soufflot
75005 Paris   Tel. 46.33.89.85
Librairie des Sciences Politiques
30, rue Saint-Guillaume
75007 Paris   Tel. 45.48.36.02
P.U.F.
49, boulevard Saint-Michel
75005 Paris   Tel. 43.25.83.40
Librairie de l'Université
12a, rue Nazareth
13100 Aix-en-Provence   Tel. (16) 42.26.18.08
Documentation Française
165, rue Garibaldi
69003 Lyon   Tel. (16) 78.63.32.23
Librairie Decitre
29, place Bellecour
69002 Lyon   Tel. (16) 72.40.54.54

GERMANY – ALLEMAGNE
OECD Publications and Information Centre
August-Bebel-Allee 6
D-53175 Bonn   Tel. (0228) 959.120
Telefax: (0228) 959.12.17

GREECE – GRÈCE
Librairie Kauffmann
Mavrokordatou 9
106 78 Athens   Tel. (01) 32.55.321
Telefax: (01) 36.33.967

HONG-KONG
Swindon Book Co. Ltd.
13–15 Lock Road
Kowloon, Hong Kong   Tel. 366.80.31
Telefax: 739.49.75

HUNGARY – HONGRIE
Euro Info Service
Margitsziget, Európa Ház
1138 Budapest   Tel. (1) 111.62.16
Telefax : (1) 111.60.61

ICELAND – ISLANDE
Mál Mog Menning
Laugavegi 18, Pósthólf 392
121 Reykjavik   Tel. 162.35.23

INDIA – INDE
Oxford Book and Stationery Co.
Scindia House
New Delhi 110001   Tel.(11) 331.5896/5308
Telefax: (11) 332.5993
17 Park Street
Calcutta 700016   Tel. 240832

INDONESIA – INDONÉSIE
Pdii-Lipi
P.O. Box 269/JKSMG/88
Jakarta 12790   Tel. 583467
Telex: 62 875

ISRAEL
Praedicta
5 Shatner Street
P.O. Box 34030
Jerusalem 91430   Tel. (2) 52.84.90/1/2
Telefax: (2) 52.84.93
R.O.Y.
P.O. Box 13056
Tel Aviv 61130   Tél. (3) 49.61.08
Telefax (3) 544.60.39

ITALY – ITALIE
Libreria Commissionaria Sansoni
Via Duca di Calabria 1/1
50125 Firenze   Tel. (055) 64.54.15
Telefax: (055) 64.12.57
Via Bartolini 29
20155 Milano   Tel. (02) 36.50.83
Editrice e Libreria Herder
Piazza Montecitorio 120
00186 Roma   Tel. 679.46.28
Telefax: 678.47.51
Libreria Hoepli
Via Hoepli 5
20121 Milano   Tel. (02) 86.54.46
Telefax: (02) 805.28.86
Libreria Scientifica
Dott. Lucio de Biasio 'Aeiou'
Via Coronelli, 6
20146 Milano   Tel. (02) 48.95.45.52
Telefax: (02) 48.95.45.48

JAPAN – JAPON
OECD Publications and Information Centre
Landic Akasaka Building
2-3-4 Akasaka, Minato-ku
Tokyo 107   Tel. (81.3) 3586.2016
Telefax: (81.3) 3584.7929

KOREA – CORÉE
Kyobo Book Centre Co. Ltd.
P.O. Box 1658, Kwang Hwa Moon
Seoul   Tel. 730.78.91
Telefax: 735.00.30

MALAYSIA – MALAISIE
Co-operative Bookshop Ltd.
University of Malaya
P.O. Box 1127, Jalan Pantai Baru
59700 Kuala Lumpur
Malaysia   Tel. 756.5000/756.5425
Telefax: 757.3661

MEXICO – MEXIQUE
Revistas y Periodicos Internacionales S.A. de C.V.
Florencia 57 - 1004
Mexico, D.F. 06600   Tel. 207.81.00
Telefax : 208.39.79

NETHERLANDS – PAYS-BAS
SDU Uitgeverij Plantijnstraat
Externe Fondsen
Postbus 20014
2500 EA's-Gravenhage   Tel. (070) 37.89.880
Voor bestellingen: Telefax: (070) 34.75.778

NEW ZEALAND
NOUVELLE-ZÉLANDE
Legislation Services
P.O. Box 12418
Thorndon, Wellington   Tel. (04) 496.5652
Telefax: (04) 496.5698

NORWAY – NORVÈGE
Narvesen Info Center – NIC
Bertrand Narvesens vei 2
P.O. Box 6125 Etterstad
0602 Oslo 6   Tel. (022) 57.33.00
                         Telefax: (022) 68.19.01

PAKISTAN
Mirza Book Agency
65 Shahrah Quaid-E-Azam
Lahore 54000   Tel. (42) 353.601
                         Telefax: (42) 231.730

PHILIPPINE – PHILIPPINES
International Book Center
5th Floor, Filipinas Life Bldg.
Ayala Avenue
Metro Manila   Tel. 81.96.76
                      Telex 23312 RHP PH

PORTUGAL
Livraria Portugal
Rua do Carmo 70-74
Apart. 2681
1200 Lisboa   Tel.: (01) 347.49.82/5
                        Telefax: (01) 347.02.64

SINGAPORE – SINGAPOUR
Gower Asia Pacific Pte Ltd.
Golden Wheel Building
41, Kallang Pudding Road, No. 04-03
Singapore 1334   Tel. 741.5166
                         Telefax: 742.9356

SPAIN – ESPAGNE
Mundi-Prensa Libros S.A.
Castelló 37, Apartado 1223
Madrid 28001   Tel. (91) 431.33.99
                         Telefax: (91) 575.39.98

Libreria Internacional AEDOS
Consejo de Ciento 391
08009 – Barcelona   Tel. (93) 488.30.09
                         Telefax: (93) 487.76.59

Llibreria de la Generalitat
Palau Moja
Rambla dels Estudis, 118
08002 – Barcelona
        (Subscripcions) Tel. (93) 318.80.12
        (Publicacions) Tel. (93) 302.67.23
                         Telefax: (93) 412.18.54

SRI LANKA
Centre for Policy Research
c/o Colombo Agencies Ltd.
No. 300-304, Galle Road
Colombo 3   Tel. (1) 574240, 573551-2
                      Telefax: (1) 575394, 510711

SWEDEN – SUÈDE
Fritzes Information Center
Box 16356
Regeringsgatan 12
106 47 Stockholm   Tel. (08) 690.90.90
                         Telefax: (08) 20.50.21

Subscription Agency/Agence d'abonnements :
Wennergren-Williams Info AB
P.O. Box 1305
171 25 Solna   Tel. (08) 705.97.50
                         Téléfax : (08) 27.00.71

SWITZERLAND – SUISSE
Maditec S.A. (Books and Periodicals - Livres
et périodiques)
Chemin des Palettes 4
Case postale 266
1020 Renens   Tel. (021) 635.08.65
                         Telefax: (021) 635.07.80

Librairie Payot S.A.
4, place Pépinet
CP 3212
1002 Lausanne   Tel. (021) 341.33.48
                         Telefax: (021) 341.33.45

Librairie Unilivres
6, rue de Candolle
1205 Genève   Tel. (022) 320.26.23
                         Telefax: (022) 329.73.18

Subscription Agency/Agence d'abonnements :
Dynapresse Marketing S.A.
38 avenue Vibert
1227 Carouge   Tel.: (022) 308.07.89
                         Telefax : (022) 308.07.99

See also – Voir aussi :
OECD Publications and Information Centre
August-Bebel-Allee 6
D-53175 Bonn (Germany)   Tel. (0228) 959.120
                         Telefax: (0228) 959.12.17

TAIWAN – FORMOSE
Good Faith Worldwide Int'l. Co. Ltd.
9th Floor, No. 118, Sec. 2
Chung Hsiao E. Road
Taipei   Tel. (02) 391.7396/391.7397
                         Telefax: (02) 394.9176

THAILAND – THAÏLANDE
Suksit Siam Co. Ltd.
113, 115 Fuang Nakhon Rd.
Opp. Wat Rajbopith
Bangkok 10200   Tel. (662) 225.9531/2
                         Telefax: (662) 222.5188

TURKEY – TURQUIE
Kültür Yayinlari Is-Türk Ltd. Sti.
Atatürk Bulvari No. 191/Kat 13
Kavaklidere/Ankara   Tel. 428.11.40 Ext. 2458
Dolmabahce Cad. No. 29
Besiktas/Istanbul   Tel. 260.71.88
                         Telex: 43482B

UNITED KINGDOM – ROYAUME-UNI
HMSO
Gen. enquiries   Tel. (071) 873 0011
Postal orders only:
P.O. Box 276, London SW8 5DT
Personal Callers HMSO Bookshop
49 High Holborn, London WC1V 6HB
                         Telefax: (071) 873 8200
Branches at: Belfast, Birmingham, Bristol, Edin-
burgh, Manchester

UNITED STATES – ÉTATS-UNIS
OECD Publications and Information Centre
2001 L Street N.W., Suite 700
Washington, D.C. 20036-4910 Tel. (202) 785.6323
                         Telefax: (202) 785.0350

VENEZUELA
Libreria del Este
Avda F. Miranda 52, Aptdo. 60337
Edificio Galipán
Caracas 106   Tel. 951.1705/951.2307/951.1297
                      Telegram: Libreste Caracas

Subscription to OECD periodicals may also be
placed through main subscription agencies.

Les abonnements aux publications périodiques de
l'OCDE peuvent être souscrits auprès des
principales agences d'abonnement.

Orders and inquiries from countries where Distribu-
tors have not yet been appointed should be sent to:
OECD Publications Service, 2 rue André-Pascal,
75775 Paris Cedex 16, France.

Les commandes provenant de pays où l'OCDE n'a
pas encore désigné de distributeur devraient être
adressées à : OCDE, Service des Publications,
2, rue André-Pascal, 75775 Paris Cedex 16, France.

9-1994

PRINTED IN FRANCE

•

OECD PUBLICATIONS
2 rue André-Pascal
75775 PARIS CEDEX 16
No. 47555
(10 94 02 1) ISBN 92-64-14292-4
ISSN 0376-6438

•